The National Trust
COUNTRYSIDE
HANDBOOK

A SELECTION
OF THE NATIONAL TRUST'S
COUNTRYSIDE PROPERTIES

THE NATIONAL TRUST

36 Queen Anne's Gate · London SWIH 9AS

Registered Charity No. 205846

Compiled by Celia Spouncer
Illustrations by Marcus Beaven

Front cover: The Lledr Valley, Gwynedd. Photo: National Trust Photographic Library/
Kevin Richardson

Back cover: A children's study group at Robin Hood's Bay, N. Yorkshire. Photo: National Trust
Photographic Library/Mike Williams

© The National Trust 1993
ISBN 0 7078 0143 5

First published in Great Britain in 1993
by National Trust Enterprises Ltd,
36 Queen Anne's Gate, London SW1H 9AS

Designed by Pardoe Blacker Ltd, Lingfield, Surrey
Phototypeset in Monophoto Lasercomp Bembo Series 270
by Southern Positives and Negatives (SPAN), Lingfield, Surrey (8452)
Printed in England by Clays Ltd, Bungay

Contents

Introduction

'These fields may be bought now, or they may be built over; which is it to be?' Octavia Hill asked this question in 1875 during a determined campaign to save Swiss Cottage Fields. The campaign failed, and this area, which she hoped would be an air-hole for the labouring lungs of North London, was lost to bricks and mortar. But Octavia Hill, with like-minded colleagues, continued her efforts to preserve countryside from development, and so the National Trust was born.

The intentions of the National Trust as laid out in 1895 by its three founder members, Octavia Hill, Robert Hunter and Canon Hardwicke Rawnsley, were to preserve 'Places of Historic Interest or Natural Beauty'. Today the National Trust is often thought of as the guardian of great country houses, but, with two exceptions, these in fact did not begin to come to the Trust until the late 1930s. Originally places of historic interest meant small buildings like the fourteenth-century Clergy House at Alfriston in Sussex, bought for £10 in 1896, and the Old Post Office at Tintagel in Cornwall, which came to the Trust in 1903. The emphasis from the first was the acquisition and protection of countryside. A look at the backgrounds of the founders confirms this: Octavia Hill and Robert

Hunter had been closely involved in the Commons Society, while Canon Rawnsley had created the Lake District Defence Society.

When the National Trust was given its first piece of countryside, $4\frac{1}{2}$ acres (2 ha) of clifftop of Dinas Oleu in North Wales, Octavia Hill posed another question: 'We have got our first piece of property, I wonder if it will be our last?' Today's organisation would surely astound her. The Trust is now the largest private landowner, owning more than 550,000 acres (222,585 ha) of countryside in England, Wales and Northern Ireland. This very large landholding contains within it an incredibly rich variety of landscapes: sunken green lanes and small field patterns in Devon and Cornwall; the bleak, open, heather-clad moors of Yorkshire and Derbyshire; the rugged crags of the Lake District and Snowdonia; and in complete contrast, the designed landscape parks of great country houses, like Stourhead in Wiltshire.

It may appear from such an expansive estate that the Trust is positively acquisitive for more property. With one important exception, this is not the case. That exception is Enterprise Neptune, launched in 1965 to acquire and protect the remaining stretches of unspoilt coastline. Dinas Oleu had been followed by other fine parts of the coast, like the Farne Islands in Northumberland and the Giant's Causeway in Northern Ireland. A survey carried out in the early 1960s showed that some 1000 miles of still unspoilt coastline of outstanding beauty was under threat from future development and other pressures, and it is Enterprise Neptune's goal to bring as much as possible of these 1000 miles into the care of the Trust. In the ensuing quarter of a century, 530 miles have been acquired by gift and purchase, and £17 million has been raised for the acquisition of coastal properties.

The philosophy which underlies the National Trust's approach to the conservation of the countryside in its ownership is one of integrated management. The Trust's primary duty is to preserve the natural characteristics of the landscape and, as far as possible, its animal and plant life. In managing its properties the Trust needs, therefore, to give due weight and consideration to a great variety of interests (sometimes in conflict with each other) and, in particular, to agriculture, woodland, nature conservation, archaeology, industrial archaeology, vernacular buildings and, of course, public enjoyment and recreation.

The major influence on the appearance of most of the British landscape remains that of farming. The National Trust is the largest farming landowner in the country, letting some forty per cent of its land on agricultural tenancies. The profound changes now taking place in farming, reinforced by the changes in the European Common Agricultural Policy and in environmental legislation, bring to the Trust both fresh challenges and opportunities. This has provided the opportunity to reappraise traditional farming regimes and to introduce, in co-operation with tenant farmers, practices which help to conserve the landscape and its natural history. Financial help from various government environmental and stewardship schemes has enabled the Trust to give priority to conservation of wildlife and landscape, and to contribute to the welfare of rural communities. This work takes a high priority in the Trust.

A visit to almost any part of the countryside of the United Kingdom today will provide evidence of past human occupation and working of the landscape. The National Trust owns over 40,000 archaeological sites – about six per cent of the national total (see notes on page 13). These sites are identified and recorded in a survey by the Trust's archaeologists, and then managed to ensure their long-term preservation: this survey should be complete by the millennium. The Trust also owns thousands of vernacular buildings: in the Lake District alone it looks after 1500 farms, barns and cottages. The National Trust is gradually carrying out comprehensive landscape surveys, in order to record all the known features and historical evidence on its properties.

The natural history interest on the Trust's estate as a whole is of great significance. The Trust owns over ten per cent of the designated Sites of Special Scientific Interest (SSSIs) in England and Wales and a further eighteen Areas of Special Scientific Interest (ASSIs) in Northern Ireland. Over the last twelve years a comprehensive biological survey has been undertaken by a team of specialists, forming the material for a complete database of knowledge about the flora and fauna on Trust properties and thus the essential information to prepare appropriate management plans for the protection of habitats. The surveys have been carried out on properties as diverse as Brownsea Island in Poole Harbour, Calke Abbey Park in Derbyshire, and the Crom Estate in Co. Fermanagh, Northern Ireland.

It is often assumed that, whereas historic houses and gardens cost money to maintain, the countryside requires no such investment. Countryside management, however, is both vital and demanding of resources. The National Trust currently employs a full time workforce of wardens, foresters and building staff, complemented by many thousands of volunteers. It is also important to remember that approximately forty per cent of Trust land is managed by tenants. Over £23 million is spent annually on its coast and countryside properties. This money comes from a variety of sources: most vital is the contribution, through subscription and donations, of the Trust's own two million members. Other important contributors to essential income are legacies and bequests; the proceeds of fund-raising appeals; income from the Trust's enterprises including shops and catering; grants from public agencies including the Countryside Commission, English Heritage and English Nature; Employment Training Schemes, and, not least from sponsors. British Gas, for example, have generously made possible the publication of this Handbook as part of their £500,000 sponsorship over the next five years for Trust wardens in the countryside. These funds will be used for projects ranging from moorland regeneration in the Peak District and an education centre in Snowdonia, to careership training schemes. The projects will take their place in the Trust's conservation programme: the rehabilitation of lowland heath and chalk downlands, the restoration of dune systems, the repair of footpaths and the recladding of areas of serious erosion. The Trust has always to strike a balance between public access and the preservation of the countryside, otherwise visitors would lose precisely what they had come to enjoy.

And come to enjoy they do. Every year, the National Trust welcomes millions of visitors into its countryside. Wherever you live in England, Wales and Northern Ireland, there is bound to be National Trust countryside within easy access for day visits or for longer holidays. This gazetteer, it is hoped, will provide you with sufficient information and inspiration to get out the map, put on the boots, and discover the delights of what the National Trust has to offer in the countryside.

Angus Stirling

How to use this Handbook

The properties featured in this Handbook are a selection of the most accessible and outstanding areas of National Trust countryside. A brief description of these selected places is given, identifying features of wildlife and historic interest together with practical information on access and facilities. The Handbook has been divided into nine sections: South-West England; Southern England; Wales and the Welsh Borders; London, Thames Valley and Chilterns; Central England; Eastern Counties; North-West England; North-East England; and Northern Ireland. Within these sections the entries are arranged in alphabetical order, giving the county and nearest town or village with brief directions. The location of each property is shown on the maps covering the nine areas.

Location and Map Reference

An Ordnance Survey map reference, measured to the centre of the property, together with a brief location description, are provided for every entry to assist in finding the properties. The boundaries of the majority of Trust properties are shown on OS maps.

Access

Access within the countryside has long depended on traditional routes linking communities together – green lanes, drove roads, bridleways and footpaths. This network of paths is now identified on Ordnance Survey maps as definitive rights of way. When the National Trust acquires a property this includes the statutory rights of access. In many instances the Trust has also established additional routes, usually permitted (where the owner has given consent for the path to be used by the public), to provide greater variety and enhance your visit.

Each entry specifies how accessible the property is, listing foot-paths, bridleways and waymarked paths, access for the disabled and, wherever possible, local stations and bus services. It is worth noting the following points when visiting a property:

* Access is free, as with anyone walking in the countryside, but in some cases there may be a charge for car park facilities or information leaflets.

* On Trust farmland please follow footpaths, whether statutory or permitted, close gates and keep dogs on a lead at all times. Please prevent your dogs from fouling paths, or clear up after them in the interests of other visitors and public hygiene.

* It is important to pay attention to local information; for example, avoid walking on crops, disturbing grazing livestock or ground-nesting birds on moorland.

Parking

At most properties car parking facilities have been specially provided. Some car parks have a car entry charge – the money is used for the upkeep of the property. Where lay-by or roadside parking is permitted, visitors are asked not to obstruct gateways or the main highway.

Facilities

All properties in this Handbook are open throughout the year, although some facilities may be closed during the winter, such as National Trust shops and restaurants. For information about opening times refer to *The National Trust Handbook* which is published annually and issued free to all National Trust members, but is also available from National Trust shops and bookshops (1993 edition, £3.95). Information boards, viewpoints, education facilities and local leaflets are also mentioned, and more information can be obtained from regional offices (see page 299).

For leaflets on bed and breakfast accommodation and camping facilities please send a s.a.e. to the London office. Leaflets are also available at Trust properties. For a brochure of National Trust cottages send a s.a.e. (75p postage) to the Mail Order Customer Services Manager, PO Box 101, Melksham, Wiltshire SN12 8EA.

Disabled visitors

This Handbook identifies those properties where access is available. A special free booklet entitled *Information for Visitors with Disablities* is produced each year and is available by post from the Trust's London office (please send a stamped addressed adhesive label, minimum postage), and from properties, Trust shops and information centres. It is advisable to check details of facilities with the property manager before your visit.

Getting involved

Membership of the National Trust

Membership subscriptions are an increasingly vital source of the National Trust's income. As a member you will contribute to its conservation work and the protection of its gardens, historic buildings and outstanding countryside. Your membership card will give you free entry to most properties in the Trust's care, and each year you will receive the members' Handbook, three colour magazines, a mail order catalogue, the annual report and two regional newsletters. For details of subscription rates and a membership leaflet please contact The National Trust Membership Department, PO Box 39, Bromley, Kent BRI INH (tel. 081–464 IIII in office hours, 9–5 Monday to Friday).

Volunteers

Volunteers provide an important resource for the National Trust: over 10,000 people of all ages and from all walks of life assist each year with the management of the Trust's coast and countryside properties. Voluntary tasks range from the highly skilled or professional to those where energy and an enthusiasm for the National Trust are the most important qualifications. The Trust's developing volunteer programme offers a constructive partnership of volunteers and staff working together to achieve the Trust's aims.

Tasks undertaken by volunteers range from wardening, archaeological and woodland surveys, and conservation work, including scrub, pond or litter clearance, footpath repairs, educational projects or the provision of access for the disabled. Some tasks call for a regular commitment while others require short-term or occasional assistance. There are a growing number of opportunities for long-term volunteers and in some cases, accommodation is provided.

If you are interested in helping the Trust individually or through one of the fifty National Trust volunteer or property-support groups, please contact the Regional Volunteers Co-ordinator at your nearest regional office (see page 299).

The Trust also organises over 400 inexpensive week-long and weekend residential working holidays for all ages from sixteen years. Full details of these are given in a brochure, *National Trust*

Acorn Projects and other Working Holidays. For a copy please send a s.a.e. (34p postage) to The National Trust Volunteer Office, 33 Sheep Street, Cirencester, Gloucestershire GL7 1QW.

The Trust has forty basecamps with hostel-type accommodation, available free of charge for volunteers and outside groups willing to help with conservation projects. Some are available for recreation and education purposes for a commercial charge.

Notes on Wildlife and Archaeology

Wildlife

The wildlife interest of some National Trust properties is overwhelmingly obvious. The clifftop flora along the Cornish coastal paths in May, the huge numbers of breeding seabirds on the Farne Islands in June, heather and gorse on the southern headlands in July, or the wildfowl and waders on the North Norfolk saltmarshes in winter, cannot fail to impress. But in many cases the importance of certain habitats and species for nature conservation is not so obvious. Some are assumed to be widespread because forty years ago they were, but this is no longer the case. Some of our rarest species are small and not very noticeable unless you know where to look. This Handbook will provide a guide to the special nature conservation interests of National Trust properties.

We are fortunate in this country in being able to base our assessments of wildlife interest on a wealth of information. The Nature Conservancy Councils have identified important habitats throughout most counties, and sponsored a National Vegetation Classification, which describes the distribution of over 250 plant communities. Other organisations and individuals have provided distribution Atlases for birds, mammals, most plants and many of the insect groups. We have Red Data Books for birds, vascular plants and insects, listing the rarest and most threatened species and the National Trust's own Biological Survey of its properties is continually updated.

WILDLIFE HABITATS AND THEIR MANAGEMENT

There are three key attributes which determine the nature conservation value of a site, and which must guide management decisions. The first is continuity. The most valuable habitats in this country are ancient. Some woodlands, wooded commons and deer parks have had a cover of native trees and shrubs since the 'wildwood' covered Britain. Many heathlands, grasslands, moorlands and mires have been open habitats, with approximately the same plants present since the wildwood was cleared in the neolithic period or Bronze Age. These ancient habitats are the richest in specialist species, that is species with extracting requirements for their survival which are localised or rare as a result. Some seventy per cent of our flora and fauna falls into this category – only thirty per cent of our wildlife is common.

The second pre-requisite for most habitats of nature conservation value is infertility. Diversity of species will only occur where natural soil infertility prevents a small number of aggressive and competitive species from becoming dominant. Grazing is crucial in helping in the process of suppressing dominant species. Without grazing there would be virtually no species-rich grasslands, heathlands, mires or sand dunes and ultimately, of course, they would all progress into woodland. Lacking the continuity of ancient woods, such secondary woods will never be as rich in species, and not nearly as rare or special as the habitats they replace. Much nature conservation management is about securing grazing regimes which keep habitats open, allow flowering and seeding and are sustainable for farmer or grazier.

Thirdly, lowered water tables are affecting the quality of the countryside and the wildlife value of many habitats in Britain today. The Trust owns many superb rivers, lakes, wet heaths and mires which are becoming too dry for their specialist species to thrive.

Many agricultural soils and water bodies are now too rich in nutrients, polluted or eutrophic. Air pollution, too, is damaging sensitive lichen communities, chalk downlands and heaths, with much the same effect as fertilizer enrichment.

Those using this Handbook will discover many examples of habitat management, some obvious, some less so, carried out by the Trust to safeguard sites of prime wildlife importance. Some of the factors influencing communities, such as grazing and restricting the use of fertilizers, may be under the Trust's control, but others, such as maintaining water levels or an acceptable quantity of water, air or soil, may not. On the coast the Trust has little or no control over what goes on in the sea, in terms of pollution or sea level rise. It is now obvious that sites of nature conservation importance cannot be managed in isolation from the wider environment. The Trust's Environmental Audit is addressing the concerns of agricultural pollution and water quality and conservation among many other subjects, as they affect National Trust property and wildlife. Increasingly, therefore, the Trust has to work with others to protect the environment beyond its boundaries.

Archaeology

Archaeology is the study of the material remains of past human activity, from the time before written records, called prehistory, through later periods when material remains survive together with documentary sources. Visible signs of the historic past mark the rural landscape in familiar forms: in the composition of woods and fields, walls and hedgerows, farms, villages of industrial sites, continuing in use or abandoned long ago. Each historic element contributes to the character and diversity of the British landscape. Archaeology aims both to study and to preserve the historic interest of the countryside.

The extent of the influence of one specific species, man, on the landscape and environment is now so great that it is easy to overlook the very long period of prehistory when a quite different balance existed. Against an evolving physical background and the effects of climate, the human species slowly changed and evolved, developing the range and geographical spread of its activities, and occupying parts of the British Isles over a time span of about half a million years.

Throughout almost all of this time human impact on the landscape was small, but archaeological evidence does survive, showing the ways in which early technology, culture and man's relationship with his environment grew.

Radical changes in the relationship began to occur only about 10,000 years ago, after certain species of plants and animals had begun to be more closely managed by man. For the first time farming communities grew up in various parts of the world, in-

13

cluding Britain and Europe. Forerunners of today's familiar farm-yard animals and crops were among the earliest domesticated species. Other changes in this period of prehistory, from the mesolithic to the Iron Age, involved new technologies, new forms of economy and social organisation, and a growing human population becoming settled on the land.

The result of these developments was a changed landscape. Native forests were progressively cleared or managed; peat began to form in the uplands; and soils were eroded. Lands were occupied, cultivated and abandoned and extensive moorlands and heathlands were developed. From the later neolithic periods, Britain had an inhabited countryside of dwellings, fields, farms, trackways and ritual monuments.

Each later period of history has contributed its own changes, and while much of the past is inevitably lost, it is these fragments of surviving evidence which are so important for study today, and which reveal to the observer the enormous depth of time which the countryside contains.

EVIDENCE OF THE PAST

Archaeological evidence survives in a great variety of forms, as visual elements of landscape, features buried below ground, or in the fabric of buildings or standing structures. Environmental evidence in the form of buried soils, preserved pollen and other organic remains can provide an important source of information on historic land use and settlement. Artefacts reveal apsects of culture, technology and economy and, for prehistory, dating evidence. Scientific techniques can be applied to archaeological deposits to produce further dating information.

Many of the undisturbed landscapes and historic sites protected by the Trust contain such a range of evidence, and it is vital that these areas should remain undisturbed: they hold the key to exciting opportunities for future research.

ARCHAEOLOGY OF THE COUNTRYSIDE

Research and survey provide the means to investigate the full range of evidence, but by simple observation we can see many visible indications of historic activities which have exploited and shaped the countryside.

Most of inland Britain has been altered by land use, with newly created landscapes succeeding the old. In the *lowlands*, the arable and cultivated farmland, woodland, heathlands and grasslands are the product of continuing farming practices which began about 6000 years ago.

In the *uplands*, land use in more recent historic times has been less intense but this has provided good conditions for the preservation of extensive surviving evidence for past settlement and agriculture which was possible during warmer climatic periods in the Bronze Age and later in the medieval period.

Coastlands, *estuaries*, *rivers* and *wetlands* have been much exploited from earliest times, and contain an enormous range of historic sites; however, the overall shape and form of these landscapes has not been altered as much as other habitats, and here the effects of natural forces predominate. Britain's island status and maritime history have nevertheless ensured that farming, fishing, industry and defence have contributed greatly to the settlement and exploitation of the coastal zone, and it is not surpising that the historic character of coastlands is particularly strong.

The essential natural resources, particularly minerals and water as a source of energy, also provide a useful basis for predicting the different kinds of archaeological features which can be found.

Table of Historic Sequence

*c.*500,000BC	PALEOLITHIC	Settlements in camps or caves.
		Hunters and gatherers.
		Intermittent occupation of Britain during inter-glacial periods.
*c.*10,000BC	MESOLITHIC	Post-glacial woodland development.
		Developments in hunting and fishing, herding and some woodland clearance. Separation of Britain from mainland Europe by rising sea levels.
*c.*4,000BC	NEOLITHIC	Permanent settlements and monuments.
		First farmers, woodland clearance, new flint and stone tool industry.
*c.*2,000BC	BRONZE AGE	Defended settlements and intensive upland settlement.
		Organised, farmed and settled landscape.
		Introduction of metal working. Climatic changes.
*c.*700BC	IRON AGE	Rapid growth of defended settlements.
		Diverse regional patterns of agricultural and grazing land.

AD43	ROMAN	New towns and industries; villa estates.
		Military roads and engineering works.
AD450	DARK AGES	Reversion to pre-Roman settlement pattern.
		Anglo–Saxon settlement, regrowth of villages and towns.
AD900	VIKING	Viking raids.
AD1066	NORMAN	Norman invasion.
AD1200	MEDIEVAL	Expansion of towns, increased population, intensified rural industries, growth of enclosures. Uplands again extensively occupied (as in Bronze Age).
AD1540	POST MEDIEVAL	Agricultural and industrial revolution, growth of towns, roads and railways. Decline of rural industries and crafts.

South-West England

CORNWALL · DEVON · DORSET · SOMERSET

The outstanding beauty and historical interest of the south-west peninsula is reflected in its diversity of protected landscapes. One third of 'Heritage Coast' designated in England includes the dramatic cliffs and inlets of the north Cornish and Devon coast, and the limestone cliffs of the Purbeck coastline. Inland the landscape is equally impressive and varied, ranging from the bleak moorland and open expanses of the Exmoor and Dartmoor National Parks to the mellow chalk downland and lowland heaths of Dorset.

The region encompasses eight designated Areas of Outstanding Natural Beauty (AONB). The coastal scenery of the Lizard and Land's End in the Cornish AONB includes spectacular cliffs, sandy coves and beaches, fishing hamlets, oak-fringed estuaries and the ruins of the tin-mining industry so typical of southern Cornwall. There are three main AONBs in Devon's contrasting landscape which include the high cliffs and deep valleys of North Devon, the steep wooded combs of the Heddon Valley to the east and the softer estuarine coastline, notably the Salcombe Estuary, in the south. To the east, on the border with Wiltshire, Cranborne Chase and the Wiltshire Downs embrace a belt of chalk downland stretching across southern England. Further north towards Somerset and Avon, the ridge of the Mendips rises above the Somerset Levels, creating a classic limestone landscape, while to the south of the Levels, the Quantocks – a narrow gently curving twelve-mile ridge – gives a surprising air of wilderness. The heathland and oak woodland to the east is of particular wildlife interest and wild ponies and deer have traditionally roamed this common land.

The landscape we witness today has been moulded by centuries of farming practices, but rapid agricultural improvement has led to the loss of many of these traditional features. Consequently West Penwith, a classic Cornish landscape west of St Ives with its unique pattern of drystone walls and archaeological remains, and the Somerset Levels and moors, a low lying wetland internationally renowned for its bird life and wetland plants, have been designated Environmentally Sensitive Areas (ESA), where farmers are given incentives to maintain a traditional form of agriculture management.

ARLINGTON COURT

2780 acres (1125 ha) 7m NE of Barnstaple, off A39, Devon [180:SS611405]

This is a large and historic estate in the deeply incised and wooded valley of the River Yeo, with views across to Exmoor and north to the coast. The house was built in the nineteenth century and is surrounded by parkland in which pockets of 'wilderness' were created as part of the original design, contrasting with the mature broadleaved woodlands that cover areas of the estate farmland.

There was a medieval deer park here and the woods are ancient semi-natural. As a result the lichen, bryophyte and invertebrate communities are very rich, with many rare species found only in sites associated with the wildwood. The parkland consists of ancient oak, ash and lime trees, which support rare and nationally important lichens and invertebrates. Shetland ponies and Jacob sheep can be seen grazing in the park.

A lake, made at the same time as the house, is an important habitat for an interesting variety of birds such as teal, pochard and tufted duck. Disused and choked leats, relics of a former system of water meadows, can be found near Smallacombe Bridge.

The Trust is controlling the invading rhododendrons in the mature oak woods along the valley sides, where there are numerous wet flushes, rich in mosses, lichens and ferns. Red deer can be seen grazing in the woodland glades. Many plants and butterflies (including marsh and silver-washed fritillaries) can be seen in the grassy pockets and meadows along the edges of the woods. Pied flycatcher, tawny owl, redstart and tree creeper nest among the trees, and dipper and kingfisher feed along the river. There is a large heronry in the woods near the lake.

ACCESS: Grounds open daily during daylight hours; house open seasonally; network of footpaths from house along river valleys; longer walks on west side of river giving views of house; walks to local hamlets, including Loxhore; circular walks; local station at Barnstaple and Barnstaple–Lynmouth bus service.

PARKING: Car park at house.

FACILITIES: NT shop and refreshments; WCs; leaflet; information boards; birdwatchers' hide over lake; limited disabled access.

BEDRUTHAN AND PARK HEAD

282½ acres (114 ha) SW of Padstow, W of B3276, 8m NE of Newquay, Cornwall [200:SW849692 and 845710]

This is a wild, convoluted stretch of coast with dramatic cliffs, isolated rock stacks and secluded coves and beaches. Bronze Age burial mounds, Iron Age headland forts and prehistoric earthworks scattered along the cliffs and on the plateau of Park Head promontory are evidence of previous civilisations that have defended the forbidding coastline. There are also remains of two nineteenth-century iron mines.

At Bedruthan, a steep flight of steps used to be the only descent to the popular beach, but the Trust was forced to close the steps in 1990 because of the danger of falling rock. A coastal path follows the line of the cliff and passes Diggory's Island, a classic example of a sea stack or pinnacle of rock separated from the mainland.

Wildlife includes grey seals in the secluded coves, marine life in rock pools and sea birds breeding on the cliff ledges. Plants growing in the rock crevices and on the maritime grassland include rock samphire, wild thyme, thrift, kidney vetch and the rare Babington leek, a tall and striking leek-like plant. Gorse scrub is important for birds such as linnet, stonechat and yellowhammer. The cliffline is backed by fields bounded by traditional Cornish hedges of small stones and cushions of thrift and stonecrop.

ACCESS: Coastal path along the cliffline (part of the South-West Coast Path).

PARKING: Car parks at Bedruthan and Pentire Farm.

FACILITIES: NT shop (originally the counting house for the local mine) and café at Bedruthan; WCs; leaflet; emergency telephone at top of steps and in Bedruthan car park.

BOSCASTLE HARBOUR AND THE VALENCY VALLEY

300 acres (121 ha) 3½m NE of Tintagel, on B3263 Bude road, Cornwall
[190:SX0990 to 1191]

Boscastle's position at the end of a sheltered, sinuous channel, one of the few natural inlets in a tortuous stretch of coastline, led to its development as a port serving this remote part of Cornwall. Several of the buildings are owned by the Trust, and it is an area of historic and ecological importance. Beyond the outer breakwater a blow hole throws a plume of spray across the harbour entrance from beneath Penally Point. Iron Age earthworks are visible across the neck of the promontory at Willapark, and there is a nineteenth-century whitewashed look-out tower on its summit.

A path follows the steep, wooded Valency Valley to the church of St Juliot, noted for its Victorian restoration with the young Thomas Hardy as architect. Peter's Wood to the south of Newmills, now leased by the Cornwall Trust for Nature Conservation, has some interesting ferns and invertebrates under a dense coppiced oak canopy and is an important feeding area for bats.

To the north of the village stand the cliffs of Pentargon, with coastal grassland and heath, and nesting razorbill, guillemot and fulmar. To the south, on Forrabury Common, can be seen surviving medieval strip fields, still in use, with forty-two curving plots or stitches. Traditionally, tenants may crop the stitches individually from Lady Day (25 March) to Michaelmas (29 September), with grazing permitted from 1 November to 28 February. The banks or baulks between the strips support many species of wild flowers.

Grey seal breed in the sheltered caves along the coast, and there are other important areas of coastal grassland and heath.

ACCESS: Cliff and valley walks; coastal path leads up from village to headlands; South-West Coast Path.

PARKING: Car parks at Boscastle.

FACILITIES: NT shop and information; WCs; leaflets; guidebooks; guided walks; viewpoints.

BRANSCOMBE, SALCOMBE REGIS AND SIDMOUTH

835 acres (338 ha) S of A3052, 3m E of Sidmouth, Devon
[192:SY2188 and 1588]

Lying within a stretch of Heritage Coast, this area of flat-topped hills, deep-cut valleys leading to the sea, copses and hedges, shingle beaches and thatched buildings is one of the most spectacular parts of the east Devon landscape. On the high ground are pockets of scrub and heath behind cliffs which are unstable and liable to landslip.

The undercliff system, dry calcareous grassland slopes, deep combe sides and marshland pockets are of immense nature conservation importance. A number of rare flowers grow, including Nottingham catchfly, several orchids and a local abundance of blue gromwell. Three species of violet-feeding fritillary butterfly occur, and colonies of the scarce wood white occupy the combe bottoms and adjoining undercliff slopes. A number of extremely rare mining bees occur, making Branscombe a top national site for these insects. The bands of woodland add further diversity, offering a delightful spring ground flora and habitat for numerous small birds. Buzzard soar overhead.

The landscape also contains evidence of past industries, including lime kilns and pits, potato-growing and milling, particularly in Branscombe village where there is an old smithy, baking-room (now a museum) and a gypsum mill (now a café) where traces of a wheel–pit are still visible. The stone quarries at Beer date back to Roman times.

Over the cliff tops towards Sidmouth, Weston Cliff falls away to Weston Mouth, a secluded wooded combe. Salcombe Hill to the east and Peak Hill to the west of Sidmouth are also protected by the Trust. There is a prehistoric enclosure at Berry Cliffs.

ACCESS: South Devon Coastal Path linking all Trust properties; connecting paths inland.

PARKING: Car parks at Peak Hill, Salcombe Hill, Weston Mouth, Branscombe Mouth and in Branscombe village.

FACILITIES: NT shop in Sidmouth; leaflet and information panels at Branscombe, Weston Mouth, Salcombe Hill and Peak Hill; information centre at Branscombe Bakery.

BREAN DOWN

159 acres (64 ha) 2m SW of Weston-super-Mare, S of Weston Bay, via Branscombe village, Somerset   [182:ST2959]

This dramatic headland of hard limestone is joined to the mainland by a narrow neck of low-lying marsh, one of the main landmarks of the Bristol Channel. At one time it was suggested as the point for the proposed Severn Barrage.

The peninsula (designated an SSSI and an SAM) has been used as a site of settlement, ritual and defence for thousands of years. Sites include Bronze Age barrows, Bronze and Iron Age settlements and field systems, an Iron Age promontory fort and a Roman temple. There are also some medieval 'pillow' mounds. The tip of the promontory is dominated by a fort built in 1867 as part of the Bristol Channel defences, and there are also some twentieth-century gun emplacements.

The continual process of erosion in the sand cliff adjoining the beach is endangering the Bronze Age and early Christian remains, and blocks have been placed along the beach in an effort to contain the problem. The sand cliff has also revealed evidence of mammals dating from the Ice Age.

The narrow promontory is also of great geological and ornithological interest, and is used as a landing-stage (together with nearby Sand Point) for migrant birds. Oystercatcher and dunlin can be seen along the foreshore and estuary, and the scrub is important for migrant birds such as thrush, redstart, brambling, redpoll and reed bunting. Resident populations include dunnock, robin, whitethroat and linnet. The south-facing slope is particularly attractive to butterflies, such as chalkhill blue and dark-green fritillary.

Exposure to wind, rain and salt spray, and the shallow soil, have strongly influenced plant communities. A number of scarce plants occur, often in unusual juxtaposition. Sea lavender and rock samphire grow in the more saline areas. The open grassland supports rare plants such as white rockrose and Somerset hairgrass (which is unique to the Mendip area), as well as more typical calcareous grassland species. Unusual lichens occur on the foreshore rocks.

ACCESS: 2 footpaths with steep steps.

PARKING: Car park at Tropical Bird Garden.

FACILITIES: Information boards at steps and gate; statutory bird protection notice.

BROWNSEA ISLAND

500 acres (202 ha) 1½m SE of Poole, in Poole Harbour, Dorset
[195:SZ0288]

Although located within one of the largest natural harbours in the world, Brownsea Island is far removed from the commercialism of the boating marinas and maritime traffic. Its charm lies in the great diversity of its wildlife and its unusual historical remains.

Expanses of heath are relics of the extensive heathland once widespread across the county, and provide a habitat for heathland specialists such as silver-studded butterfly, Dartford warbler and sand lizard.

The woodland, which now covers parts of the island, is managed as a nature reserve by the Dorset Trust for Nature Conservation and is a mixture of pine (where red squirrel can be seen) and deciduous trees.

The island's heronry is one of the largest in Britain, and many other waders and sea birds are attracted to the lagoon, with greater and lesser black-backed gulls, herring gull, shelduck, curlew, oyster-catcher, dunlin, greenshank, bar-tailed and black-tailed godwits, common and spotted redshanks, avocet, wigeon, teal and pintail. Sandwich and common terns use the small gravel islets specially created for their breeding, and the reed beds and alder carr attract many small birds, including reed and sedge warblers.

Among the historical sites are Branksea Castle, with the remains of a Tudor blockhouse, built in the reign of Henry VIII for the defence of Poole, and some old pottery, brick and tile works.

ACCESS: By boat from Poole Quay and Sandbanks; private boats may land at Pottery Pier, at the west end of the island; seasonal access to nature reserve; station at Poole and foot ferry from Sandbanks to Poole.

PARKING: Car parks in Poole.

FACILITIES: NT shop; restaurant; WCs; leaflet; contact Dorset Trust for Nature Conservation about guided walks; public birdwatchers' hide with views over lagoons; wheelchair access around quay (paths hilly and rough); no accommodation; no dogs.

BUCKLAND

287 acres (116 ha) 6m S of Tavistock, 11m N of Plymouth, Devon
[201:SX487667]

Set within the tranquil valley of the River Tavy, Buckland Abbey has a rich 700-year history dating back to its establishment as a Cistercian monastery in the thirteenth century. In the sixteenth century it was converted to a country house for the Grenville and, later, the Drake families; on display are the period rooms and exhibitions on monastic life, Sir Francis Drake and the development of the estate. There is also a massive barn and other medieval buildings and craft workshops in the ox sheds.

The Abbey stands on the eastern side of an extensively wooded valley, with the ecologically important Fishacre Woods (under the management of the Forestry Commission) stretching for two miles along the western side of the Tavy. In the woodlands of sessile oak the damp conditions are ideal for rare mosses, lichens, liverworts and ferns, with other ground plants such as the great woodrush, bilberry, bluebell, yellow archangel, sweet woodruff and wood anemone flourishing under the dense canopy. The dead wood provides a habitat for many beetles, snails, woodlice and other invertebrates.

Flowers thrive along the side of the streams where there is more light, and the alder carr and marshlands along the alluvial flats are rich in wetland plants, with marsh violet, flag iris, valerian, meadowsweet, sedges and grasses. Butterflies, such as silver-washed and pearl-bordered fritillaries and purple hairstreak, flourish in the glades and along the woodland edges. Buzzard are often seen circling overhead, and blackcap, chiff-chaff, willow warbler and wren are some of the many birds nesting in the woodlands.

ACCESS: Abbey open seasonally and at weekends during winter; walks and circular paths on the estate; Forestry Commission paths through Fishacre Woods (not directly accessible from NT property); site steep and difficult for disabled; local station at Bere Alston and bus service from Yelverton.

PARKING: Car park at the Abbey; special car park for disabled.

FACILITIES: NT shop, restaurant and tea-room; WCs (including disabled); working craft workshops; scented herb garden; audio-visual introduction; education centre; museum with period display rooms; motorised buggy (sometimes) and wheelchairs (for lower floors of house only) available; Braille guide and special leaflet with disabled facilities available on request.

BUDE TO MORWENSTOW

1096 acres (443½ ha) off A39(T), Cornwall [190:SS205153 and 202085]

The Trust owns three tracts of this dramatic west-facing Cornish coast near the Devon border. Here Celtic Cornwall merges with

Saxon England, with small fields bounded by earth banks, old farm-steads, hamlets and isolated churches. Between Henna Point and Higher Sharpnose near Morwenstow the contorted rocks (the cause of several wrecked vessels) form a ragged, uncultivated cliffline of maritime grassland, gorse, heath and woodland, with thrift and other cliff plants clinging to the ledges.

To the south Sandy Mouth, Duckpool and Maer Cliff surround beaches and a boulder-strewn shore with access along narrow lanes. Inland, wild herbs on sheltered grassy slopes and yellow flag grow-ing in damper locations attract a variety of butterflies, including blues, gatekeeper and speckled wood. The heathlands are of par-ticular ecological interest, supporting many insects, and the wood-land of the Tidna Valley is renowned for its unusual lichens. Other places of interest include Hawker's Hut where Parson Hawker, a well-known local figure in the nineteenth century, meditated and wrote his poetry; and St John's Well at Morwenstow.

ACCESS: Difficult to get to by road; narrow lanes; coastal path.

PARKING: Car parks at Sandy Mouth, Northcott Mouth, Steeple Point, Morwenstow and Crooklets Beach.

FACILITIES: Seasonal refreshments at Sandy Mouth and Morwen-stow; WCs at Crooklets Beach, Sandy Mouth and Steeple Point car parks; disabled WCs at Crooklets Beach and Sandy Mouth; view-point at Steeple Point; leaflet.

CASTLE DROGO
AND TEIGN VALLEY WOODS

611 acres (247 ha) at Drewsteignton, 4m NE of Chagford, 4m S of A30 (signposted from A30 at Cheriton Bishop turning and off A382 from Sandy Park); Teign Valley Woods 8m W of Exeter, 3m NE of Moretonhampstead, both sides of B3212, Devon
[191:SX721900 and 199:SX795885]

This imposing granite 'fortress' was designed by the architect Edwin Lutyens at the beginning of this century. It overlooks the wooded gorge of the River Teign, which flows down from the granite mas-sif of Dartmoor National Park.

Riverside, hilltop and woodland paths lead from the estate. The hunter's path, following the north side of the Teign, passes through heathland and overlooks the gorge and the Iron Age hill forts of Prestonbury and Cranbrook castles (not owned by the Trust). Nearby Fingle Bridge was the site of skirmishes during the Civil War. On the heath, ivy-leaved bellflower and flax-leaved St John's wort can be found, as well as stonechat and grayling butterfly. The Trust has recently introduced pony grazing to help counter the development of scrub and to conserve the important heathland. Riverside wet flushes are rich in sedges, *Sphagnum* moss, marsh pennywort and tormentil.

To the south of the river, Whiddon Park House is surrounded by farmland, ancient oak woodlands (once coppiced for tanning bark and wood for local industries such as charcoal) and an old deer park, where the remains of a nine-foot high granite surrounding wall dating from the sixteenth century, earlier drystone walls and a seventeenth-century deer-culling hut can still be seen. The parkland consists of ancient oak, ash and beech trees set in open bracken and wet grasslands. The woodlands are rich in wildlife and the mature trees within the park support nationally rare communities of lichen and moss.

There are good views across the valley from the outcrops of rock breaking through the dense oak canopy, and many plants typical of these ancient woodlands are found, including greater woodrush, wood sorrel, wood anemone and primrose, with impressive displays of wild daffodil and bluebell in the spring. Warbler, tree creeper, pied flycatcher, nuthatch, redstart and tawny owl nest in the woods, and green woodpecker can be seen often eating the wood ants which make movable nests out of piles of twigs and leaves. Dipper and kingfisher frequent the river, and raven nest on the crags of Sharp Tor. Buzzard soar above the valley.

ACCESS: Castle open seasonally; paths from Castle Drogo; circular walks starting from Fingle Bridge along or above river valley; other paths to the west; local station at Yeoford and bus service from Exeter.

PARKING: Car parks at Castle Drogo, Drewsteignton village and Fingle Bridge, Steps Bridge and south entrance to Meadhaydown Woodland on Dunsford and Drewsteignton road.

FACILITIES: NT shop and refreshments at Castle Drogo; WCS (including disabled) at Castle Drogo, also at Drewsteignton and Fingle Bridge; leaflet; Dartmoor National Park information centre; viewpoint; fishing by permit only (details from regional office or at Castle Drogo).

THE CHEDDAR CLIFFS

375 acres (152 ha) 8m NW of Wells, on B3135, Somerset [182:ST468543]

Much of the land around one of Britain's most spectacular and popular sights is managed by the Trust for its superb nature conservation interest. The dramatic limestone gorge, famous for its potholes and caves, has evidence of palaeolithic and neolithic occupation. The road winds down between high vertical cliffs, with outstanding views from the top (on a clear day) of the Somerset Levels, the Quantock Hills and across the Bristol Channel to Wales.

The cliffs and scree slopes have recently undergone an extensive rock-safety and scrub-clearance programme, grant-aided by English Nature, to conserve the complex mosaic of open habitats so beneficial to the geological, entomological and botanical interest of this SSSI. Specialist plants found here include the famous Cheddar pink (also found in south-east France but nowhere else in Britain), three endemic hawkweeds, and good populations of green-winged orchid and autumn lady's tresses. Also present are butterfly rarities such as green hairstreak and marbled white.

The grass and woodland of Black Rock and Black Rock Drove are leased to the Somerset Trust for Nature Conservation which manages them as nature reserves. A circular walk from the B3135 road at Black Rock Gate passes through plantations, natural woodland and rough downland.

ACCESS: Footpath from Black Rock car park to permitted path along top of property down to Cufick Lane; station at Worle (about 10m away).

PARKING: Car parks at Cheddar end of gorge; small car park at Black Rock.

FACILITIES: Local facilities and information at Cheddar.

THE CORFE CASTLE ESTATE

7294 acres (2952 ha) 5m NW of Swanage, 4m SE of Wareham on A351,
Dorset [195:SY959824]

Commanding a prominent position in the Purbeck Hills, this ruined castle is one of the most important historical sites in Trust ownership. The ruins date from the time of the Norman Conquest to the fourteenth century, and the property is known to have been a royal fortified site since the days of the Anglo-Saxon times. It was destroyed in the Civil War after a dramatic siege and spirited defence by Lady Mary Bankes, widow of Charles I's Attorney-General. Much of the stone was used to build houses in the village, but the ruin remains one of the most spectacular in the country, particularly when viewed from a distance.

The extensive estate encompasses a section of the Dorset coast line from Poole Harbour, through Studland Bay, Old Harry Rocks, Ballard Down, Belle Vue and the Seacombe Valley.

This part of the country, known as the Isle of Purbeck, is interesting for its geological variation and for its landscape, which has changed little since it was used as a setting for the novels of Thomas Hardy. The famous Purbeck stone is quarried here and has been used for centuries in local buildings, including the castle itself.

Around the castle lie areas of damp grassland, fen and mire of particular importance for insects and plants such as various sedges, southern marsh orchid and meadow thistle. The mound itself also has some interesting flora, including the bee orchid, and holds a famous colony of the Lulworth skipper, a butterfly virtually restricted to Purbeck.

Studland and Godlington heaths, partly managed as a National Nature Reserve, are extensive tracts of lowland heath, remnants of a habitat that fifty years ago covered a large part of the southern shores of Poole Harbour. Heathland destruction has been so horrendous that the surviving habitat is now a vitally important reserve for rare and endangered heathland specialists, including all six British reptiles, hobby, Dartford warbler and a whole host of Red Data Book insects.

Many habitats, unique to the coast, are found on the cliffline around the Isle of Purbeck, with associated plants such as thrift, kidney vetch, samphire and campion. Clifftop birds include peregrine, puffin, cormorant and buzzard. Studland 'peninsula', overlooking Poole Harbour, is made up of dunes, heath, saltmarsh and a lagoon with some important plants, insects and overwintering birds. The upper marsh areas and meadows include royal fern, sundews and meadow thistle. Ailwood Down and Old Harry, south of Studland, have some oak, ash and hazel woodlands (possibly of ancient origin).

Around the peninsula and inland, the chalk and calcareous grasslands on Ballard Down, Ailwood Down, Belle Vue and the Seacombe Valley are rich in orchids, moths and butterflies, including adonis and chalkhill blues; and Middlebere Heath and Hartland Moor (also a National Nature Reserve) to the north-west of Corfe include some important lowland heaths. North-west of Studland village some old ball-clay ponds now provide a wetland and fen habitat attracting many insects, including scarce dragonflies. There are also some ancient field enclosures, prehistoric field patterns and sites such as Nine Barrow Down, a Bronze Age cemetery.

ACCESS: Castle open seasonally; network of footpaths; long-distance coastal path; local station at Wareham and Poole–Swanage bus service.

PARKING: Car and coach park in West Street, Corfe (not NT).

FACILITIES: NT shop and restaurant; guidebooks; dogs allowed on leads.

COTEHELE

1289 acres (522 ha) on W bank of the Tamar, 2m W of Calstock, by footpath, 9m SW of Tavistock, Cornwall   [201:SX422685]

Among the wooded fringes of the River Tamar stands one of the best preserved medieval houses in the country, surrounded by an estate which has substantial remains of a former working landscape centred on a riverside quay. Now renovated by the Trust, with small tea-rooms, a maritime museum and the restored Tamar sailing barge, *Shamrock*, the quay has witnessed the passage of barges carrying various cargoes, from soft fruit grown on the rolling sheltered slopes of the river valley during the late nineteenth century to copper and arsenic from inland mines, and limestone brought in to supply the local lime kilns. Several of these kilns can still be seen near the quayside, and were once an important part of an intensively industrial scene.

Also near the quay are an eighteenth-century mill, wheelwright's and carpenter's shops, a cider press (the old orchard is still visible), a forge, saw pit and old mine workings in the Danescombe Valley, all of which bear witness to what was once a self-contained community housed in small hamlets nearby, such as the small village of Bohetherick which has good examples of vernacular buildings.

Some important wildlife habitats are to be found in this exceptionally mild part of the country. Damp and shaded oak woodlands are of interest, with some areas thought to be ancient woods, and harbouring a rich variety of plants, mosses, insects and lichens. Sparrowhawk, barn owl and lesser spotted woodpecker can be seen. The brackish marsh along Morden Mill stream supports an unusual combination of freshwater and coastal plants, with associated birds sheltering in the reed beds. The thick hedge banks along the old lanes are lined with wild flowers attracting butterflies and birds.

ACCESS: House and mill open seasonally; garden open all year; walks throughout the estate; local station at Calstock.

PARKING: Car parks at quay and house.

FACILITIES: NT shop at house (no shops on Quay); refreshments (seasonal) in the Barn on Quay; WCS (including disabled); limited facilities for disabled (only Quay and part of gardens level enough for wheelchairs).

CRACKINGTON HAVEN

814 acres (329 ha), 6m NE of Boscastle, 8m SW of Bude, Cornwall
[190:SX142968]

On either side of the tiny port of Crackington Haven is a distorted cliffline of fractured rocks (the cause of several shipwrecks) with spectacular fissures, landslips, caves and arches, and geologically important contorted folding visible in the cliff faces.

To the north, Dizzard Point is of note for its wind-clipped thicket of twisted sessile oaks, wild service and holly trees, which struggle to reach a height of twenty feet. They support an interesting variety of lichens and mosses. There are many areas of coastal grassland and heath all along the cliffs and undercliffs, which must provide some of the best examples of natural vegetation, unmodified by man, in the South West.

The outline of an Iron Age castle can be detected at Castle Point, and there is much of prehistoric interest in the area, with earthworks and barrows, as well as signs of medieval strip field systems, particularly near St Genny's Church.

The headland of Cambeak projects west from Tremoutha Haven and commands outstanding views along the coast beyond the natural rock archway of Northern Door. Behind the coastline, small hamlets and farms are scattered around the valleys. Trevigue Farm is an example of a building style typical to north Cornwall, with its large locally quarried random slates. Penkenna and Castle Point are dominated by heath, with wind-blown shrubs of heather and bell heather attracting linnet, whitethroat and stonechat.

ACCESS: Via small roads (crowded in peak season); footpaths along cliffline.

PARKING: Car parks at Trevigue, High Cliff and Rusey Cliff (very limited), and Crackington Haven.

FACILITIES: Seasonal refreshments at Trevigue Farm; WCs at Crackington Haven; leaflet; viewpoints.

CRANTOCK BEACH TO HOLYWELL BAY

1138 acres (460½ ha) SW of Newquay, W of Crantock, Cornwall
[200:TW790610, SW7961 and 7760]

Sandy beaches, headlands with deep inlets and collapsed caves, common land, stream valleys, broad expanses of dunes and the tidal estuary of the Gannel make up this varied and more sheltered stretch of Cornish coast, which is steeped in historic associations and curiosities. The Gannel lies between the headlands of Pentire East and West Points, where sailing vessels used to travel up the inlet with cargoes of limestone and coal. Notable populations of waders and wildfowl can be seen on the saltings and mudflats of the Gannel, part of a complex estuarine and dune habitat; over 700 curlew overwinter here, along with other species such as oystercatcher, lapwing, ringed and golden plovers, turnstone, bar-tailed godwit, redshank, dunlin and heron.

The sand dunes rise to the plateau of Rushy Green, an area of sandy grassland rich in lime-loving plants. Kelsey Head, where the low bank and shallow ditch of a cliff castle can be seen, is backed by a series of historic field boundaries known as the Outer, Middle and Inner Kelseys. Fulmar, shag, herring gull and kittiwake nest along the cliffs of Kelsey Head, an important site for the passage of birds, and many auks, including razorbill and puffin, can be seen just offshore on Carter's Rocks (not owned by the Trust). Fulmar nest on the Chick, off Kelsey Head, and grey seal are found along the coast.

Porth Joke is a beautiful, secluded beach, isolated from the intrusion of cars, and small fields in the Porth Joke valley support a rich variety of flowers and grasses. A walk follows the stream to Treago Mill. The fragile and unstable dune system (the largest within the Trust's Cornish holdings) behind the broad expanse of Holywell Bay is colonised by plants such as sea holly, sea bindweed and henbane, and between the more stable dunes a rich grassland supports many flowers such as thyme, eyebright, cowslip, hairy violet and pyramidal orchid, with butterflies, including the uncommon dark-green fritillary.

Cubert Common is an undulating stretch of sandy grassland which contains lime-loving plants such as cowslip. There is a fine Bronze Age barrow on the southern side of the common.

ACCESS: The Gannel can be reached from road S of Newquay; free access to beach at Crantock; Holywell coastal paths and boardwalks; no right of way from Trevemper to Penpol Creek on S shore of the Gannel, but footpath through Treringey to head of the creek.

PARKING: Car parks at Crantock, Cubert Common, Treago Mill, Holywell and West Pentire.

FACILITIES: Seasonal refreshments at Crantock; WCs; leaflet; viewpoint from Kelsey Head.

NOTE: The Gannel may be crossed at low tide by both tidal bridges between end May and mid-September, in winter by Trethellan Bridge only; crossing at high tide only by rounding from Trevemper; wading is not recommended; bathing is unsafe at the Gannel end of Crantock Beach.

THE DODMAN AND NARE HEAD

518 acres (210 ha) 10m SW of St Austell and 4m S of Megavissey, Cornwall [204:SX916370 and SX0039]

These two prominent headlands between the Lizard and Fowey can be explored on spectacular circular walks with dramatic views of coves, beaches, rock archways and crumbling cliffs covered with relic heath, coastal grassland and scrub. Small marshes and reed beds in the valleys are the habitat of damp-loving plants such as meadowsweet, yellow flag and sedges, and there are a few areas of unimproved grasslands in enclosures with magnificent stone-faced hedgebanks.

Covered with archaeological remains, this unspoilt coastline has a great feeling of history. On Dodman Point a massive earthwork defines an Iron Age cliff castle, and within the enclosure can be seen traces of a medieval strip field system. There are also Bronze Age barrows, a stone cross and an eighteenth-century watch house. Walks radiate from the hamlet of Penare to the Dodman, Hemmick Beach, Vault Beach and Maenease Point.

To the west of Nare Head, Pendower Beach merges with Carne Beach, and the irregular pattern of fields, bounded by traditional Cornish stone walls, extends to the cliff edge. The valley behind Pendower Beach is wooded and can be explored on a sheltered walk. The Trust has worked closely with local tenant farmers to ensure that the modern farming methods on Nare Head do not intrude on this beautiful part of the country.

Near Nare Head can also be found Veryan Castle on the side of a steep valley, an Iron Age settlement on an oval platform cut into the hillside, and Carne Beacon, a Bronze Age barrow. Gull Rock, to the south-east, was the film set for *Treasure Island* in the 1950s, and is now a sanctuary for nesting sea birds, including guillemot, cormorant and shag. Kiberick Cove is backed by landslips, including Slip Field, thought to have slipped as recently as the last century.

ACCESS: Nare Head accessible from both sides; network of circular paths at Nare Head and Dodman Point.

PARKING: Car parks at Nare Head, Carne Beach and Pendower Beach, Penare and Lamledra.

FACILITIES: Leaflet; viewpoint path with access for wheelchairs at Nare Head; beaches suitable for families (no steep slopes except at Kiberick and Paradoe coves).

DUNSLAND

62 acres (25 ha) 4½m E of Holsworthy, 9m W of Hatherleigh to N of A3072, Devon   [190:SS409051]

Dunsland is a pre-Norman manor, with a remarkable survival of ancient woodland and pasture, and an interesting ecological system associated with the wildwood. The Tudor house, altered and enlarged in the seventeenth century, was tragically destroyed by fire in 1967 after extensive restoration work by the Trust, but the park still carries the historic interest of the site, one of the best in England for lichens of the Lobarion community.

Outhouses remain, including a granary, stables and a generator shed. Cadiho Well, a spring covered by a well-head, is where the first Cadiho, the Norman owner of the house, reputedly killed the previous Anglo-Saxon incumbent. There are some overgrown and disused fishtanks (possibly medieval) which now provide a valuable habitat for wildlife.

The present park landscape was planted in 1795, and includes an area of flower-rich grassland, and a pocket of tall plants where the dominant meadowsweet supports a varied population of invertebrates, including damselflies and dragonflies. In the woods, the ancient oak, ash, beech, aspen and willow trees are encrusted with lichens, with many rare species. Broadleaved helleborine can be found in the valley woodlands. Ponds, where willow carr is beginning to be established around the margins, provide a valuable habitat for newts and many invertebrates including springtail.

ACCESS: Footpaths.

PARKING: Car park and informal parking.

FACILITIES: Local facilities.

FONTMELL AND MELBURY DOWNS

730 acres (295 ha) 6m S of Shaftesbury, between Shaftesbury and Blandford, Dorset [183:ST884184]

This estate covers an important stretch of ancient chalk downland within the Cranborne and West Wiltshire AONB. The downs, which include Fontmell Down, Melbury Beacon and Melbury Down, are cut by steep-sided valley coombes, and the surrounding hamlets have witnessed little change in the land-use pattern over the years. Sheep-grazing continues the traditions of local farming, with cattle in some areas. There is much of historical interest, notably two Iron Age cross-ridge dykes, Celtic field systems, medieval strip lynchets and a Saxon trackway. On Melbury Down is a Bronze Age barrow and an Armada beacon.

Fontmell Down, with its magnificent views over the Blackmore Vale and Cranborne Chase, was bought by the Trust to commemorate the evocative landscapes of Thomas Hardy. It is now leased to the Dorset Trust for Nature Conservation. All three downs are of great importance for their butterfly populations.

A great diversity of chalk-loving grasses and flowers reflects the downs' long standing as an area of unploughed and largely unimproved grassland, and species include cowslip, milkwort, stemless thistle, clustered bellflower, horseshoe vetch, bastard toadflax, squinancywort and quaking grass. The wide range of butterflies feeding on the grassland plants includes chalkhill and adonis blues, silver-spotted skipper, Duke of Burgundy and dark-green fritillary.

In places, scrub is invading the downland, with blackthorn and wayfaring trees smothered in wild clematis (old man's beard), attracting many birds. Over fifty-five species have been recorded, including nightingale, grasshopper warbler, sparrowhawk, kestrel, buzzard and hen harrier. The hedgerows are lined with wild arum, primrose, cow parsley, yellow archangel and herb robert.

37

ACCESS: Path and access for disabled from car park.

PARKING: Small car park at Spread Eagle Hill on B3081.

FACILITIES: Facilities at nearby Compton Abbas Airfield; information panels in car park.

FOWEY AND LANTIC BAY TO SHARROW POINT

374 acres (151 ha) surrounding village of Fowey (accessible from both sides of estuary) and from mouth of River Fowey to Looe, Cornwall
[200:SX127545 and 140510, and 201:SW390525]

The Trust owns a number of properties around the historic harbour of Fowey and along the coast to Sharrow Point. On and around the secluded Fowey Estuary they include Gribbin Head, Pont Pill, St Saviour's Point at Polruan, St Catherine's Point which is crowned with a castle (under the guardianship of English Heritage), Coombe, a coastal farm west of St Catherine's Point, and Station Wood. A recent Enterprise Neptune appeal for Townsend Farm has helped to save the valuable landscape by effectively containing the town of Polruan, which was in danger of engulfing this beautiful estuary. Behind St Catherine's Castle is Covington Wood, a hanging wood with many ferns, mosses and liverworts.

This busy commercial harbour includes a mosaic of estuarine and coastal habitats, with scrubby woodlands of oak, ash and hazel growing in old field sites fringing the estuaries, small areas of un-improved grassland, and in places a narrow fringe of herb-rich maritime grassland on the cliffs where thrift, sea campion and ox-eye daisy thrive. Traveller's joy is a distinctive plant of the wood-land edge. Along the secluded shores heron, redshank, oystercatcher and occasional kingfisher can be seen.

This is a quiet and gentler coastline of scattered hamlets, sheltered sandy coves and both high and low cliffs which provide a home for raven, peregrine, kestrel and jackdaw. Pencarrow Head separates Lantic and Lantivet bays, and commands impressive views of the coast. Inland, behind a tiny cove on Lantivet Bay, the isolated hamlet of Lansallos nestles above a wooded coombe. Lanes and paths connect the scattered communities, and the cliffs at Polperro conceal the well-known fishing village, adorned with colourful gardens. Stories of smugglers and maritime tales add to the rich history of this coastal landscape. From Polperro, Downend Point and Hore Point enclose Talland Bay, which is the site of one set of large black and white panels used by the Royal Navy to mark out the length of a nautical mile. Other sites of interest are the isolated Lanteglos Church and Tregantle Fort (not owned by the Trust), which is still in use and is one of a number of nineteenth-century forts in the area. Firing ranges operate on the cliffs nearby.

The cliffs in the Pencarrow Head area have a characteristic bevelled profile. Except on the Head itself, they have not been grazed for many years, so that much of the cliff-slope vegetation is dense bracken, blackthorn scrub and even incipient sycamore woodland. Since these cliffs are more sheltered than those on the north coast, maritime vegetation associated with salt spray and wind is found only along the very edge of the coast. There are some interesting features, however. Sand and shingle beaches, including some fine examples of storm beaches, have local plants such as sea holly, sea bindweed and sea kale. Brackish pools on the wave-cut platform at the foot of the cliffs are also of interest.

Grasslands in the fields above the cliffs have a rich flora which includes wild thyme, pale flax and centaury. The striking tree mallow, a Cornish speciality, grows in rough or waste ground along the coast.

Sunken lanes and paths to the beaches were once used by pack horses carrying sand and seaweed up to the fields. Not only was grazing once much more extensive, but so was cultivation: old bulb fields occur at Polperro, now filled with scrub.

ACCESS: Via small roads; footpath along Pont Pill and at Coombe Haven; Hall Walk opposite Fowey; steep climb down to Lantic Bay; access to Polperro cliffs difficult (narrow path); network of paths linked to coastal path and inland.

PARKING: Car parks at Coombe, Fowey, Pencarrow Head, Lansallos, Sharrow Point, Hore Point, Talland Bay and Polperro.

FACILITIES: Local facilities at Fowey, Polperro and Polruan; leaflets; 3 viewpoints at Lantic Bay, also at Nealand Point, Downend Point and Hore Point.

GLASTONBURY TOR

66 acres (27 ha) SE of Glastonbury, off A361, Somerset
[182 and 183:ST512386]

Renowned for its ecclesiastical, secular and legendary associations, the unmistakable profile of Glastonbury Tor is a dominant feature in the landscape with splendid views over the Somerset Levels, once a wide area of lake and marshland surrounding the tor. The conical hill, made up of horizontal layers of rock, has been a defensive strong-hold throughout history. Built on the site of at least two former places of worship, the fifteenth-century St Michael's Tower on the summit, scheduled as an SAM has now been restored.

On the slopes of the tor, the terraces are the strip lynchets or cultivation terraces of medieval farming (there are fields on the east side of the tor still called Lynches).

The grassland on the slopes has suffered from the effects of erosion caused by the number of visitors, but wild thyme grows in places. Hedgerows, trees and small orchards create cover for a variety of birds.

ACCESS: By foot only from SW and NE.

PARKING: Limited parking at top and bottom of Wellhouse Lane.

FACILITIES: Interpretation panels at both access points; leaflet.

GODREVY TO PORTREATH

751 acres (304 ha) N of B3301, Cornwall   [203:SW6043]

The Trust owns most of the coastline from Godrevy Head round to Navax Point, east of St Ives Bay, and along the cliffline of Hudder and Reskajeage downs to Western Hill, west of Portreath Beach. The cliffs are high and sheer, and their tops support gorse, and some of the best maritime heath in the country, indeed in Europe, with heather, bell heather, western gorse, yellow rattle, sheep's bit, golden rod, devil's bit scabious, betony, dyer's greenweed and the unusual pale dog violet, with many other species. Royal fern, primrose, bluebell and sea spleenwort grow in the cliff gullies and on the rocks. Guillemot, razorbill, fulmar, cormorant and shag breed on the cliffs. The area is rich in wild flowers, and interesting species also occur along old hedgebanks.

The sand dunes at Gwithian, a place popular with surfers, are known as 'towans', and have preserved a string of archaeological remains of settlements from the Mesolithic era onwards. The more stable dunes, despite excessive pressure from holiday-makers, support a great range of maritime plants such as blue fleabane, sea fern grass, sand cat's tail and field madder.

Behind the coast is the country park of Tehidy Woods, which is managed by the County Council. Other points of interest are an Iron Age cliff castle and localised quarries. Godrevy Lighthouse (not owned by the Trust) was the inspiration for Virginia Woolf's novel *To the Lighthouse*. The local names spell out the curious maritime history of the area, and the traditional stone walls, gateposts, stiles and buildings all add to the sense of a historical landscape, but sadly the unspoilt nature of the coastline is being affected by the removal of sand and the effects of waste from tin extraction discharged into the river.

ACCESS: Footpath routes linked with Tehidy Country Park; coastal footpath.

PARKING: Car parks at Gwithian, Godrevy, Portreath and along coast.

FACILITIES: Seasonal refreshments; WCs; leaflet; viewing platform for disabled at Reskajeage.

GOLDEN CAP

1974 acres (799 ha) between Charmouth and Bridport, off A35, Dorset
[193:SY4092]

This eight-mile stretch of coast, part of the dramatic west Dorset coastline of blue lias clays capped with sandstone, contains the highest cliff on the south coast. At 618 feet, Golden Cap is so called because of the 'cap' of golden sandstone and gorse which can be seen on the cliff face.

The estate is made up of a number of long hills, covered in gorse and trees, and incised with coombes which run down to the cliffs. Small fields of mainly permanent pasture and herb-rich meadows are linked by ancient hedgerows. The stone and brick farmsteads and the partly deserted village of St Gabriel's, with the ruins of its thirteenth-century chapel, nestle among these windswept valleys, protected by gnarled hedges and trees.

There are other interesting historical sites, including some Bronze Age bowl barrows on the Cap, a Roman road, medieval pillow mounds and strip lynchets, old lime kilns, an Admiralty signal station dating from the Napoleonic Wars and a listed farmhouse.

The landscape of undulating hills and valleys is a maze of more than twenty-five miles of footpaths and bridleways, meandering over the gorse and heather, down through some of the most extensive herb-rich neutral meadows owned by the Trust, and along the coastline. In the unimproved meadows plants such as adder's tongue fern, green-winged orchid, dropwort and pepper saxifrage can be found. The scrubby hedgebanks are fringed with flowers and ferns.

The cliffs are highly unstable and decidedly hazardous. They contain a large number of fossils, although their extraction is discouraged. The landslip terraces and dangerous mid-flows along the undercliff sections are important for a great range of specialist insects, mainly beetles, semi-aquatic flies, mining bees and digger wasps, including many national rarities.

Tangled thickets of willow and thorn scrub below the cliffline attract many migrant birds, and pockets of remnant heath provide important habitats for Dartford warbler, stonechat and linnet. There are several small woods with evidence of old ash and hazel coppicing (now being reintroduced) and some ancient boundary banks.

ACCESS: By minor roads; some open access; coastal path; network of footpaths and bridleways.

PARKING: Car parks at Stonebarrow Hill and Langdon Wood; public car parks at Lyme Regis, Charmouth, Seatown and Eype.

FACILITIES: NT shop and WCS (including disabled) at Stonebarrow car park; information panel; viewpoints at Stonebarrow, Langdon and Golden Cap; Dorset Heritage Fossil Centre at Charmouth Beach; camping; base camp for volunteers.

HENTOR, WILLINGS WALLS, TROWLESWORTHY WARRENS AND GOODAMEAVY

3739 acres (1513 ha) 2m N of Buckfastleigh, 1m S of A384, reached by narrow minor roads off A38 or A384, 6m NE of Plymouth, 2m S of Yelverton, Devon
[202:SX575645/600655/615680/726684 and 201:SX5464]

This area (much of it in the guardianship of English Heritage) covers a large tract of open moorland above the wooded River Plym, cut by steep-sided brooks and lying partly within the Dartmoor National Park. Numerous archaeological remains exist, including settlements comprising hut circles and surrounding enclosures, and burial chambers or cists dating back to the Bronze Age. The underlying granite of the Dartmoor massif is visible in this rock-strewn prehistoric landscape, much of it formed as a result of the erosive forces of the Ice Age.

The distinctive outline of the tors, granite blocks of uncertain origin, dominate the warrens where rabbits were extensively bred for fur and meat from the Middle Ages to the nineteenth century. Lee Moor leat is crossed by stone bridges for use by the warreners. Medieval farmsteads can be seen at Hentor and Willings Walls warrens. The area is important for the extraction of high quality granite, and there are old quarries at Trowlesworthy, Dewerstone and Cadworthy Woods, with the remains of old tramways once used for haulage now followed by footpaths.

Heaths occur on the mineral soils and shallow peat, supporting a variety of plants such as purple moor grass, heather, bog cotton, *Sphagnum* moss, lesser spearwort, sedges, bog pimpernel, marsh pennywort and bog asphodel. Goodameavy, to the south west, is an important prehistoric moorland and wooded landscape rising above the Plym. In the woods are many birds such as tree creeper, jay and green woodpecker. Skylark, meadow pipit, wheatear and stonechat can be seen on the moors, with raven, crow and jackdaw inhabiting the rocky outcrops.

The woods are rich in wildlife, and are especially important for the rare mosses and lichens which flourish in the damp air.

ACCESS: Networks of tracks across open land to Castle Drogo; marked circular walks link to tracks.

PARKING: Car parks at Hentor, Goodameavy, Shaugh Bridge and Trowlesworthy.

FACILITIES: Local facilities; leaflets.

THE HOLNICOTE ESTATE

12,443 acres (5036 ha) 4m W of Minehead, each side of A39, Somerset
[181:ss920469]

There can be few estates of such landscape variety as Holnicote. The gentle Vale of Porlock, with its fertile farms and attractive villages, separates two dramatic upland areas. To the north, the coastal heathland of Bossington Hill and Selworthy Beacon (1000 feet) stretches for three miles between the mouth of Grexy Combe in the east and Hurlstone Point in the west.

The rugged, north-facing cliffs with their 'hog's back' profile fall steeply to the Bristol Channel some 800 feet below. To the south, an extensive stretch of wild heather moorland rises to the skyline, dominated by Dunkery Beacon, at 1705 feet the highest point of Exmoor. Virtually the whole of the Horner River system is within the estate, from high-level moorland springs down to the sea. It emerges on Bossington Beach, one of the best examples of shingle storm beach in the country.

One of the largest blocks of entirely semi-natural woodland in England lies on the steep valley sides of the Horner Water. In contrast, nearby are beautiful conifer plantations established by Sir Francis Acland in the 1920s.

Such diversity of land forms ensures a wide variety of habitats, supporting rare and locally specialised flora and fauna. It is not surprising that two-thirds of the estate has been designated an SSSI. The predominantly sessile oak woods of Horner support a lichen flora of international importance; more than 170 species are present, including many rarities. A rich birdlife includes breeding populations of pied flycatcher, wood warbler, redstart and dipper. The open nature of the wood allows the growth of violets, the food plant for an abundance of silver-washed fritillary butterflies.

The vast expanse of heather moorland represents the most important heathland remaining on Exmoor. Plant species of national and regional interest include lesser twayblade, Cornish moneywort, fir club moss, cranberry, crowberry, ivy-leaved bellflower and dodder. The dwarf shrub supports six nationally rare spider species and the largest British colonies of the rare heath fritillary butterfly. Nesting moorland birds include red grouse, ring ouzel, wheatear, stonechat, whinchat, raven and buzzard. Britain's smallest bird of prey, the merlin, regularly nests here. Herds of wild red deer wander freely over the uplands.

Signs of man's early history are evident throughout the landscape in the form of Bronze Age barrows, tumuli, cairns, beacon sites and Iron Age hill forts. The development of agricultural life can be appreciated by the mills and accompanying leats, the dovecote at Blackford, the remnants of old cider orchards, packhorse bridges and signs of the tanning industry in Horner Wood. The estate includes the majority of the attractive stone or colourwashed houses and buildings of Selworthy, Luccombe, Allerford, Bossington and Horner. Over 125 buildings are listed.

ACCESS: Open access.

PARKING: Car parks and lay-bys on moorland. Car parks with WCs at Horner, Bossington, Allerford, Selworthy and Luccombe.

FACILITIES: NT shop and information centre at Selworthy Green; restaurants at Selworthy, Bossington, Allerford and Horner; information boards; footpath leaflet; educational study centre at Piles Mill (contact Head Warden for information about booking).

ILFRACOMBE AND LEE TO CROYDE

1336 acres (541 ha) NE of Barnstaple, access off A361 Barnstaple to Ilfracombe road, via B3231 to Croyde and B3343 to Woolacombe, Devon
[180:SS5047 to 4241]

Despite their popularity as seaside resorts, the coast between Ilfracombe and Woolacombe (mostly in Trust ownership) remains unspoilt. From Ilfracombe the North Devon Coastal Path overlooks the coastline to Morte Point, thought to be one of the most dramatic headlands in the West Country. From Lee Bay the path rises to

Damage Cliffs, renowned for its flowering primroses and orchids in the spring and a number of prehistoric remains, including some standing stones on Lee Down. At the top of the Tors Walk is a disused lime kiln, dating from the late nineteenth and early twentieth centuries. There are also signs of medieval strip field systems.

The tranquillity of Combesgate Valley offers a refreshing contrast to the windswept coastline, and the extensive sands of Woolacombe Beach, behind Morte Point, are also sheltered by dunes and grassland where autumn lady's tresses and yellow wort grow (much work has been done to control the erosion caused by walkers, and to rescue the flower-rich grassland by clearing the privet scrub). At Morte Point sea thrift, rock samphire, bird's foot trefoil, heather and plantain grow, and rock pipit, wheatear and stonechat are frequently seen along the cliffs, nesting among the scrub and heath.

Baggy Point, best approached from Croyde Bay, is unlike Morte Point in appearance because of the different rock structure, and its vertical cliffs, popular with climbers, provide nesting ledges for numerous sea birds, including fulmar, shag and cormorant. The uncultivated grassland along the cliff edge supports a wide variety of plant species, with associated insects, and the inlet of Bennett's Mouth is one of an important series of habitats along the Bristol Channel for migrating, breeding and overwintering birds.

ACCESS: Network of walks along coast.

PARKING: Car parks at Ilfracombe, Mortehoe village, Croyde, Woolacombe, Marine Drive and Vention.

FACILITIES: Local facilities; wcs by Marine Drive; leaflet; viewpoint; blue flag beach; swimming; climbing; part of coastal path from Croyde car park accessible to wheelchairs.

IVYTHORN AND WALTON HILLS

88½ acres (36 ha) 1m S of Street, W of B3151, Somerset [182:ST474348]

This wooded, south-facing scarp lies on a ridge known as the Polden Hills, above the Somerset Levels. Walton Hill is covered with an ash-scrub woodland, chalk grassland and oak woodland, probably of ancient origin.

Part of the woodland, an SSSI, on Ivythorn Hill is of particular interest for its ancient oak coppicing, and traditional methods of woodland management are now being reintroduced to maintain the original character of the wood. Standard and mature trees are scattered throughout the coppice.

In the woods there is evidence of badgers, and in pockets of blackthorn on the margins the elusive brown hairstreak butterfly can be seen. Bluebell, dog's mercury, violet, lords and ladies, primrose and wood aven grow among the trees. There are some old boundary banks in the woodlands.

The woodland merges with scrub and a limestone grassland, rich in flowers and grasses, which provides a valuable habitat for a variety of unusual butterflies among plants such as pyramidal orchid and woolly thistle. In the old and overgrown quarry pits are sheltered corners with lime-loving plants.

ACCESS: Network of footpaths.

PARKING: Car park at Walton Hill; 2 car parks at Ivythorn Hill near youth hostel.

FACILITIES: Information panel in the car park at Walton Hill; youth hostel.

KILLERTON

6388 acres (2585 ha) 7m NE of Exeter, each side of B3181 Exeter to Cullompton road, Devon [192:SX9700]

Set within the fertile river landscapes of the rivers Clyst and Culm, this large estate encompasses an eighteenth-century house and gardens, deer park and parkland originally designed by John Veitch, the famous nurseryman and landscape designer. There is a nineteenth-century chapel. Killerton Clump, a prominent volcanic hill sheltering the house and the site of the Dolbury Iron Age hill fort, is part of the estate. Also of interest is Marker's Cottage, built in the fifteenth century and containing some mid-sixteenth century paintings on a wooden screen. An arboretum is laid out on the slopes, with some rare and unusual trees introduced by Veitch. The surrounding farmland is bounded by hedges and woodland.

White Down Copse was planted in the nineteenth century, and Ashclyst Forest (managed partly by the Forestry Commission and partly by the Trust) includes ancient woods as well as nineteenth-century plantings on the former open common land. The woods are now a mixture of broadleaved trees and conifers, with ancient oak pollards supporting rare lichens and invertebrates. Some areas of conifer are being restored to open heath, and other areas are being converted to woodland dominated by oak and ash. Roe deer can be seen grazing in the forest glades. Over thirty-five different species of butterflies breed here, including many hairstreaks, skippers, fritillaries and browns. Birds such as redstart, wood warbler, woodpeckers, tree creeper and buzzard can be seen, as well as many wild flowers including bluebell, primrose, bugle and orchids.

Forest Cottage housed a gamekeeper in the second half of the century, and other cottages were for the use of foresters. The tracks for shooting were cut between 1876 and 1879.

ACCESS: Park and garden open all year during daylight hours; house open seasonally; open access to Ashclyst Forest, White Down and Paradise Copse; way-marked trails through forests; footpath through estate and along wooded slopes; stations at Pinhoe, Whimple, Exeter Central and St Davids, and regular local bus service from Exeter.

PARKING: Car parks at Killerton House, Columbjohn and Killerton chapel; 4 car parks on road running N–S through Ashclyst Forest and Paradise Copse; special parking for disabled.

FACILITIES: NT shop and refreshments; WCs (including disabled); information centre at house car park; motorised buggies.

THE KINGSTON LACY ESTATE, INCLUDING BADBURY RINGS

8795 acres (3559 ha) 2m NW of Wimborne Minster, on each side of B3082 Blandford road, Dorset   [195:SY978014]

This substantial agricultural estate surrounds the historic seventeenth-century mansion of Kingston Lacy. Located in low-lying chalk downland between the River Stour and its tributaries, the property encompasses fourteen farms, parts of the villages of Shapwick and Pamphill, Holt Heath National Nature Reserve and to the north-west the Scheduled Ancient Monument of Badbury Rings.

The house is set in an eighteenth-century naturalistic landscaped park, where historic records show that there was once a medieval house and deer park. The mature trees support good lichen and invertebrate communities typical of a long-established woodland site. Small copses and woods are scattered over the farmland, and the marginal woodland belts also include some ancient sites with interesting ground flora.

The slow-moving river is the haunt of kingfisher, mute swan and little grebe, and some of the unimproved riverside meadows on the wide alluvial plains are rich in wild flowers, with the few remaining areas of permanent pastures providing good feeding grounds for wading birds such as lapwing and redshank.

The chalk grasslands over the Badbury Rings are rich in plants such as the greater butterfly, frog and bee orchids, bastard toadflax, adder's tongue fern and knapweed broomrape, and support a number of butterflies. The Rings themselves form one of the best-known Iron Age hill forts in Britain. The circular, grassy mound with its wooded clump shows signs of the different stages of the fort's construction, with three concentric ramparts and ditches.

Also of historical interest on the estate are some prehistoric round burial barrows, a Roman road and settlement, and evidence of Celtic field systems.

ACCESS: Network of footpaths and bridleways; access to estate all year; house and park open seasonally; station at Poole and local bus service to Wimborne Square.

PARKING: Car park at house; special parking for disabled by arrangement with the Administrator; other small informal car parks around estate; large free car park at Badbury Rings.

FACILITIES: NT shop and restaurant at house; WCs (including disabled); wheelchair access to garden only; dogs allowed on leads in north park only; picnics in north park only.

LANHYDROCK

911 acres (369 ha) 2½m S of Bodmin on Lostwithiel road, Cornwall
[200:SX085636]

This delightful Victorian house, a Grade I listed building of monastic origins with a seventeenth-century wing and gatehouse, is set in a medieval deer park enclosing remains of the ancient woodland overlooking the valley of the River Fowey. The boundaries of the park can be seen along the Maudlin Valley, and an old gate post on the way to Brownqueen Farm. Station Drive follows the line of the original carriage-drive from Bodmin Station to the house. A network of paths leads from the shrub gardens of magnolia, rhododendron and camellia through the luxuriant natural woodlands to the river.

Lanhydrock is approached by a famous avenue of beeches and sycamores, some of the latter planted as long ago as 1648. The oak woodlands, with the individual trees within the park, are also of great conservation importance. Despite recent storm damage, they represent a long history of woodland continuity and support many interesting insects and lichens. The woods are also important for flowers and ferns, including royal fern. Many birds are found here. All three species of woodpecker are present, as well as dipper, grey wagtail, owls (little, barn and tawny), nuthatch and tree creeper. There are extensive badger setts, and otters are thought to use the River Fowey.

Evidence of tin-streaming can be seen throughout Higginsmoor.

ACCESS: Free public access to park; network of footpaths and circular walks; house and garden open seasonally; local station at Bodmin Parkway.

PARKING: Car parks at Respryn and Lanhydrock house.

FACILITIES: NT shop and restaurant at house; WCs (including disabled); NT regional office within park; information boards in car parks; estate maps in guidebook; education material; disabled visitors may be driven to house (special parking available through car park attendant);

LANYON QUOIT

1½ acres (½ ha) 4m NW of Penzance, 2m SE of Morvah on N road between Morvah and Penzance, Cornwall [203:SW430337]

One of several quoits in the South West, this trio of granite uprights supporting a huge granite slab (the remains of a megalithic chambered tomb dating from 2000 to 1600BC) is one of the most famous prehistoric sites in Cornwall. Rising prominently from the open moorland, Lanyon Quoit was probably the ceremonial tomb for a local community. The stones were re-erected in 1824 after collapsing in 1815.

ACCESS: Short footpath.

PARKING: Small lay-by beside road.

FACILITIES: Local facilities.

THE LIZARD (EAST): LIZARD POINT TO ST KEVERNE AND THE HELFORD RIVER

1010 acres (409 ha) SE of Helston, off A3294, and 3m S of Falmouth, Cornwall [203:SW716130, 204:SW770165, 797278 and 728257]

The Trust owns a number of properties along the dramatic coastline of the Lizard, a prominent and broad, flat-topped peninsula which terminates at Lizard Point, the southernmost extremity of mainland Britain. The Point was acquired through the Enterprise Neptune appeal.

To the east of the point is a spectacular collapsed sea cave. The Lizard peninsula is unique for its complex geology of serpentine, gabbro, granite and gneiss. Serpentine was once worked at Carleon Cove (a significant part of the Lizard's economic history), and there are still stiles made of this smooth, polished rock. Today's visitors see only ruined walls, floors and chimneys of the old workings. The soil overlying these rocks, together with the very mild oceanic climate, result in a flora unlike that of any other in the country. The cliffs in the area have been invaded by the rampant Hottentot fig, imported from South Africa at the turn of the century, which threatens to swamp the finer native plants for which the Lizard is internationally renowned.

Cadgwith is a fishing cove with some charming examples of Cornish vernacular buildings (many of thatch in a county where slate is more common) and old pilchard cellars. An unusual wood of dwarf elms, thought to have been planted originally for cheap fuel, covers the promontory to the Devil's Frying Pan, a collapsed cavern through which the sea crashes at high tide.

Beagles Point, Black Head and Lowland Point are three isolated properties, the last with much of archaeological interest. Kildown Point to Enys Head is an exceptional area for plants, and Beagles Point is another excellent locality for its variety of insects and plants, including Cornish heath and western gorse. The Poltesco valley, where Babington's leek was first identified, and evidence of 'lazy beds' (mounds created by cultivation in areas of thin or poor soil, with drainage ditches in between) in the Downas Valley are also notable.

The estuarine channels and the northern entrance of the Helford River around Mawnan Smith are of great marine ecological importance. The rich, muddy intertidal belt is exposed at low tide, and many birds can be seen feeding on the mudflats, including heron, cormorant, shelduck, mallard, curlew and kingfisher. A network of ancient natural woodlands lines the creeks, with abundant ground flora. From Tremayne Wood, which encompasses Vallum Tremayne Creek, there are attractive views across to Merthen Wood (not owned by the Trust), an ancient woodland of particular interest. Frenchman's Creek also has notable oak woodlands.

Many of these ancient woodlands, with their old boundary banks still visible, have been coppiced over the years for firewood, charcoal, ship-building and bark for leather-tanning. They support a variety of ground plants such as bluebell, bilberry, wood anemone, mosses, ferns and lichens, and many woodland invertebrates, as well as greater spotted woodpecker, buzzard and tree creeper. Rosemullion Head has interesting coastal grassland, with early purple and green-winged orchids. The valley garden of Glendurgan lies behind the quiet hamlet of Durgan, and Mawnan Church overlooks the mouth of the river, linked to Rosemullion Head (the possible site of a prehistoric fort) by a coastal footpath. There is a Bronze Age settlement at the Herra, on Gillan Harbour, and St Francis's Chapel at Pengwedhen (built in 1930) is also worth a visit.

ACCESS: Coastal footpaths on the Lizard linked to inland paths; access to Helford River by small roads and paths, with several circular paths running inland (eg from Porth Saxon along wooded valley to Carwinion, around Pengwedhen Wood from Penarvon Cove); network of paths around Mawnan Smith; from Helford running W to Pengwedhen and Frenchman's Creek; foot ferry from Helford Passage to Helford.

PARKING: Car parks at Mawnan Church, Bosveal, Glendurgan, St Anthony-in-Meneage and Helford; for Lizard, car parks at Poltesco, Cadgwith, Inglewidden, Landewednack Church and Coverack.

FACILITIES: Facilities at Helford, Manaccan, Helford Passage, Mawnan Smith and Lizard Town; leaflets; viewpoints.

THE LIZARD (WEST): FROM GUNWALLOE CHURCH COVE AND KYNANCE COVE

853 acres (345 ha) S of Helston, minor roads off A3083, A3293 and A3294. Kynance Cove 1m NW of Lizard Town, reached on foot or by toll road (A3083), Cornwall [203:SW690133]

The coastline on the west of the peninsula is more exposed than the gentler east side, with rocky coves, sea stacks, blow holes, cliffs and beaches, structures unique to the Lizard of schist, gneiss, gabbro and serpentine. These rocks, the soil derived from them, the oceanic climate and historical land use have led to a remarkable mosaic of heaths, grasslands and cliffs.

The Lizard has been a mecca for botanists for a long time. The serpentine, in particular, supports plant species not found on any other rock type and many not found elsewhere on mainland Britain. The Cornish heath, a robust, bright pink heather found commonly on the heaths, cliffs and hedgerows, is one such speciality. Many other plants are found in the grasslands and heaths, such as kidney vetch, common milkwort, thyme, bloody crane's bill, lady's bed-straw, dropwort, great burnet and burnet rose. The large, unculti-vated tracts of heath on the Lizard plateau and cliffs are one of its main features, and one of the largest surviving areas of heathland in lowland Britain.

Heathland plants include bell heather, gorse, saw wort, prostrate dyer's greenweed, heath spotted orchid and devil's bit scabious, as well as the Cornish heath already mentioned. Unusual rushes (such as the black bog rush, and some very rare dwarf rushes), sedges and royal fern can be seen in damp areas, valleys, cart tracks and around pools on the heath. Small migrant birds nest among the thickets of scrub, and the variety of invertebrate species is also of international importance. Much of this heath is now in National Nature Reserves, or is managed primarily for its wildlife and historic landscape value by conservation organisations, and in parts by the Ministry of Defence, who own the largest helicopter station in western Europe at Culdrose.

The church of Gunwalloe Church Cove lies next to Winnianton Farm, once a royal Anglo-Saxon manor and the last remnant of a Dark Age settlement which once occupied the land between the farm, cliffs and church. A path leads from the church past the golf course to Poldhu Cove, which is backed by a series of eroded sand dunes. Further south, Mullion Cove provides a valuable harbour for the local fishing community, where there are good examples of ver-nacular buildings and an old net store. Iron Age field systems can be seen on the Predannack cliffs, and the farm, with typical ver-nacular buildings, has field boundaries unchanged at least since the Lanhydrock Atlas of 1695.

The rocky clefts and ledges around Predannack are ablaze with cliff flowers, such as blue spring squill, in April and May, and thrift, sea campion, green-winged orchid, dropwort, kidney vetch and patches of Cornish heath cover the Mullion cliffs. Kynance Cove has been a destination for day trips since the the eighteenth century's fascination for the picturesque. The characteristic, multi-coloured, metamorphic serpentine rocks have been cut and polished for many years, now mainly for the local craft and souvenir industry. The secluded cove is also of great interest to the ecologist for its variety of plants and invertebrates, particularly moths and unusual spiders in the grasslands, and a great range of plants on the cliff edges and in the heath behind. A Bronze Age settlement with barrows, hut circles and enclosures (not owned by the Trust) can be seen in the Kynance Valley, and there are also some medieval peat-drying platforms and field patterns near the farms.

ACCESS: Coastal path; linking paths across farmland; toll road; path from clifftop car park (past viewpoint for disabled visitors) descends to Kynance Cove via Goose Curtain Brook.

PARKING: Car parks at Winnianton, Carrag-a-pilez, Poldhu Cove, Mullion Cove, Predannack and Kynance.

FACILITIES: Seasonal café and WCs at Kynance Cove and Gunwalloe; leaflets from local outlets; viewpoints (wheelchair access to viewpoint at Kynance Cove).

NOTE: Care should be taken when bathing at Kynance Cove which is cut off at high tide.

THE LOE AND GUNWALLOE

1554 acres (629 ha) 2m S of Helston, 1m E of Porthleven, Cornwall
[203:SW645250]

Loe Pool is an elongated freshwater lake, the largest natural lake in Cornwall, with flooded river valleys forming creeks round its edge. It is renowned for its populations of water birds, including mallard, tufted duck, mute swan, coot, wintering pigeon, teal, shoveler, red-throated diver and red-necked grebe.

At the mouth of the River Cober where it flows into the lake is Loe Marsh, a rich wetland of alder and willow, which can be crossed by a causeway following a historic route. It provides an important habitat for many invertebrates (particularly damselfly and dragonfly), for marshland birds such as sedge and reed warblers and water rail, and for its variety of wetland plants (yellow flag, valerian, hemlock water dropwort, marsh marigold and many sedges). Gentle wooded slopes partly fringe the margins of the lake, which is separated from the sea by a shingle bar linked to Porthleven Sands. Sea bindweed and sea rocket thrive along the shingle.

To the east the beach rises to a cliffline (with a colony of sand martins) from Gunwalloe Fishing Cove (used by local fishermen),

Hazelphron Cliffs and Castle Mound where there is an Iron Age cliff castle. Other sites of historical interest are Bronze Age barrows on Pedngwinian, the pattern of an ancient strip-field system at Chyvarloe, the fourteenth-century church at Gunwalloe and old silver and lead mine workings at Wheal Pool. To the east of the Loe, in the surrounding undulating farmland, lies the Penrose estate, which has had a significant influence on the area with notable plantings of tall palms, tree ferns, bamboo groves and exotic conifers in the nineteenth-century landscaped park.

ACCESS: Footpaths round lake, behind shingle bar, and along cliffs beyond Loe Bar to Gunwalloe Church.

PARKING: Car parks at Helston, Penrose, Highburrow, Degibna, Chyvarloe and Winnianton.

FACILITIES: Leaflet; birdwatchers' hide accessible for wheelchairs at Helston Lodge; patrolled swimming at Gunwalloe (summer months); excellent sea fishing from Loe Bar to Gunwalloe; emergency telephone at Bar Lodge.

NOTE: Bathing, boating and other water sports are not permitted on Loe Pool in the interests of the wildlife. Bathing off Loe Bar is dangerous because of strong currents.

LYDFORD GORGE

117 acres (47 ha) W of Lydford village, off A386 Okehampton to Tavistock road, Devon [191 and 201:SX509846]

This well-known deep, wooded ravine in the Dartmoor National Park was gouged out by the erosive powers of the River Lyd, the result of 'river capture', earth movements which diverted the flow of the river. A series of smooth potholes have been carved out by the water, and a tributary stream plunges ninety feet down White Lady waterfall, which can be reached by a circular walk returning along a narrow and dramatic path leading to the Devil's Cauldron, a spectacular amphitheatre of rock. Footbridges cross the river, with views of the steep-sided gorge and its mantle of trees enveloped in mosses, lichens and ferns.

The oak woodlands surrounding the river and falls have delightful names indicating their historic origins – Smalland, Lambhole and Old Cleave. Their maturity is reflected in the variety of plants to be seen from the wetter margins to the valley tops. Lady, male and hart's tongue ferns, woodrush, ramson and ivy cover the gorge, as well as more unusual plants such as pink purslane. The rocks and trees are covered with many types of rare mosses, lichens and liverworts. Kingfisher, heron, grey wagtail and dipper feed along the river, and the greater spotted woodpecker, tree creeper, pied flycatcher and nuthatch can be seen among the trees.

The nearby village of Lydford with its castle is of interest as a 'burh' dating from the time of King Alfred. The remains of the Anglo-Saxon town bank, an earth rampart, and a Norman fort embankment can be seen. There is a disused railway line to the south.

ACCESS: Entrances at Lydford Bridge and on Brentor road (seasonal opening); station at Bere Alston and local bus service to Lydford.

PARKING: Car parks at both entrances.

FACILITIES: NT shop; refreshments; WCs; leaflet; guidebook; viewpoint.

NOTE: The gorge is often slippery and steep in parts; stout footwear essential and unsuitable for disabled visitors.

LYNMOUTH: FORELAND POINT, COUNTISBURY HILL AND WATERSMEET

1500 acres (607 ha) E of Lynmouth, each side of A39, access from A39, Devon [180:SS7449]

This is an extensive and varied property around the deeply incised valleys of the East Lyn River and Hoar Oak Water, descending from Exmoor to the sea along the Somerset border. The fast-flowing peat-stained rivers, waterfalls and steep hillsides covered with oak woodlands form part of Exmoor National Park.

The coastline is backed by open hill country, and the uncultivated cliff edge of heath, gorse and grassland contrasts with the agricultural land. Foreland Point is Devon's most northerly point, and site of the Foreland lighthouse. The land rises inland to over 1000 feet at Countisbury Hill above the hamlet with its charming stone buildings, while to the east of Chubhill Combe, above the sheer cliff tops, a predominantly oak woodland covers the coastline.

Of archaeological interest is the massive earthwork on Wind Hill, known as Countisbury Camp. There are also prehistoric barrows on Countisbury Common, and a standing stone, possibly Bronze Age, west of the footpath crossing Myrtleberry North Camp. The latter, together with Myrtleberry South Camp, is the remains of Iron Age enclosures. Lloyds Signal Station, on Butler Hill, is now used to house electrical equipment and as a shelter for walkers. Other interesting historical features are the two disused nineteenth-century lime kilns which can be seen at Watersmeet.

The woodlands are of particular ecological interest, with birch, rowan and ash among the sessile oak, as well as a number of scarce trees including some species of whitebeam (*Sorbus devoniensis, S. subcutanea* and *S.vexans*). The flora is rich and varied with some unusual plants such as Irish spurge, Wilson's filmy fern, wood vetch, wood stitchwort and nettle-leaved bellflower. Ferns and rare woodland mosses and lichens thrive in the moist and unpolluted atmosphere, and the woods provide important cover for buzzard, redstart, pied flycatcher and wood warbler. Woodland butterflies are common along the paths and in openings among the trees, and dark-green fritillary can be seen on the bracken-covered slopes. In July silver-washed fritillary feed on the brambles.

On the deep river pools and waterfalls a keen eye may spot dipper, grey wagtail and kingfisher.

ACCESS: North Devon Coastal Path; network of paths along coast and inland; high-level paths above valleys.

PARKING: Car parks at Watersmeet, Hillsford Bridge, Countisbury, Lynmouth and Barna Barrow.

FACILITIES: Shop; refreshments; WCs; leaflet; information point and self-service restaurant at Watersmeet House (seasonal opening); viewpoints; fishing permits obtainable locally; swimming; riding; Exmoor base camp (used for conservation projects and holidays) at Countisbury.

THE MENDIPS: CROOK'S PEAK, WAVERING DOWN AND SHUTE SHELVE HILL

725 acres (293½ ha) 10m SW of Weston-super-Mare, off A38 on minor roads, Somerset [182:ST387558]

On the western slope of the Mendip Hills, this extensive area of downland rises above the Somerset Levels. The Trust owns the southern steep slopes, coombes and spurs of this rolling limestone landscape, which has been grazed for centuries as commonland, largely by sheep. As well as the grassland, habitats include heathland, woodland and scrub, containing an immense variety of wildlife.

The open grassland is rich with flowers and herbs such as thyme, stemless thistle and rock rose. Butterflies include chalkhill blue, dark-green fritillary and brown argus. Pockets of heathland occur over leached soil, and here the plants differ from the limestone grassland with bell heather, heather, tormentil and heath bedstraw. The craggy outcrops support some delightful ferns, including the maidenhair spleenwort. Glow-worm beetles prey on the abundant snail population.

Among the woodlands are an unusual pocket of yew on Cross Plain, and signs of a long history of land use within King's Wood, a notable ancient woodland site, such as old pollards, boundary banks and a characteristic association of plants and invertebrates. There are some magnificent small-leaved lime trees and an exceptionally rich ground flora, including toothwort, sanicle, yellow archangel, woodruff, bluebell, ransom and dog's mercury. Birds such as the green woodpecker, buzzard, blackcap, chiff-chaff and cuckoo can also be seen.

ACCESS: Footpaths; bridleways; West Mendip Way crosses site.

PARKING: Small car park at Kingswood and limited parking along Webbington Road.

FACILITIES: Local facilities; leaflet; interpretation panels.

MONTACUTE

303 acres (123 ha) 4m W of Yeovil, S of A3088, 3m E of A303, Somerset
[183 and 193:ST498170]

This manorial estate is dominated by a grand Elizabethan house built of warm yellow stone. The historic parkland surrounding the well-documented house and formal gardens includes St Michael's Hill (the 'pointed hill' or *mons acutus* that gave the house and village its name) with the gatehouse of a former twelfth-century priory at its foot (not owned by the Trust) and an eighteenth-century 'pepperpot' tower on its summit, the remains of a mill, a copse and some post-medieval field patterns which have now been modified by modern agricultural practices. Old fish ponds can be seen near Abbey Farm.

There are ancient woodlands around St Michael's Hill, and interesting lichens on the parkland trees.

ACCESS: Park and St Michael's Hill open all year; house open seasonally; walks in park and to St Michael's Hill; Ladies' Walk; local stations at Yeovil Pen Mill, Yeovil Junction and Crewkerne.

PARKING: Car park.

FACILITIES: Facilities at house; WCS (including disabled); Braille guide; dogs allowed in park on leads.

PLYM BRIDGE WOODS

190 acres (77 ha) 3½m NE of Plymouth, via minor road between B3432 roundabout and B3416, Devon
[201:SX522595]

These luxuriant oak woodlands border the River Plym and contain fascinating archaeological remains to the south of Shaugh Bridge, many dating from the seventeenth century when the area was exploited for tons of slate cut from the exposed rock. Quarries, spoil heaps and the remnants of now disused modes of transport (including stone sleepers which are evidence of early tramways) litter the woods, creating new habitats for wildlife but hidden dangers for visitors.

The present bridge over the Plym was built in the eighteenth century over the remains of an earlier one damaged by flood, but there is known to have been a bridge here – for centuries the lowest crossing point of the river – since 1238. A disused railway line runs from Plymouth to Tavistock, and there is a weir on the river.

The woods are at their best in spring when a carpet of flowers covers the ground before the dense canopy casts its shade. Wood anemone, bluebell, wild garlic and primrose are common. Foxglove flourish in openings where the disturbance of quarrying has created ideal growing conditions, and mosses, woodrush, lady and male ferns, St John's wort, red campion and toadflax also occur. The clean atmosphere and continuity of woodland here encourage the growth of rare lichens. In the lush vegetation mammals and birds thrive, with lesser spotted woodpecker, marsh tit, redstart, pied flycatcher, nuthatch and tree creeper. Heron, wagtail and dipper breed along the river, and the woods are known for moths and butterflies with fritillaries, hairstreak and peacock. Damselflies and dragonflies settle on the reeds and grasses along the riverside.

ACCESS: Extensive network of paths, including cycle path.

PARKING: 3 car parks including one in former quarry.

FACILITIES: Leaflet; guidebook; information board at SW of property; bathing and picnics along river.

POLZEATH TO PORTQUIN BAY

723 acres (293 ha) 6m NW of Wadebridge, off A39, Cornwall
[200:SW968805]

This property covers six miles of the dramatic coastline between New Polzeath and Port Quin, incorporating the headlands of Pentire and the Rumps, and the smaller promontories of Com Head, Carnweather and Doyden Points, and overlooking Padstow Bay at the mouth of the Camel Estuary. Sheltered bays and coves provide access to the foreshore with its rock pools and lichen-clad rocks. The small fields are bounded by characteristic Cornish hedges of herringbone-pattern stone filled with earth, and the lanes are bordered by primrose, bluebell, pink campion, stitchwort and hogweed. The precipitous cliffs provide ledges for nesting sea birds such as fulmar, gull and cormorant, and the short turf of the clifftops, kept smooth by grazing sheep recently reintroduced by the Trust, is studded with spring squill during May, followed by a carpet of sea thrift, bladder campion, stonecrop, violet, thyme and kidney vetch.

The unmistakable outlines of elaborate Iron Age defensive earthworks span the neck of the Rumps, and old lead mines and waste tips near Pentireglaze bear witness to the later industrial exploitation of the area's mineral wealth. Lundy Bay is the site of the natural rock archway of Lundy Hole, one of the many distinctive features of the coast, and is bordered by thickets of hawthorn, blackthorn and gorse scrub which provide ideal nesting habitats for birds such as stonechat, linnet, wren, finch and thrush.

There are many vernacular buildings in the area, some with slate-hung walls, and a range of barns built of local stone, as well as a Gothic tower on Doyden Point and a Bronze Age bowl barrow (burial mound) visible from the cliff path at Pentire Haven. Other barrows are masked by gorse.

ACCESS: Coastal footpath linked by network of paths across farmland, including good circular walks.

PARKING: Car parks at New Polzeath, Pentireglaze lead mines, Pentire Farm (limited), Port Quin and Lundy Bay.

FACILITIES: Local facilities; leaflet; viewpoints along coast.

THE QUANTOCKS: BEACON HILL AND BICKNOLLER HILL

626 acres (253 ha) ½m S of West Quantoxhead, off A39, Somerset
[181:ST116411]

These hills form an area of open moorland, rising from 500 feet to 1000 feet at the northern end of the Quantock Hills AONB. The land is dissected by three major east–west running combes: Long Combe, Bicknoller Combe and Weacombe Combe, the last two with small streams and adjacent wet flushes. The hill slopes have a covering of bracken with scattered hawthorns and other woody species. The open summits are heath-dominated, either by vigorous dwarf shrub heath or grass heath.

The whole property lies within the Quantock Hills sssi. It is a fine example of semi-natural landscape supporting a community of four characteristic dwarf shrubs (heather, bell heather, bilberry and western gorse) together with associated plants such as dodder and green-ribbed sedge. Red deer are common, with upland birds such as meadow pipit, stonechat and raven.

This magnificent walking country offers splendid views over the Bristol Channel, the Vale of Taunton Deane, the Brendon Hills and Exmoor. A fairly rich scattering of archaeological sites includes Bronze Age bowl barrows on Beacon Hill and an Iron Age enclosed camp at Trendle Ring, overlooking Bicknoller.

ACCESS: Open access.

PARKING: Car park at Staple Plain.

FACILITIES: Local facilities.

THE ROSELAND PENINSULA

600 acres (243 ha) 10m SW of Tregony (by road), 2½m E of Falmouth (by ferry), Cornwall   [204:SW8632]

Curving round St Mawes Harbour and overlooking the historic town of Falmouth, the Roseland Peninsula is a delightful blend of beaches, cliffs, creeks, woods and farmland, and ideal for circular walks. The former strategic importance of St Anthony Head is apparent from the numerous military associations and remains. The Armada was sighted from here, and the headland was fortified during the Napoleonic Wars. St Anthony Battery was the site of a late nineteenth-century gun emplacement, later to be used during both World Wars. The Trust has mended the scars of the military buildings and is encouraging the natural vegetation to become established and flourish.

Sea birds nest along the craggier cliffs, and towards the cliffline the grasslands are at their most colourful in May and June with sea thrift, sea campion and other maritime species. The stretch of coast south of St Just-in-Roseland as far as Newton Cliffs is included in the Roseland Voluntary Marine Conservation Area which protects some unusual calcareous seaweed known as maërl. Footpaths skirt the sinuous creeks of the picturesque Percuil River, some of which were exploited in the Middle Ages as tide mills. The cliffs of Porthmellin Head, on the seaward side of the indented headland, are bordered by the beaches of Towan and Porthbeor.

ACCESS: Network of footpaths; path to St Anthony Head with access for wheelchairs; path to viewfinder.

PARKING: Car parks at Portscatho, Porth, St Anthony Head, St Mawes, Castle Point, Percuil and St Just.

FACILITIES: WCs at Portscatho, Porth, St Anthony Head, St Mawes Castle and St Just; leaflet; viewfinder; picnics.

ST AGNES AND CHAPEL PORTH

428 acres (173 ha) W and NW of St Agnes, Cornwall [203:SW710504]

From St Agnes Beacon, a heather-covered ridge between the coast and the village of St Agnes, there are spectacular views along the coastline. The tall chimneys, miners' trackways and remains of engine houses at the head of tin and copper mine shafts bear witness to the centuries of industrial exploitation of the area. The remains of Great Wheal Charlotte, Wheal Coates and the engine house of Towanroath stand proud against the cliffline, and the rocks, home of basking adders and lizards, are pitted with a honeycomb of mine shafts.

The scarred landscape is now softened by the purple, green and brown hues of the heath, which is of very great wildlife importance, with herbs and flowers such as the pale dog violet, spring squill and bloody crane's bill flourishing near the cliff edge. Grey seal and basking shark can be seen around the coastline, and birds such as fulmar, razorbill, guillemot and gannet nest in the cliffs. Rare and localised plants can be seen at Chapel Porth (where the remains of the eleventh-century chapel still exist), with lime-loving plants such as cowslip at Mulgram Hill and damp-loving plants in the hollows.

A number of heathery mounds on St Agnes Beacon are Bronze Age burial mounds, and the remains of a small Iron Age cliff castle adorns the promontory of Tubby's Head. Traditionally, bonfires were lit on the Beacon for celebrations or as a warning signal. South of Chapel Porth, ancient field patterns are masked by heather and taller vegetation inland. Chapel Coombe, a sheltered valley with scrub of willow, gorse and elder, attracts birds and butterflies (clouded yellow, painted lady and common blue).

ACCESS: Network of paths; South-West Coast Path.

PARKING: Car parks at Chapel Porth, St Agnes Beacon and Head.

FACILITIES: Seasonal refreshments and WCs at Chapel Porth; viewpoint from St Agnes Beacon.

SALCOMBE (EAST): MILL BAY TO PRAWLE AND WOODCOMBE POINT

600 acres (243 ha), access via minor roads from Kingsbridge or by ferry from Salcombe, Devon [202:SX740375]

Overlooking the picturesque harbour of Salcombe, the coastline to the west of the Kingsbridge Estuary extends from Mill Bay round a dramatic series of points to Prawle Point, the southernmost tip of Devon and used as a coastal lookout.

To the west, Maceley and Elender coves are shielded by the rocky headland of Gammon Head, which commands superb and unspoilt views along this Heritage Coastline. The jagged cliffs, the rocks encrusted with orange, black and yellow lichens, are ideal for bird-watching, with sea birds such as fulmar, kittiwake and gull nesting along the undisturbed stretches. (The stepped appearance of this part of the coast is the result of the lowering of the sea level, with the 'steps' being the ancient clifflines and the level land raised beaches.)

The cliff edges beyond the bounds of cultivation support a mosaic of herb-rich grasslands, heath, gorse and thorn scrub, with sea thrift, campion, rock samphire, bloody crane's bill, spring and autumn squills, rock spurrey, stonecrop and kidney vetch. Prawle Point is an extremely important landfall site for migrating birds, and is very popular with ornithologists. The rare cirl bunting breeds in the area. Butterflies include dark-green and small pearl-bordered fritillaries and silver-studded blue.

Of interest is a Bronze Age wreck (classified a historic wreck) which has been identified off the coast. A circular whitewashed stone lookout hut stands on Gara Rock, and ancient field boundaries, defined by upright slabs of rock, can still be seen. Rickham Common Entrenchments are defensive earthworks with the remains of a gun battery.

ACCESS: Network of paths and lanes for circular walks.

PARKING: Car parks at East Portlemouth, Rickham Common, Gara Rock Hotel, Prawle Point and East Prawle.

FACILITIES: WCs at East Prawle; leaflet; swimming at Mill Bay and Sunny Bay off Limebury Point.

SALCOMBE (WEST): BOLT HEAD TO HOPE COVE

1055 acres (427 ha), 7m S of Kingsbridge, off A381, access on minor roads, Devon [202:S7236–6639]

To the west of Salcombe, at the mouth of the Kingsbridge Estuary, the Trust owns six miles of rugged coastline consisting of a series of headlands and coves extending to Hope Cove.

The maritime history of the area is reflected in the local names, and over forty vessels have been wrecked along the coastline, including a four-masted Finnish barque, which struck the Ham Stone and which can sometimes be seen in the sands of Starehole Bay.

Sharp Tor is succeeded by the more prominent Bolt Head, an important location for sea birds such as fulmar, kittiwake and gulls. Bolt Head and the Warren are rich in butterflies, including sizeable colonies of silver-studded blue. A path leads inland along the sheltered Starehole Bottom, where damp hollows harbour plants which include hemlock water dropwort, hemp agrimony, angelica, marsh St John's wort, marsh pennywort and lesser spearwort. At Bolberry Down, ancient field patterns are defined by slabs of rock containing plates of mica. The path continues to Bolt Tail, a spectacular headland complementing Bolt Head and the site of Bolt Tail Camp, an Iron Age promontory fort. Another site of interest is a mound of earth and stone, known as Grant's Grave since the eighteenth century.

On the cliffs the rocks and scree are important for rare lichens, and the coastal heath habitat supports a variety of plants such as sea thrift, sea campion, rock samphire, bloody crane's bill, spring and autumn squills and kidney vetch, as well as many ants, grasshoppers and beetles. Butterflies flourish, and skylark, greater spotted woodpecker, willow warbler, chaffinch, stonechat, linnet and white-throat are seen.

ACCESS: South Devon Way along coast linked to inland paths; circular routes around Bolt Head and Starehole Bay.

PARKING: Car parks at Overbecks Museum, Soar Mill Cove Hotel and Outer Hope.

FACILITIES: Local facilities at Salcombe; NT shop, refreshments and displays about local natural history at Overbecks (seasonal opening); leaflets; viewpoints from headlands; path suitable for wheelchairs from Bolberry Down.

SALTRAM PARK

470 acres (190 ha) 2m W of Plympton, 3½m E of Plymouth between A38 and A379, Devon [201:SX520557]

A welcome green island in Plymouth's grey sprawl, this estate provides a vital open space for visitor and local alike. It comprises 200 acres of parkland surrounding a prestigious eighteenth-century mansion and garden, located near the tidal creek of the Plym Estuary.

The estuary is a regionally important site for its winter population of waders, which include black-tailed godwit and the occasional avocet, along with large flocks of dunlin, curlew and redshank. The amphitheatre, a relic of the opulent Georgian past, is an ideal point from which to watch these birds. Blaxton Quay is also of historical interest.

Dotted around the rest of the park are various habitat types which give a great deal of variety from ponds to butterfly meadows and ancient oak woodlands. Mature oak and sycamore in the parkland carry a rich lichen flora.

ACCESS: Network of footpaths; cycle track which starts at Saltram and leads up the Plym Valley to the southern reaches of Dartmoor;

house open seasonally; no public right of way; local bus service from Plymouth.

PARKING: Car park.

FACILITIES: NT shop, restaurant and other facilities in house; for conservation reasons dogs restricted to certain areas.

SOUTHDOWN CLIFFS, COLETON FISHACRE, DARTMOUTH AND THE DART ESTUARY

1313 acres (531 ha) $\frac{1}{2}$m S of Brixham, N of Dart Estuary, 3m S of Dartmouth, E of Little Dartmouth, Devon
[202:SX927540 and 878506 to 880490]

The Trust acquired these properties as a result of the Dart and Start Bay Appeal and Enterprise Neptune, in order to protect the valuable coastline on either side of the Dart Estuary.

To the west of the ancient town of Brixham, a series of promontories shelter sandy bays, and the unstable cliffs of Southdown and Woodhuish are covered with scrubby vegetation, ideal for small migratory birds. Plants include sea campion, thrift, rock samphire, heather and autumn squill.

The garden of Coleton Fishacre, sheltered in Pudcombe Bay, is run by the Trust and open to the public, and the Trust also owns a string of woodland properties along the east side of the estuary, including Long Wood, a typical Devon oak woodland with evidence of traditional coppicing, once used for the tanning industry and the production of charcoal. Bluebell, dog's mercury, ramson and ferns flourish, and several of the woods contain active badger setts. The hedgerows around Brownstone and Coleton are rich in flowers such as primrose, red campion, cow parsley and honeysuckle.

There are some disused lime kilns in the area, as well as remains from the Second World War.

Scabbacombe Head, with its more jagged rocks, attracts large numbers of sea birds with fulmar, gull, shag and cormorant nesting on the ledges where the outcropping rocks are covered with lichens, including some rarities. The dramatic headlands of Outer and Inner

Froward Points overlook Mew Stone, another haven for sea birds and seals. The Trust has introduced pony grazing to the clifftop grasslands at Froward Point, which has greatly enhanced the nature conservation interest by countering the invasion of rank vegetation.

Overlooking the east bank of the Dart Estuary, the Trust also owns much of the coastline along the western approach to Dartmouth. Dyer's Hill is a steep wooded rise where an old rope walk (with remains of the rope works) passes through the dense sycamores. Gallant Bower is also a wooded mound with good views of the Britannia Royal Naval College and crossed by a network of paths. On the summit can be seen the earthworks of a Royalist fort built in 1645. The surrounding woodlands are varied and include some mature oak, sycamore and ash. The ground flora includes bluebell, ramson and dog's mercury.

Dartmouth Castle (English Heritage) defends the restricted harbour entrance, and on Blackstone Point, now the site of the coastguard lookout, is a seventeenth-century gun battery.

A path leads along the Little Dartmouth cliffs from Blackstone Point around Compass Cove to Warren Point, and visitors may notice the stone gate-posts, a characteristic feature of the south Devon landscape.

ACCESS: By foot from car park at Sharkham Point; network of definitive and permitted paths along coastline, estuary and inland; network of paths linking properties to Warren Point; footbridge across deep gully at Compass Cove.

PARKING: Car parks at Coleton Fishacre, Woodhuish, Sharkham Point, Dartmouth and Little Dartmouth.

NOTE: Informal parking causes congestion.

FACILITIES: Local facilities; NT shop in Dartmouth; WCs at Dartmouth Castle; leaflets; viewpoints.

TINTAGEL

200 acres (81 ha) off B3263, S of Tintagel village, Cornwall
[200:SX056884]

Tintagel stands on a dramatic coastline of headlands and cliffs, with castles, ancient field systems and relics of a former slate-quarrying industry. Tintagel Castle has a literary association with the Arthurian legends and is a popular place for holidaymakers. There is a Norman church near the village.

To the north, the neck of Willapark is backed by the defensive ditch and rampart of an Iron Age cliff castle, and there is also an old lime kiln. The outlines of ancient field patterns or lynchets can be traced at Bossiney Common to the east. Barras Nose, a headland overlooking Tintagel Castle and formerly owned by the Duchy of Cornwall, was bought by the Trust in 1897 after a local appeal instigated by the plans to build King Arthur's Castle Hotel. Remains from the Dark Ages on Tintagel Island, still owned by the Duchy, are under the guardianship of English Heritage.

Impressive rock fissures can be seen along the Glebe cliffline, where there is evidence of old slate quarrying in which the rocks were cut by men lowered precariously over the cliff edge. The quarried stone was used locally to build cottages with traditional slate walls, or 'hedges', constructed in a chevron design or 'curzyway'. The relics of this once industrial landscape are now colonised by a rich variety of wildlife, including coastal grass and heathlands with thrift, sea campion, rock samphire, dyer's greenweed, kidney vetch, wild carrot, betony and many other species. Grey seal breed along the rocky shore, and sea birds include shag, guillemot, fulmar and razorbill.

ACCESS: Coastal footpaths and connecting paths; bus service from Bodmin, Bude and Wadebridge.

PARKING: Car parks at Bossiney, Tintagel Church and Trebarwith Strand.

FACILITIES: Youth hostel and WCs at Tintagel, Bossiney and Trebarwith Strand; leaflet; viewpoints.

TRELISSICK

400 acres (162 ha) 5m S of Truro, on both sides of B3289, above King Harry Ferry, Cornwall　　　　　　　　　　　　　　　　　　[204:SW837396]

Trelissick is famous for its large garden with many rare sub-tropical plants, but beyond the bounds of the formal garden are parklands and areas of broadleaved woodlands covering the steep banks and shores overlooking the creeks of the Fal Estuary and Falmouth Harbour. Evidence of oak coppicing is common throughout the woods (the bark was used for tanning leather and the wood for charcoal). The dead wood, glades, clearings and small wetlands make a rich and diverse habitat. The lichens and invertebrates associated with the older oaks are particularly important and provide evidence of continuity of ancient woodland and wood pasture. Wet ground in the Lambsclose Plantation includes royal fern, a characteristic plant of wet woodland, heath and flushes.

As well as oak, other trees such as ash, pedunculate oak (a sessile oak), hazel, holly, beech and hawthorn can be seen. Birds include the greater spotted woodpecker, nuthatch, jay, chaffinch and tree creeper. Pipistrelle and brown long-eared bats roost and feed in Lodge Plantation, and the plants of Namphillow Wood include primrose, lesser celandine and bluebell. South Wood is rich in a variety of woodland plants (bluebell, herb bennet, cow wheat and ferns) as well as remnant heathland plants. Soft shield fern grow at the head of Lamouth Creek.

The estate is bounded by Lamouth Creek to the north and Channels Creek to the south, estuarine habitats which add to the ecological interest of the area. The wooded edges of the creeks provide ideal platforms for kingfisher feeding on small fish, and curlew, redshank, greenshank, oystercatcher and shelduck feed on the mudflats exposed at low tide. Historical and ecological records reveal evidence of ancient woodland, fragments of which have been modified by later planting of conifers. Also of historic interest is the well-preserved promontory fort at Cowlands Creek.

ACCESS: Garden closed in winter, but walks in park and woodland accessible throughout the year; circular walks; stations at Truro and Perranwell, and bus service from Truro.

PARKING: Car park.

FACILITIES: NT shop (with plant sales) and restaurant; WCs (including disabled); batricar; leaflets; exhibition gallery; programme of theatrical and musical events (details from Administrator or regional office).

WEMBURY BAY AND THE YEALM ESTUARY

915 acres (370 ha) 5−6m E of Plymouth, access to W of estuary from Wembury village, E via Noss Mayo, Devon [201:SX530480]

The secluded Yealm Estuary lies to the east of Plymouth and round the headland of Heybrook, sheltering the villages of Newton Ferrers and Noss Mayo. The mouth of the estuary is protected by the Trust, but Great Mew Stone, within Wembury Bay (one of the first voluntary marine nature reserves) is now owned by the Ministry of Defence.

To the west, a path leads from Wembury along the High Cliffs to Warren Point, commanding beautiful views of the estuarine landscape which includes wooded slopes, open farmland, sheltered creeks, cliffs and rocky coves. Warren Point, as its name indicates, was once associated with the breeding of rabbits for fur and meat (the Warren Wall and Warren Cottage can still be seen). To the east, paths and the Revelstroke Drive (built a century ago) follow the coastline through woodlands and along the clifftops from Noss Mayo round Gara Point to Stoke Point.

Points of interest include Wembury Mill, now converted to a café, the miller's house which is let as holiday accommodation, and Wheal Emily at Knighton Farm, a mine that was in operation until 1852.

The estuaries, where the river waters meet the sea, are rich habitats for wildlife, with waders such as redshank and greenshank sheltering and feeding along the tidal coves. The woodlands, extending from Noss Mayo to Mouthstone Point, are also of interest, dominated by mature oak, sweet chestnut and beech. The clifftops include grasslands where autumn squill, kidney vetch, rock rose and thyme flourish. Cirl bunting can sometimes be seen. The Warren abounds with butterflies, including dark-green fritillary and grayling. Stonechat, wheatear and other small birds frequent the gorse and scrub.

ACCESS: Coastal path linked to inland routes (easy walking with few steep sections); circular routes from Noss Mayo; foot ferry across the estuary in summer.

PARKING: Car parks at Wembury, Noss Mayo and East Holli-combes.

FACILITIES: Shop at Wembury; WCs and refreshments at Wembury Beach and Noss Mayo; leaflet.

NOTE: Dogs restricted on Wembury Beach from May to September.

THE WEST DORSET HILL FORTS: PILSDEN PEN, LAMBERT'S CASTLE AND CONEY'S CASTLE

289 acres (117 ha) 3m SW of Broadwindsor and 4½m E of Axminster
[193:SY414012, 370986 and 372975]

West Dorset is renowned for the series of Iron Age hill forts which dominate its steep greensand hills. Pilsden Pen (the highest point in Dorset), Lambert's Castle and Coney's Castle all provide superb views over the Marshwood Vale to the sea, and the three hills are covered with a mixture of heath, scrub, grassland, woodland and wet flushes which create a diverse landscape rich in wildlife.

At Pilsdon Pen the wet flushes, typical of the greensand, contain bog asphodel, sundews and heath spotted orchid among the many damp-loving plants. Within the ramparts of the Iron Age hill fort are the banks of medieval pillow mounds (rabbit warrens).

In a beech woodland to the north-west of Lambert's Castle dormouse have been found, and to the south-east a mixture of scrub, birchwood, hedgebanks and wet flushes provide a variety of habitats. The small pearl-bordered fritillary inhabits the bog near the castle, which can be viewed from the public footpath. Medieval field systems can be seen, as well as the site of a post-medieval fair and a telegraph station.

Damp-loving plants also thrive in springs and flushes along the base of the ridge of Coney's Castle.

ACCESS: Network of footpaths.

PARKING: Car parks at all 3 sites.

FACILITIES: Local facilities; interpretation panels at all 3 sites.

WEST EXMOOR COAST: INCLUDING THE HEDDON VALLEY AND WOODY BAY

1136 acres (460 ha) on N Devon coast between Ilfracombe and Lynton, access from A399 and from narrow minor roads N from A399 and A39
[180:SS565477 to 675487]

On the western extremity of Exmoor National Park, this series of properties contains some of the most beautiful features of the North Devon landscape, with heather moorland, cliffs, deep wooded combes, narrow lanes and isolated hamlets. The precipitous cliffs, designated Heritage Coast, are the highest in England and are the classic example of 'hog's back' cliffs. Guillemot, kittiwake, fulmar, razorbill, jackdaw and raven inhabit the cliffs.

The Little Hangman and Great Hangman, Holdstone Down and Trentishoe Down together form an extensive and important tract of coastal heath. In late summer these hills are transformed by the colours of the flowering heathers and gorse. Stonechat, linnet, tree pipit, wheatear and whinchat thrive on the heaths. Miners' tracks can be seen crossing Great Hangman, where manganese, silver, iron and copper were once extracted. There is also an old iron mine (and two prehistoric hut circles) on Holdstone Down. Trentishoe Barrows are two prehistoric burial mounds.

The hanging oak woods (with old ash pollards) and meadows of the deep Heddon Valley are a pleasant surprise for those walking the North Devon Coast Path. Important ferns, mosses and lichens flourish in the woods, which harbour many birds such as redstart, pied flycatcher, wood warbler, and lesser spotted and green woodpeckers. Buzzard are often seen circling overhead. The meadows along the bottom of the valley are important for wetland flowers, and are home to a multitude of butterflies, including Britain's three large fritillaries, the silver-washed, dark-green and the rare high-brown.

The cove of Heddonsmouth is flanked by screes, a remnant of the last Ice Age, and to the east, beyond the waterfall of Hollowbrook and Highveer Point, secretive Woody Bay is clothed with majestic oaks. Disused post-medieval lime kilns can be seen at Woody Bay and Martinhoe, and there is a path leading from Woody Bay to the Roman signal station on the knoll above Martinhoe. Thanks to the Enterprise Neptune appeal, the Trust now owns over forty per cent of the coastline in Devon. Woody Bay was one of the first of these acquisitions in 1967.

ACCESS: Network of paths along coast and valleys; circular walks of varying lengths from Hunter's Inn; North Devon Coastal Path.

PARKING: Car parks at Combe Martin, Holdstone Down, Hunter's Inn, Trentishoe Down, Martinhoe and Inkerman Bridge.

FACILITIES: Local facilities; WCs opposite car park at Hunter's Inn; leaflet; information centre at Combe Martin; viewpoints from Highveer Point to Woody Bay (good views across to South Wales).

NOTE: Dogs to be kept on lead.

WEST PENWITH: CAPE CORNWALL TO PENBERTH

276 acres (112 ha), access via St Just on B3071 or Land's End on A30, Cornwall   [203:SW351319]

This is one of the most exposed and windswept areas of the Cornish coast, where cliffs, headlands and secluded coves overlook the Atlantic Ocean to the west and are backed by a historic landscape of lanes, fields and scattered hamlets to the south.

From the prominent rocky headland of Cape Cornwall (donated in 1987 by H. J. Heinz Ltd in association with the World Wildlife Fund), the Trust owns a number of separate properties of great archaeological and ecological interest. Coastal grasslands and coastal and inland heaths provide much of the latter. The strongly maritime heath shows interesting 'waved' formations, due to constant exposure to the prevailing winds, and provides a base for plants such as heather, bell heather, western gorse, tormentil, common milkwort, heath bedstraw, gorse, spring squill, heath spotted orchid, sedges and grasses. On the seaward slopes sea campion, thrift, scurvy grass, buck's horn plantain, rock samphire and sea beet can be seen.

The coastline is also important for sea birds, with kittiwake, guillemot, razorbill, fulmar, shag, cormorant and oystercatcher present. Buzzard, peregrine and kestrel can be seen hunting, and lapwing, corn bunting and the scarce nightjar are also present.

The well-preserved engine houses scattered over the landscape date back to the region's more recent tin-mining history (the Levant engine house is a notable example). Beneath the ground there is a maze of tunnels, galleries and chambers. The sheltered Priest's Cove has been a landing place for centuries. Chapel Carn Brea, the first and last hill in England, is clad with heath and many archaeological remains. At Carn Gloose is the entrance to a Bronze Age grave. Pedn-mên-du is a historical coastguard look-out and signalling headland. Maen Castle is thought to be the earliest Iron Age cliff castle in West Penwith.

Further to the south, the granite cliffs east of Pedn-mên-an-mere have been eroded to an unusual block-shaped formation. Treen Cliff rises above the beautiful sandy cove of Pedn-vounder Beach, and Penberth Cove has been a productive fishing harbour for centuries. The slopes of the Penberth valley are covered with minute meadows or 'quillets', many now overgrown with scrub, which were once used for growing violets and daffodils for market.

ACCESS: Network of footpaths along coastline.

PARKING: Car parks at Cape Cornwall, Chapel Carn Brea, Sennen, Treen and Porthcurno.

FACILITIES: WCs at Sennen, Porthcurno and Treen; leaflet.

WEST PENWITH: ST IVES TO PENDEEN

444½ acres (180 ha) N of B3306, W of St Ives, Cornwall
[203:SW4539 and 203:SW415365]

This is a remote and unspoilt coastline of coves, headlands and rocky cliffs and plateaux towards the western extremity of Cornwall. The stunning ancient landscape of prehistoric field systems has seen relatively little change over the centuries. Its archaeological and wildlife value is now protected, not just by the Trust but also by the designation of West Penwith as an Environmentally Sensitive Area, in which farmers are encouraged to conserve historic features and farm in traditional ways.

Prehistoric cliff castles can be seen at Gurnard's Head and Bosigran. Tin-mine engine houses, such as the one at Carn Galver, and other industrial remains in the Porthmeor Valley punctuate the farmland. Unimproved cliff and commonland provide habitats for a wide variety of wildlife. Grey seal inhabit the coastline, and manx shearwater, gannet, guillemot and kittiwake can be seen along the cliffs.

There are rich bogs, mires, stream sides and small wooded valleys of great ecological importance, such as the lower Treveal Valley, where dense scrub provides resting cover for migrating birds, as well as nesting sites. Many plants of interest are found, with purple moor grass, rushes such as the black bog rush, St John's wort, southern marsh orchid and royal fern (in damp areas). Large Cornish 'hedges' or walls border the small, irregular fields, and headlands are capped by rocky granite tors. Zennor Head, a prominent granite point, is reached from the village of Zennor and is bordered by the characteristic ancient field patterns. From the summit of Carn Galver there are splendid views of the ancient landscape of small fields, narrow lanes, scattered farms and isolated cottages. To the west, the farms around Rosemergy include good examples of ribbon farmland – long narrow holdings extending down from the moors to the cliffs.

ACCESS: Network of footpaths along coastline.

PARKING: Car parks at Wicca, Zennor and Carn Galver.

FACILITIES: Viewpoints; leaflet; information centre at the Wayside Museum in Zennor.

Southern England

HAMPSHIRE · KENT · SURREY · EAST AND WEST SUSSEX
ISLE OF WIGHT · WILTSHIRE

This densely populated region embraces some of Britain's most treasured landscapes: the North and South Downs, the Weald, the Chilterns, the Thames Valley, the Surrey heathlands, the Berkshire Downs, the New Forest, the Isle of Wight and the Seven Sisters.

The pattern of land use in Southern England reflects the sequence of occupation: Roman, Anglo-Saxon and Normans. Wiltshire's ancient landscapes recall even earlier inhabitants and are particularly rich in archaeological interest, with the mysterious Avebury Ring, Bronze Age burial barrows and standing stones – some of the best preserved ancient monuments in the country.

The North Downs are notable for the variety of wildlife as well as their archaeological remains. The Surrey Hills AONB, embracing the chalk landscapes of the North Downs and pockets of remaining lowland heathland, is an important and sadly diminishing wildlife habitat. The Trust has been able to acquire areas of the South Downs in desperate need of conservation, thanks to its South Downs Appeal, re-launched in 1991. Straddling the Wiltshire, Hampshire and

Berkshire borders, the North Wessex Downs AONB is a sweep of chalk landscape above the Vale of the White Horse. To the east, the chalk ridge meets the Thames along wooded reaches of the Goring Gap, a richly farmed valley landscape.

Another area of great historic significance is the New Forest – once a medieval hunting forest and pasture woodland. Bramshaw Commons, on its north edge, contain an interesting variety of wild-life habitats.

To the south-east, Chichester Harbour, including East Head, is a haven for large numbers of sea birds. It is one of the most under-developed harbours in south England and a natural tidal inlet. The Isle of Wight – a unique area of great wildlife interest – is dominated by a central backbone of chalk: the impressive white chalk pinnacles of the Needles create a stark contrast to the grassland of Tennyson Down on West Wight.

Southern England suffers particularly badly from over-development; the continually increasing use of cars results in more roads, by-passes and motorways carving up tracts of outstanding landscape. The National Trust's presence in this region over the last century has proved vital.

ABINGER ROUGHS, PINEY COPSE AND NETLEY PARK

541 acres (219 ha) 7m W of Dorking, and 11m W of Dorking, off A25, Surrey   [187:TQ1048 and 078484]

These three North Downs properties in the Surrey Hills, which in-clude a farm and some cottages, are part of an AONB and character-ised by sloping wooded ridges overlooking valleys to the north, described by Cobbett as 'the choicest retreat for man'.

Abinger Roughs, above the hamlet of Abinger, is a central spine of woodland with scrub, grassland and plantings of beech and coni-fers. The oak, birch, beech and pine woods, with several fine old trees, provide habitats for many birds including greater and lesser spotted woodpeckers, nuthatch, tree creeper and wood warbler.

Netley is made up of grazed parkland, pasture and woodland,

79

while Piney Copse is a mixed wood (many of the woods were badly damaged in the storms of 1987 and 1990). Netley Park contains small areas of unimproved grassland and some fragments of ancient beech woodland along the chalk ridge which support a ground flora of spurge laurel, wood melick, wood sedge and nettle-leaved bell-flower.

ACCESS: Network of footpaths.

PARKING: Car park at Abinger Roughs.

FACILITIES: Local facilities.

AVEBURY

1450 acres (587 ha) 6m W of Marlborough, 1m N of A4, Wiltshire
[173:SU102700]

This much celebrated and impressive megalithic monument, designated a World Heritage Site and under the guardianship of English Heritage, is the largest prehistoric stone circle in Europe. Surrounded by an immense bank and ditch, and approached from the south by an avenue of stones, the West Kennet Avenue, it is encroached upon by the medieval village. A later thoroughfare cuts through the site, and is now a busy road.

The surrounding landscape of the Marlborough Downs is made up of sweeping arable fields, grassland and prominent clumps of beech, and is strewn with archaeological remains. Barrows can be seen nearby on Overton Hill, and there is evidence of Iron Age, Roman and medieval field systems. Among ancient routes is the post-Roman Herepath and the Ridgeway. Windmill Hill, to the north-west of Avebury, has a famous neolithic causewayed enclosure on its summit. Also notable is the sixteenth-century Avebury Manor and a seventeenth-century tithe barn.

Most of the land is intensively farmed, but remnants of chalk grassland on the earthbank slopes support a wide variety of plants such as cowslip, stemless thistle, thyme and eyebright. The sarsen stones are encrusted with lichens.

ACCESS: Open daily; network of paths; stations at Pewsey and Swindon, and bus service from Swindon, Devizes and Salisbury.

PARKING: Car and coach park; limited parking for cars only at Windmill Hill.

FACILITIES: NT shop; restaurant and inn; WCS (including disabled); museum (English Heritage but free to NT members); Wiltshire Folk Life Society and English Heritage education centre with display of rural life; craft centre.

BEMBRIDGE AND CULVER DOWNS

104 acres (42 ha) 2m E of Brading, off B3395, Isle of Wight
[196:SZ624860]

Located at the eastern end of the beautiful Isle of Wight, these downs (an SSSI and AONB) are dominated by the chalk ridge which runs across the island from east to west. The sheer cliffs rising out of the English Channel are used by nesting birds, and are of great geological interest.

The remainder of the property includes remnants of chalk grassland on the ridges of Bembridge and Culver downs, and areas of agricultural land. A mile to the north is Bembridge Windmill (also owned by the Trust), the only one on the island and an example of a tower mill, and also of interest is the nineteenth-century Bembridge Fort, commissioned by Lord Palmerston's government as part of the south-coast defence system (not open to visitors), and two late nineteenth-century gun emplacements at Culver Down. There is also the impressive stone column of the Yarborough Monument (not owned by the Trust).

The parts of Bembridge and Culver downs owned by the Trust merge with open land owned by the South Wight Borough Council. The boundaries are unmarked.

The flora is only patchily rich, since several areas of downland have been agriculturally improved. The high exposure factor ensures that many plants occur only in stunted form. None the less, a wide range of chalk specialists is found, such as yellow-wort, horseshoe vetch, squinancywort and lady's bedstraw. The insect fauna is restricted by the windswept conditions, but includes the chalkhill blue butterfly and various uncommon beetles. Scrub pockets provide a useful breeding habitat for several small birds.

ACCESS: Open access to downs; coastal path; local station at Brading; no access to fort.

PARKING: Car park at Bembridge and Culver downs.

FACILITIES: NT shop at Bembridge Windmill (seasonal opening); leaflet; display.

BLACK DOWN

602 acres (244 ha) 1m SE of Haslemere, West Sussex
[186 and 197:SU9230]

Part of the greensand ridge of the north Weald, Black Down is the highest point in Sussex and forms a prominent landmark for miles around, commanding good views across the well-wooded landscape of the Weald. The plateau was once an extensive heath created by common grazing and managed as common pasture with bracken cut for bedding and fuel collected from the woodland fringe (which contains some old wood pasture). It is now much covered by naturally regenerating Scots pine, silver birch and rhododendron, and the Trust is initiating projects to maintain and increase the remaining fragments of heath, which include some interesting small bogs.

The Victorian Poet Laureate Lord Tennyson was inspired by the landscape and built his house on the shoulder of the down.

The main summit area and other relict areas of heathland are dominated by heather and bell heather, with wetland plants such as cross-leaved heath, round-leaved sundew, common and hare's tail cotton grasses and bog asphodel. The old woodlands include Quellwood Common in the south, part of an ancient wood pasture, with oak, beech and holly woods to the south-east. Pine woodland dominates the remainder of Black Down, with rowan, birch, gorse, bramble and bilberry.

Birds include nuthatch, woodcock, the occasional crossbill, meadow pipit, linnet, yellowhammer and green, greater and lesser spotted woodpeckers. There is a strong invertebrate interest, centred on the bogs, dry heathland and older woodland areas. On its north side, the open meadows and parkland of Valewood, with its pattern of small fields, trackways and banks, offer a contrast to the woods of Black Down.

Of historic interest are old chert quarries on Black Down, and some hammerponds at Shottermill, used for smelting iron. Woodland coppices produced charcoal to supply the ironworks.

ACCESS: Network of footpaths and bridleways.

PARKING: Car park off Tennyson Lane; informal parking.

FACILITIES: Local facilities.

BOOKHAM AND BANK'S COMMON

452 acres (183 ha) 3m W of Leatherhead, just N of Bookham station, Surrey [187:TQ1256]

This large area of wooded commonland is linked by a network of ancient routes, footpaths and bridleways, and covered by extensive patches of mature woodland. Its history dates back to at least AD666, when the manor is known to have been owned by Chertsey Abbey, and the commons are listed in the Domesday Book as providing pannage (the right to graze pigs on acorns) for the monks.

The woodland contains many very fine ancient oaks, and a varied range of other trees with shrubs as younger 'infill'. Rich grasslands, a series of ancient ponds and a fragment of heath also occurs. Common grazing ceased in the 1940s, but has recently been re introduced to part of the property.

It is renowned for its insect fauna, which has been well studied and includes many national rarities, especially beetles and flies. Insects new to Britain have been discovered here. Many notable butterflies, including purple emperor and white admiral, can be seen in the semi-natural woodland, with birds such as nightingale, greater spotted woodpecker, great, long-tailed and marsh tits, tree creeper and nuthatch.

The ancient ponds, once used by the monks of Chertsey Abbey for storing fish, are an important habitat for palmate, great crested and smooth newts, with many frogs and toads. Ditches and streams support wetland plants such as water mint, bur reed, horsetail, water figwort, gipsywort, meadowsweet, great hairy willowherb and marsh woundwort, and purple moor grass and heather grow on a pocket of heathland near the ponds. The grassland is dominated by rushes and bracken.

ACCESS: Network of footpaths and bridleways; station at Bookham.

PARKING: 4 car parks.

FACILITIES: Leaflet; information boards.

BOX HILL

954 acres (386 ha) 1m NE of Dorking, 1½m S of Leatherhead, E of A24, Surrey [187:TQ1751]

Located on a prominent chalk scarp overlooking the River Mole, this important SSSI is cut by a number of dry combes to make up the attractive 'karst' or limestone scenery, a rare feature in southern Britain. The hill is named for the box trees, native to the site, and the prolific yew is also distinctive, especially on the steep slopes of the scarp. Much of the high beech wood was destroyed in the storms of 1987 and 1990, but natural regeneration and the programme of re-planting will ensure the continuity and richness of the associated wildlife.

The chalk grasslands contain many characteristic plants and in-vertebrates, including several scarce species. Over a dozen species of orchid have been recorded, and at least 400 species of other plants. More than two-thirds of the current species of British butterflies are found on the hill, relying on key larval plants such as horseshoe vetch, bird's foot trefoil, hairy violet and cowslip.

The areas of box harbour the rare box shield bug, and the pockets of juniper attract the juniper shield bug. The many species of molluscs and beetles, some listed as rare or endangered, are indi-cators of the antiquity of parts of the woodland. Scrubby areas of dogwood, wayfaring tree, yew, ash, birch, box and spindle create ideal nesting sites for many smaller birds, and there are many birds of prey such as sparrowhawk, kestrel and tawny and little owls. Kingfisher and grey wagtail can be seen near the river. Mammals include badger, roe deer, fox, yellowneck mouse, weasel and the ubiquitous rabbit.

The hill has been a centre for field study since Victorian times, and now has the Juniper Hall Centre on the site. Much information has been gathered over the years to make an important historical inventory, and the research continues. Box Hill also has literary associations, with visitors from John Evelyn and Celia Fiennes to John Keats, Jane Austen and George Meredith, and it provided a hiding-place for refugees from the French Revolution.

Also of interest are some prehistoric tumuli, field systems, the Roman road of Stane Street and Box Hill Fort, built in 1899 and now under restoration.

ACCESS: Network of footpaths; Pilgrims' Way crosses property; stations at Boxhill, Dorking and Westhumble, and bus service from Leatherhead.

PARKING: Car parks.

FACILITIES: NT shop; WCS (including disabled); leaflets for self-guided walks; information centre; maps in car parks; guidebook; educational pack; viewpoint; level walk from car park to viewpoint and beyond for disabled.

BRAMSHAW COMMONS

1404 acres (568 ha) between Bramshaw, Cadnam and Plaitford, on N edge of New Forest, just S of A36, 10m W of Southampton, Hampshire
[184 and 185:SU2717]

This very extensive network of manorial wastes and commons on the periphery of the New Forest includes Cadnam and Stocks Cross greens, and Bramshaw, Cadnam, Furzley, Half Moon, Penn and Plaitford commons. The New Forest, a Royal Forest established in the eleventh century by William the Conqueror, evolved with its own charter for enclosure, cultivation, hunting, grazing and commoners' rights.

Of interest are two Bronze Age cairns on Plaitford Common, and a twin-bowl barrow on Furzley Common.

The manorial wastes, usually heathland, provided the commoners with timber, fuel and other useful commodities. Today they represent the best surviving example of lowland heath and mire

85

in Europe, still managed by the common grazing of ponies, pigs, donkeys, cattle and sheep.

The Bramshaw heaths and mires are among the most important in the New Forest. The flora is very rich, and includes large populations of penny royal and small fleabane; long-leaved sundew, marsh St John's wort and bog asphodel occur in the mires. The dry heaths are particularly good for Dartford warbler and woodlark. The invertebrate fauna is extremely rich: the rare fairy shrimp occurs in a seasonal pool; there is an impressive list of solitary bees and wasps; rare bugs and weevils inhabit the bogs; there are some scarce dead-wood beetles along the wood pasture fringes; and standard heathland butterflies such as grayling, green hairstreak and silver-studded blue occur. The commons also provide a habitat for the scarce blue-tailed damselfly, raft spider and grasshoppers.

ACCESS: Open access; station at Southampton Parkway.

PARKING: Car park at Black Hill.

FACILITIES: Information boards in car park and at the main cross roads.

CHERHILL DOWN AND OLDBURY CASTLE

182 acres (74 ha) on A4 between Calne and Beckhampton, Wiltshire
[173:SU046694]

This ancient downland landscape overlooks the Vale of Pewsey, with a series of deeply incised sheltered coombes supporting a herb-rich chalk grassland with characteristic clumps of beech trees. At the summit of the chalk ridge is the Iron Age hill fort of Oldbury Castle and the recently restored Lansdowne Monument, built in 1845 by the 3rd Marquis of Lansdowne in memory of the economist Sir William Petty.

A white horse (not owned by the Trust) is carved into the flank of the downland, one of the many man-made features in this striking landscape, which also has Bronze Age bowl and long barrows, a cross-ridge dyke, ancient routeways, tumuli, strip field systems, earthworks and old mineral workings.

The steeper slopes to the west and south are best for chalkland flowers, with squinancywort, clustered bellflower, rock-rose, cowslip and fragrant orchid. Butterflys include chalkhill blue, marbled white, dingy skipper, marsh fritillary and brown argus. The uniform mounds left by the yellow meadow ant are typical of a long-unploughed grassland. Skylark and meadow pipit are common in summer, and hen harrier and short-eared owl in winter. Coarse tor grass is increasing to the detriment of flora and fauna.

ACCESS: Footpaths and bridleways.

PARKING: No formal car park.

FACILITIES: Local facilities.

CISSBURY RING

123 acres (50 ha) 1½m E of Findon on A24, 3m N of Worthing, West Sussex [198:TQ140082]

Set on a chalk promontory on the South Downs, with good views across to Beachy Head and the west Isle of Wight, and part of the Sussex Downs AONB, this Iron Age hill fort with its ditch and ramparts encompasses about sixty-five acres. It is the second largest in England and an SAM. Archaeological evidence shows that this strategic site was also important for flint production during the neolithic period, and was later cultivated during Celtic and Roman times (some strip lynchets can still be seen).

Also valued as an SSSI, the chalk grassland covering the earthworks supports a wide range of downland plants such as horseshoe vetch, cowslip, stemless thistle and several species of orchid (including pyramid and common spotted). Butterflies include chalkhill blue and dark-green fritillary.

A dry combe or steep-sided valley cuts into the chalk plateau, and is also rich in lime-loving flowers and grasses such as rock-rose, horseshoe vetch, quaking grass and ploughman's spikenard.

ACCESS: Open access on foot only (no bicycles); network of footpaths; station at Worthing.

PARKING: Car park off minor road to N.

FACILITIES: Information board near car park.

CLEY HILL

66 acres (27 ha) 2m W of Warminster, N of A362, Wiltshire
[183:ST838450]

This chalk hill, some six miles to the west of Salisbury Plain, consists of unimproved downland of SSSI status which supports a good range of characteristic flora and fauna, including a wide variety of rarer species. It is famous as a habitat of the chalkhill blue butterfly, and several orchids.

Like so many hilltops in Wessex the summit is crowned by an Iron Age hill fort, with two Bronze Age bowl barrows inside. It was the site of an Armada beacon, and there are some medieval strip lynchets and a disused nineteenth-century quarry.

From the summit there are fine views to the south overlooking the Longleat Estate.

ACCESS: Open access; station at Warminster.

PARKING: Car park.

FACILITIES: Archaeological leaflet.

THE COOMBES, HINTON PARVA

43 acres (17 ha) 7m E of Swindon, off B4507, Wiltshire [174:SU228828]

Situated to the south-west of the Vale of the White Horse and close to the Oxfordshire border, this area of chalk downland (an SSSI) includes a small unimproved hay meadow and a deep combe.

The herb-rich grassland, with cowslip, thyme, small scabious and rock-rose, attracts many butterflies including brown argus and marbled white. Green-veined and pyramidal orchids are numerous, and there is a winterbourne, or small intermittent stream, lined with old willow pollards. There is a fine set of medieval strip lynchets.

ACCESS: Footpath and bridleway link the property to the Ridge-way; station at Swindon.

PARKING: Small car park (not NT).

FACILITIES: Local facilities.

DITCHLING BEACON

5 acres (2 ha) 6m N of Brighton, off unclassified Brighton to Ditchling road,
East Sussex   [198:TQ333130]

Located on the South Downs Way, this prominent site has slight traces of the rampart and ditch of an Iron Age hill fort which commanded extensive views over the Sussex Weald, the mouth of the River Ouse and out to the English Channel. The Clayton to Offham escarpment is an sssi, and the whole area falls within the Sussex Downs aonb. The steep slope of the escarpment includes a fine example of quality downland. In the north-west corner of the site is an important prehistoric earthbank.

Used traditionally by local graziers as a sheep walk, the chalk grasslands on the South Downs ridge are rich in wild flowers, with marjoram, salad burnet, devil's bit scabious, carline thistle and common spotted orchid all frequent locally. There are numerous mounds of the yellow meadow ant, indicating ancient turf (see Harting Down for a more detailed explanation).

ACCESS: Open during daylight hours; South Downs Way; footpaths and a bridleway cross the site; circular walks.

PARKING: Car park at top of ridge.

FACILITIES: Information board with maps; wheelchair access to South Downs Way and Beacon from car park.

FAIRLIGHT

228 acres (92 ha) 4½m E of Hastings, off A259, East Sussex
                                                    [199:TQ884127]

This property consists primarily of a farmed landscape abutting the East Sussex cliffline, of considerable wildlife and geological interest.

The notable mudstone cliffs at Hastings are eroding fast and have been designated an sssi for their geology. Market and Stumblet woods are thought to be of ancient origin (with evidence of badgers and early woodland management), and support an attractive ground flora of primrose, bluebell, wood sorrel, moschatel and honeysuckle. The reed beds at Marsham are of great value to migrant songbirds and nesting wetland birds including sedge warbler and reed bunting, and the grazing marshes are of interest for damp-loving plants. Old anthills on the clifftop grasslands are indications of their ancient origins.

ACCESS: NT permitted and public footpaths (restricted access to reed beds); stations at Hastings and Ore.

PARKING: Car park at Cliff End behind Pett Beach, and other local authority car parks.

FACILITIES: Local facilities in Hastings and Ore; WCs in car parks; viewpoint.

FIGSBURY RING

27 acres (11 ha) 4m NE of Salisbury, ½m N of A30 London road, Wiltshire
[184:SU188338]

These distinctive earthbanks are the remains of a well-preserved Iron Age hill fort located on a chalk promontory overlooking the Vale of Salisbury. The fort consists of a single circular bank and outer ditch breached by two openings, with an internal quarry ditch forming a second ring. A continuous programme of management, together with cattle-grazing, keeps the site free from encroaching scrub and maintains its botanical interest.

The warm south-facing slopes of the banks are well suited to chalk-loving plants such as pyramidal, fragrant, bee, common spotted and frog orchids, harebell, thyme and small scabious. Twenty species of butterfly have been recorded, including adonis and chalk-hill blues and brown argus, and among other invertebrates of note is the large population of the spectacular giant robberfly *Asilus crabroniformis*, a harmless – if frightening – yellow and black fly which can be seen during late summer.

ACCESS: Over stile from car park; station at Salisbury.

PARKING: Car park.

FACILITIES: Information panel; archaeological leaflet from NT shop in Salisbury.

FRENSHAM COMMON

922 acres (373 ha) 10m S of Farnham, both sides of A287, Surrey
[186:SU8541]

This fine example of open Surrey heathland, one of the largest expanses in the Weald and designated an SSSI, consists of dry and wet heath, some woodland, scrub and ponds. It is of great importance for heathland insects and reptiles, and with the neighbouring heaths is a proposed Special Protection Area for its heathland birds, such as nightjar, stonechat and whinchat.

The common and Great Pond are leased to Waverley Borough Council which manages the area partly as a country park. The Great Pond was excavated in the thirteenth century on the site of a smaller pond, and used to supply fish to the Bishop of Winchester's Court when visiting Farnham Castle.

The Little Pond is also man-made and was formed when a dam was built in 1246. It has some important fen habitats, with fringes of yellow iris, sweet flag and common reeds, and alder and willow carr. Marsh cinquefoil, bur marigold, water mint and angelica are also found, along with many species of damselfly and dragonfly. The pond is managed partly as a bird sanctuary, and supports reed bunting, reed and sedge warbler, snipe, redshank, great crested grebe and water rail.

Both ponds were drained during the Second World War to remove distinctive identification features in the landscape, and were used for tank exercises until being refilled in 1949.

On the heathland are plants such as bell heather, ling, gorse (including dwarf gorse) and bracken in the drier areas, with mosses, sedges, common and cotton grasses and round-leaved sundew on wet ground. Sand lizards occur, along with heathland insects such as silver-studded blue butterfly, and numerous mining bees and digger wasps. The spider fauna is also rich.

ACCESS: Network of footpaths and bridleways.

PARKING: Car parks.

FACILITIES: WCs (including disabled); information room at Great Pond.

NOTE: There is a great risk of accidental fires.

FROG FIRLE FARM

348 acres (141 ha) off B2108 *Alfriston to Seaford road, East Sussex*
[TQ517012]

The farm, acquired by the Trust in 1991, lies between Alfriston and Seaford on the South Downs. Part of an AONB, it is made up of downland, water meadow beside the river and arable fields, and also contains an SSSI.

As well as features of natural beauty, this property clearly shows the influence of land use on the downs through the types of grass encouraged by traditional grazing regimes. An interesting variety of grasses also occur on and around the famous white horse which is carved out of the hillside. The Trust intends to maintain this chalk landmark, and has reintroduced traditional grazing on the downland.

There is an interesting flora along the ditches, including sea club rush, flowering rush and patches of purple loosestrife along the bank. The flora supports a very rich insect fauna, with eight species of dragonfly recorded, including the ruddy darter, emperor dragonfly and emerald damselfly.

The stretch of steep downland of High and Over has large areas of fescue turf. Creeping fescue dominates the fine turf areas, and south of the combe, areas of brome turf have a rich herb content. The slope supports important butterfly colonies, including common and chalkhill blues, and marbled white.

The property is valuable for wintering birds, with teal, snipe and wigeon on the alluvial meadows.

The farm consists of a range of nineteenth-century flint and tile buildings, including a fire-damaged barn which will be repaired and returned to agricultural use. There is one prehistoric tumulus on the site.

ACCESS: Footpaths across farm from car park and from Seaford; station at Seaford.

PARKING: Car park at High and Over.

FACILITIES: Local facilities in Seaford.

FULKING ESCARPMENT

105 acres (42½ ha) 5m NW of Brighton, S of Poynings, Fulking and Edburton, West Sussex [198:TQ2411]

This magnificent north-facing escarpment of chalk downland, within the Sussex Downs AONB, is characteristically indented by a series of dry combes, including the most spectacular one nearby, known as the Devil's Dyke, which is the largest chalkland dry combe in Britain and harbours many associated plants and butterflies.

Following the re-launch of its South Downs Appeal, the Trust is acquiring large areas of the ancient escarpment landscape, with its archaeological and ecological diversity, which has been designated an ESA to protect it from the pressures of agricultural improvement and development.

The quality of the grassland depends on the grazing regime; if there is insufficient grazing the coarse grasses can shade out less competitive plants. Sensitive management of this grassland has ensured that such plants as lady's bedstraw, ribwort plantain, cowslip, burnet saxifrage, common knapweed and orchids, which include the common spotted, bee, frog and twayblade, can thrive here.

The open grassland flora varies from area to area according to factors such as soil depth, aspect and grazing history. Butterflies include chalkhill blue (breeding on horseshoe vetch), and brown argus and green hairstreak (both breeding on rock-rose). The most notable breeding birds are skylark, corn bunting, meadow pipit and willow warbler.

Of historical interest are the remains of a Norman motte and bailey (an SAM) and the site of a deserted medieval village, some Bronze Age burial mounds and an old lime kiln. The adjacent property, Newtimber Hill, is also well worth visiting for its spectacular views over the Weald.

ACCESS: Network of footpaths; South Downs Way; station at Brighton.

PARKING: Car park by Devil's Dyke.

FACILITIES: Viewpoint.

HACKHURST DOWN AND LITTLE KING'S WOOD

73 acres (30 ha) ½m NE of Gomshall and Shere stations; 4m W of Dorking, on A25 above Gomshall, Surrey
[187:TQ092486 and 090492]

On the North Downs escarpment, with views across the valley of Tillingbourne, these two properties are part of the pastoral landscape of the Surrey Hills, and an AONB. Part of Hackhurst Down, overlying a chalk ridge, is included in a local nature reserve because of the rich diversity of its chalk-loving insects and plants such as juniper.

Also of interest are some historic field boundaries and evidence of old coppicing. The North Downs Way, an ancient drove road, runs through the properties.

The grassland supports a variety of plants such as salad burnet, wild basil and marjoram, quaking grass, hairy violet and bird's foot trefoil. This in turn supports a rich butterfly fauna. There is a notable stand of juniper at Hackhurst Down, which harbours the scarce juniper shield bug. There are also thickets of wayfaring tree, whitebeam, privet, dogwood, hazel, yew and ash; and Little King's Wood has some mature oak and beech trees.

ACCESS: By footpath from Abinger Hammer; North Downs Way; stations at Dorking, Gomshall and Shere.

PARKING: Car parks at Abinger Roughs and Ranmore, and on local council parking areas.

FACILITIES: Information board; local facilities.

HALE PURLIEU

512 acres (207 ha) 3m N of Fordingbridge, off B3080, Hampshire
[184:SU200180]

Situated on the northern side of the historic royal hunting ground of the New Forest, this former manorial waste is still grazed under the traditional commoners' rights, and is made up of dry and wet heath, mires and scrub.

Heathland plants include dwarf gorse, purple moor grass and bog asphodel, with two types of sundews, marsh St John's wort, meadow thistle and two species of cotton grass occurring in the wet heath. Birds such as Dartford warbler, nightjar, snipe, stonechat and redshank can be seen, and many insects, including the black darter dragonfly, inhabit the ponds and streams.

Millersford Plantation, leased to the Forestry Commission, includes Corsican and Scots pines, and there are some mixed woodlands of oak, holly, birch and beech. Greater spotted woodpecker and woodcock can be seen.

Of historical interest are some old boiling pits (for heating stones to warm food or for saunas) and some prehistoric barrows.

ACCESS: Network of footpaths.

PARKING: Car park at Lady's Mile.

FACILITIES: Local facilities.

NOTE: There is a high risk of fire.

HAREWOODS

2034 acres (823 ha) 3m SE of Redhill, E of A22, Surrey   [187:TQ3347]

This agricultural estate in an unspoilt part of the Surrey countryside contains a variety of landscape features, such as ancient woodland, unimproved meadows, hedges, marl pit ponds and streams, which makes it of considerable conservation interest.

The meadows support plants including fleabane, sneezewort, self-heal and strawberry clover, and the semi-natural oak and ash woodlands, which also contain hazel and wild service tree (an indicator of their antiquity), have a rich ground flora with wood spurge, yellow archangel and spurge laurel. Outwood Common, long ungrazed, has important ancient trees and is reverting to a broadleaved woodland of oak, ash and hornbeam.

ACCESS: Network of footpaths and bridleways.

PARKING: Informal parking at Outwood Common.

FACILITIES: Local facilities.

HARTING DOWN

520 acres (210 ha) 4m SE of Petersfield, off B2146, West Sussex
[197:SU8018]

One of the largest areas of ancient chalk downland owned by the Trust, this SSSI is an important habitat for the variety of plants and invertebrates it supports. Sheep have traditionally grazed the downland, and the continued grazing is vital to maintain the range of species. The Trust, in liaison with the County Council and local graziers, has reintroduced grazing after a gap of about ten years.

Small hummocky mounds, the nests of yellow meadow ants, are a sign that the grassland has not been ploughed for a long time, if ever, and those areas of downland that were ploughed in the early 1970s are now reverting to pasture. The area is part of the South Downs ESA, in which farmers and landowners are encouraged to farm the downs 'traditionally', by maintaining sheep or cattle grazing and by avoiding the use of artificial fertilisers.

The sward on the steep slopes is dominated by rather rank upright brome grass, and rarities, such as chalk milkwort and musk orchid, are restricted to the skeletal soil areas. There is a tiny area of chalk heath and an excellent juniper stand. Invertebrates include Duke of Burgundy and grizzled skipper butterflies, the exquisite blue carpenter bee and the rare cheese snail.

Of historical interest are an Iron Age hill fort (an SAM), some earthworks and cross-ridge dykes.

ACCESS: Network of footpaths; South Downs Way.

PARKING: Car park.

FACILITIES: Picnic area (leased by West Sussex County Council).

HIGHDOWN HILL

52 acres (21 ha) 1m N of Ferring, 3m NW of Worthing, West Sussex
[197 and 198:TQ092043]

On this ancient chalk knoll bounded by Worthing, the sea and the South Downs, archaeological remains have revealed evidence of the successive civilisations that have occupied the site. The ditch and rampart of an Iron Age fort is obvious, but the remains of an earlier Bronze Age settlement, a Romano-British settlement and a Anglo-Saxon cemetery also exist here. A fifteen-foot raised beach, created as a result of a fall in the sea level, forms the southern boundary.

The grassland includes some important wildlife habitats, and plants associated with the old chalk grassland include cowslip, common spotted orchid, kidney vetch, vervain, rock-rose and chalk milkwort. The carthusian snail, a rare mollusc associated with fine unimproved grassland, has been found, and there are many birds such as whitethroat, linnet, goldfinch and willow warbler which nest in thickets in the old chalk pits.

ACCESS: Open access; network of footpaths and bridleways; station at Worthing.

PARKING: Car park (not NT).

FACILITIES: Local facilities.

HINDHEAD

1394 acres (564 ha) NW of Haslemere, E of A3 and A287 junction, Surrey
[186:SU8936]

Hindhead Commons include some extensive areas of lowland heath in an AONB of importance for its large expanses of undeveloped countryside. The slopes of the Devil's Punchbowl, a large natural amphitheatre, are covered with heath, small streams and areas of woodland.

The Punchbowl was formed by springs cutting down and back from their sources, and is the largest spring-formed feature in Britain. The process can still be seen in miniature around the springs in the bottom of the bowl.

Until the First World War, the bowl was inhabited by 'broom squires', who made brooms from the surrounding birch trees.

Gibbet Hill, a sandstone hill with views across the Weald, marks the site where three footpads (highwaymen on foot) were hung after murdering a sailor on the then wild wastelands of Hindhead Common. It was also the site of the original London to Portsmouth road, which explains why the sailor was there – the Sailor's Stone commemorates the event.

Grazing of the heathland by commoners ceased around 1900, which allowed the spread of birch, pine and bracken over the heather, but this encroachment is now being reversed by a programme of active reclamation.

The heath is dominated by heather, bell heather and dwarf gorse, with bracken and common gorse and grasses such as purple moor grass. Older woods and wood pastures of oak, holly, ash and beech coppice occur in places, as in Highcombe Copse, and alder, willow and bog bean grow along the stream at Highcombe Bottom, with a series of small mires. Green, greater and lesser spotted woodpeckers can be seen in the woods, with nightjar and stonechat around the commons. The valley bottom supports a rich insect fauna, including rare craneflies.

ACCESS: Network of footpaths and bridleways.

PARKING: Car park.

FACILITIES: Café; information board; leaflet for self-guided walks.

HOLMWOOD COMMON

650 acres (263 ha) 1m S of Dorking, both sides of A24, Surrey
[187:TQ1746]

This large area of ungrazed commonland is crossed by a network of paths and rides which are popular with walkers. Its ownership can be traced back to Edith, widow of Edward the Confessor, from whom it passed to William the Conqueror. There is a history of squatters, smugglers, sheep stealers and highwaymen. The first road through the area was a toll road along the western edge, built in 1755 on the Horsham–London route.

The Trust is actively encouraging the present balance of open grassland, scrub, bracken and pockets of old woodland, which attract a wide range of birds and insects, including numerous moths and some unusual species of butterfly such as purple and brown hairstreaks and white admiral. The streams are bordered by water mint, lady fern, yellow flag, water figwort and fleabane.

ACCESS: Network of footpaths and bridleways; station at Dorking.

PARKING: 5 car parks around the common.

FACILITIES: Local facilities; viewpoint with panorama of the North Downs.

HYDON'S BALL AND HEATH

126 acres (51 ha) 3m S of Godalming, 1½m W of B2130, Surrey
[186:SU978396]

This area of heath, designated an AONB, with a steep, wooded south-facing slope commanding fine views across the Surrey landscape, is a memorial to Octavia Hill, one of the founding members of the National Trust.

The woodland is a mixture of planted species with natural regeneration, and includes oak, rowan, holly, birch, pine and chestnut. Bilberry and bracken grow on the common. Amelanchier and gaultheria, two alien shrubs, were planted by Gertrude Jekyll and are therefore of historic interest.

The remaining area of heath on the summit is small, and its value has declined seriously over the years, but the diversity of woodland, scrub and open grassland is ideal for a range of birds such as nightingale, lesser, greater spotted and green woodpecker, and sparrowhawk. Redpoll, siskin and brambling visit the common in winter.

ACCESS: Network of permitted paths and bridleways.

PARKING: Car park.

FACILITIES: Local facilities.

THE LACOCK ESTATE

350 acres (142 ha) 3m S of Chippenham, E of A350, Wiltshire
[173:ST910684]

Lacock is one of the best-preserved medieval wool towns in England. The cottages, barns and houses, vary in architectural styles dating from the fourteenth to the eighteenth centuries, but many have medieval timber-framed cores. The River Avon meanders close to the thirteenth-century nunnery of Lacock Abbey (the cloisters still exist), which was converted into a house in 1539 after the Dissolution of the Monasteries and later became the home of the Talbot family, who gave the Abbey and town to the Trust in 1944. A museum at the Abbey gate commemorates the achievements of William Henry Fox Talbot, the famous early Victorian pioneer of photography.

The surrounding countryside contains traces of field cultivation, historic boundaries, pack-horse bridges and features associated with the former monastic communities. A Roman road runs along the southern boundary of the estate.

The steep-sided riverbanks, with occasional pollards, are the haunt of kingfisher, dipper and sand martin, and owls, jackdaw, nuthatch and spotted flycatcher can be seen among the ornamental parkland trees around the Abbey. In places, the grassland of Bewley Common supports a variety of plants such as yellow rattle, ragged robin, marsh arrowgrass, sedges and rushes.

ACCESS: Abbey open seasonally; open access to town; station at Chippenham and local bus service from Chippenham and Trowbridge.

PARKING: Car park; special parking for disabled.

FACILITIES: NT shop in town; WCs (including disabled) at Abbey; guidebooks for Abbey and town; wheelchairs available from museum.

LEITH HILL

860 acres (348 ha) 4m SW of Dorking, NW of A29, Surrey
[187:TQ139432]

The highest point in the south-east of England, this hill is covered by woodland on its slopes, and open heathland on Coldharbour Common. Many of the woodlands have been replanted, but there are still interesting semi-natural oak, hazel and alder woods, and some actively worked hazel coppice.

A fortified folly built in 1766 dominates the hilltop, and commands magnificent views across the North and South Downs. On the southern slopes of the hill is Rhododendron Wood, planted by Josiah Wedgwood, grandson of the famous potter, which is a mass of colour in spring and early summer.

Many of the woodlands contain plants which indicate their antiquity, particularly parts of Mosses Wood and Frank's Wood. The oak and hazel conceal a ground flora of typical woodland herbs such as yellow archangel, wood spurge and sweet woodruff. The elusive white admiral butterfly can be seen. Other woods of interest include Etherley Copse (part of Leith Hill Copse) and Church Wood. In spring, Mosses Wood has a fine array of bluebell and rhododendron. Woodland birds include nuthatch, tree creeper and wood warbler, and the open heathland is home to tree pipits and reptiles such as the common lizard and adder.

ACCESS: Network of paths and bridleways; 2 waymarked circular walks; station at Dorking.

PARKING: 6 car parks (3 NT, 3 County Council).

FACILITIES: Refreshments and information room in tower; fine panoramic views from the top.

LIMPSFIELD COMMON

340 acres (138 ha) 18m E of Reigate, 2m SE of Oxted, off B2026, Surrey
[187:TQ090492]

Lying on a greensand ridge on the Kent border, Limpsfield Common is part of the North Downs AONB. The string of commons, dominated by woodland, include the Chart, Moor House Bank and Common, Scearn Bank, West Heath and Little Heath. This is a popular venue for walking, and includes a network of paths and rides and the course of a Roman road. Ecological surveys have been carried out over many years, highlighting changes to this rich wildlife site (an SSSI), particularly to the western half of the common.

The woodland of oak, birch and sycamore has largely colonised the former open heathland, although small areas of heathland remain, with pine plantations and holly, hazel and elder shrubs in pockets of ancient oak and beech woods. Woodland birds such as woodcock, nightingale, lesser spotted woodpecker and nightjar can be seen.

ACCESS: Network of footpaths and bridleways across (unconnected) sites.

PARKING: Lay-bys.

FACILITIES: Local facilities.

LUDSHOTT COMMON AND WAGGONERS' WELLS

705 acres (285 ha) 1½m W of Hindhead, S of B3002, Hampshire
[186:SU855350]

One of the largest remaining areas of lowland greensand heath in the western Weald, and part of the East Hampshire AONB, Ludshott Common was first recorded in the Domesday Book. For centuries it was exploited by local commoners for peat, thatch, gorse and grazing, and since the nineteenth century it has been a valuable open space in the area. A severe accidental summer fire in 1980 affected more than 400 acres of the common and eliminated much of the invading Scots pine. Although the heather is beginning to recover, the gorse is again very vigorous and invasive.

Waggoners' Wells consist of a series of man-made ponds fed by a stream, which were originally hammerponds serving an iron foundry known as Wakeners' Wells, on the site. They are of great wildlife interest and contain a variety of fish.

Heather, bell heather, dwarf and European gorse, and the bristle-leaved bent characterise the heathland. The scrubby vegetation provides a habitat for linnet, stonechat, woodlark, nightjar, visiting great grey shrike and the scarce Dartford warbler; there are a great many spiders and butterflies (including silver-studded blue, grayling and green hairstreak).

Pockets of semi-natural sessile oak woodland occur along the valley sides, and the mature trees lining the ponds to the east of the property harbour fascinating lichen communities with other plants characteristic of an ancient site. Nightingale, redpoll, woodcock, spotted flycatcher and tawny owl use the marginal scrub, and kingfisher, coot and other wildfowl inhabit the ponds.

ACCESS: Network of footpaths and bridleways.

PARKING: Car park.

FACILITIES: Leaflets; nature trails.

NOTE: Accidental fires are a hazard.

NEWTIMBER HILL

238 acres (96 ha) 5m NW of Brighton, between Pyecombe and Poynings, S of A281, West Sussex [198:TQ2712]

Adjoining the Fulking Escarpment, this is one of several Trust properties on the ancient chalk downland, and part of the Sussex Downs AONB. From the summit there are spectacular views over the Weald and out to sea.

The open grassland contains a number of scarce plants, notably the rare red star thistle which is restricted to the eastern South Downs; there are also some quality downland herbs such as dropwort, clustered bellflower and round-headed rampion. Butterflies include grayling, green hairstreak, and adonis and chalkhill blues. Small pockets of chalk heath and larger areas of gorse scrub can be found on the acidic hilltop plateau. Juniper scrub is present along the slope.

The ancient woodland contains old coppice stools among the oak, ash and beech trees, with ground flora of wood spurge, wood anemone, goldilocks and twayblade. Birds such as green woodpecker, nuthatch and tree creeper can be seen.

In the Dew Pond are found all three species of British newt (great crested, palmate and smooth).

Of historical interest are a cross-ridge dyke, prehistoric tumuli, and some lynchets on the south and west slopes.

ACCESS: Open access; South Downs Way; station at Brighton.

PARKING: Informal parking; car park (not NT) 1m away near Devil's Dyke Hotel.

FACILITIES: Local facilities.

OLDBURY HILL AND STYANT'S WOOD

153 acres (62 ha) N of A25, NW of Ightham, 3m SW of Wrotham, Kent
[188:TQ582561]

On the summit of Oldbury Hill, commanding a powerfully defensive position, is one of the finest Iron Age hill forts in the Medway, with substantial earth ramparts two miles in length. Ancient woodland, scrub and relic heathland, typical of the prominent greensand ridge, disguise its complete outline.

The woodlands support oak, birch and Scots pine (the pine originally planted but now reseeding naturally in appropriate areas), with a variety of fungi and plants colonised from the former heathland, such as heather and bilberry. Sizeable areas of oak coppice are systematically being reworked, making this one of the few Kentish woods where this traditional Wealden management is being practised.

The hill and wood are a Greensand Ridge Special Landscape Area, and part of the Metropolitan Green Belt, managed by the Kent County Council. The small caves and shallow rock shelters in the sandstone ridge were probably used by paleolithic man.

ACCESS: Open access from road; footpaths and bridleways; stations at Borough Green and Wrotham, and local bus service from Sevenoaks and Tunbridge Wells.

PARKING: Car park.

FACILITIES: Information panel and map; picnic area in car park; caravan and camp site.

ONE TREE HILL

34 acres (14 ha) 2m SE of Sevenoaks, between Underriver and Bitchet Common, Kent
[188:TQ560532]

The storms of 1987 badly damaged the wooded plateau of this Special Landscape Area of the Greensand Ridge, which lies within the North Downs AONB. Located on the crest of a sandstone escarpment with panoramic views across the Medway Valley, it is part of the One Tree Hill and Bitchet Common SSSI, containing the remnants of a former more extensive ancient woodland. (The name of One Tree Hill originally referred to a large beech tree that grew near the summit until 1924, since replaced with a copper beech.)

Only the scarp slope is truly ancient woodland, however, since there is evidence that the plateau area was put to agricultural use during the eighteenth and nineteenth centuries. The intention of the Trust's foresters and ecologists is to leave the damaged areas of woodland to regenerate naturally, although there has been some token planting and the changing ecology will be closely recorded. The extensive storm damage of 1987 would have been a common occurrence in the larger primeval woods, with the glades rejuvenating themselves and thus continuing the woodland cycle.

The northern part of the property consists of a developing secondary oak and birch woodland. Oaks are locally frequent, with stands of sweet chestnut and a dense band of blackthorn scrub. Old ash coppice is evident on the steep scarp slope (originally this would have been a wych-elm and ash woodland), with a good shrub layer and a range of ground flora species characteristic of the base-rich soils. The woods support a good bird population, with lesser and greater spotted woodpecker, blackcap, chiff-chaff, nuthatch and tree creeper.

On the summit is the supposed site of a Roman cemetery, and an old Anglo-Saxon woodland boundary bank can be seen.

ACCESS: Footpaths across plateau and bottom of escarpment; Greensand Way crosses property; one permitted bridleway (fenced); station at Sevenoaks.

PARKING: Car park.

FACILITIES: Viewpoint; informal picnic areas; path (steep) to main viewing area passable by wheelchairs.

OXTED DOWNS

68 acres (27½ ha) 1m NW of Oxted, Surrey [187:TG374538]

This distinct Surrey chalk landscape of rounded hills, steep valleys and 'hanging' beech woodlands (Gangers Hill, Whistler's Steep,

Hanging Wood and South Hawke) on the slopes of the North Downs, is part of the Surrey Hills AONB.

Although storm damage has taken its toll of the magnificent mature trees, the woodlands are now gradually regenerating, and the ground flora of bluebell, dog's mercury and sanicle is flourishing. There are some important areas of chalk downland and scrub on the slopes, with many downland plants such as cowslip, violet, autumn gentian, ploughman's spikenard, basil thyme, harebell and dwarf thistle. The grassland slopes support typical downland butterflies and grasshoppers.

ACCESS: North Downs Way.

PARKING: Small car park above South Hawke on ridge at Woldingham.

FACILITIES: Local facilities.

PEPPERBOX HILL

72 acres (29 ha) 5m SE of Salisbury, N of A36, Wiltshire
[184:SU215248]

Located at Brickworth Down, a chalk ridge above the River Avon, this hill is named after the seventeenth-century folly on its summit. The curious Jacobean tower was possibly built to provide ladies with a viewpoint from which to follow the progress of falconry and the hunt. The hill commands spectacular views across to Hampshire and the Isle of Wight.

It is one of the few downs where juniper thrives (attracting some special insect fauna such as the juniper shield bug), and is of much wildlife interest in the mixture of wood, scrub and grassland. In addition to juniper there is much whitebeam, dogwood, hawthorn, wayfaring tree, yew, guelder rose and wild privet. White and broadleaved helleborines are found in the areas of beech.

Seven species of orchid grow on the chalk grassland, with greater knapweed, dropwort, field fleawort and chalk milkwort, and the large numbers of butterflies and moths include the chalkhill blue and brown argus. Corn bunting, quail and nightingale can also be seen or heard. Harvest mice occur.

There are remains of Celtic field systems, with downland banks and lynchets.

ACCESS: By track.

PARKING: Car park.

FACILITIES: Information panel; view finder.

PETTS WOOD AND HAWKWOOD

338 acres (137 ha) between Chislehurst and Orpington, W of A208, Kent
[177:TQ450687]

This assemblage of ancient woodland, copses, hedgerows, streams and farmland provides a much-valued green area on the edge of London. The woodlands have played a significant part in the region's economy, with the sound timbers used for shipbuilding until the nineteenth century, when a fire destroyed the oaks which were replaced with exotic trees. These give the area a unique quality; among the crowned oak are birch, rowan, alder, ash, Scots pine, European larch, hornbeam and sweet chestnut. The uncommon wild service tree grows in the old hedgerows.

Petts Wood includes one of the few remaining areas of ancient woodland in London, with evidence of old earthwork boundaries (between the wood and St Paul's Common), and plants such as lily-of-the-valley (rare in the region) and wood anemone. Many birds make their home here, including lesser spotted woodpecker, tawny owl, tree creeper and jay. The river banks, rich in wildlife, are bordered by old willows, although the storm damage of 1987 destroyed large numbers of these trees.

A point of interest in Petts Wood is the monument to William Willett, the inventor of British Summer Time.

A number of ponds, two of which (in Pond Wood and Flusher's Wood on the Hawkwood Estate) are man-made, provide a habitat for newts and frogs.

ACCESS: Open access to Petts Wood off A208; permitted paths cross both estates; no public access to farmland or woods on Hawkwood Farm.

PARKING: Informal parking.

FACILITIES: Horse riding only permitted on the public bridleways; way-marking only on bridleways; short section only of path suitable for wheelchairs (slopes and uneven surfaces).

POLESDEN LACEY, RANMORE COMMON, DENBIES HILLSIDE AND WHITE DOWNS

1625 acres (658 ha) 2m NW of Dorking, Surrey [187:TQ1451]

Lying mainly to the south of the nineteenth-century Regency villa of Polesden Lacey is a beautiful and varied landscape of mature woodlands, beech walks, wooded commons, chalk downland and chalk scrub. The parkland around the mansion has been influenced by the tastes of various owners over the years, and before the Second World War a large golf course was laid out. Old grassland plants grow in the lawns near the house.

From the lawns and long walk of Polesden Lacey there are fine views across the valley to Ranmore, a wooded common on the slopes of the North Downs which can be reached from the house by numerous paths.

The scarp slope paddocks of Denbies Hillside and White Downs contain some of the richest chalk grassland in Britain. The paddocks are separated by blocks of woodland, including yew woods. The grassland flora is most impressive, highlighted by rarities such as man orchid and species indicative of quality old downland, such as basil thyme, clustered bellflower and round-headed rampion. Nearly every British chalk grassland butterfly occurs, including colonies of adonis blue and silver-spotted skipper. There are also rare moths, notably the straw belle, a North Downs specialist, and the orange-tailed clearing, whose larvae bore in the stems of wayfaring tree. The invertebrate interest extends to micro moths, beetles, bees and snails.

The property contains several blocks of ancient woodland which hold characteristic plants such as columbine, nettle-leaved bellflower and early dog violet. Secondary woodland of beech, oak and ash has been colonising both the clay plateau heath and downland for the last century, with a flora of columbine, white helleborine, bluebell, foxglove and wood anemone. Butterflies, including purple hairstreak, white admiral and silver-washed fritillary, can be seen in the rides and clearings, and birds such as sparrowhawk and green, lesser and greater spotted woodpeckers.

ACCESS: From Westhumble; minor road N of railway line from Dorking; network of footpaths at Ranmore Common; walks round Polesden Lacey grounds and gardens; house open seasonally; stations at Boxhill and Westhumble ($2\frac{1}{2}$m walk from Polesden Lacey) and bus service from Guildford.

PARKING: Car parks at Polesden Lacey, Ranmore Common and Denbies Hillside.

FACILITIES: NT shop and restaurant; WCs (including disabled); open-air theatre (for details contact Administrator); picnic site by main car park at house; youth hostel on estate.

REIGATE AND GATTON PARK

340 acres (138 ha) between Reigate Hill and Banstead Heath; and 1$\frac{1}{2}$m NE of Reigate, just N of A242 on W side of Gatton Park, Surrey
[187:TQ250520 and 265522]

Rising steeply to the north of Reigate is the chalk downland that comprises Colley and Reigate hills. The area, in the Surrey Hills AONB, is a mixture of open grassland and woodland, and has excellent views over the neighbouring countryside. Part of its historical interest is a late nineteenth-century 'mobilisation centre', known as the Fort, and some old firestone and hearthstone mines.

Gatton Park lies to the east, across the A27. The land was originally used as a park in 1449, and was one of the first to be landscaped by 'Capability' Brown. It is only partially owned by the Trust, with the eastern section belonging to the school set up by Sir Jeremiah Colman, the former owner.

One of the original owners was Leofwin Godwinson, brother of King Harold II, and the estate was later given to Anne of Cleves by Henry VIII as part of their divorce settlement. It was described by William Cobbett in his *Rural Rides* as the third most rotten borough in England.

Both properties are an important part of the Mole Gap to Reigate SSSI, of which the scarp slope here is of national importance for its chalk downland habitat of short turf with associated wildlife species. Grassland plants include stemless thistle, harebell, orchids, thyme and salad burnet, with butterflies such as brown argus, green hairstreak and chalkhill blue. Gatton has a small but valuable area of long chalk sward and scrub.

Margery Wood, now separated from the escarpment by the M25, was named by the Anglo-Saxons and is almost certainly ancient woodland, as are Great Buck Wood and Nut Wood in Gatton Park, with beech, elm, yew, Midland hawthorn, broad-leaved helleborine, common spotted orchid, bluebell, primrose and wood spurge.

Gatton has one of the highest bird counts in the London area.

ACCESS: 8 access points to both sites; footpaths; station at Reigate.

PARKING: Car parks at Reigate Hill (A217) and at Margery Wood.

FACILITIES: WCs between Reigate and Gatton; guided walks and talks.

RUNNYMEDE

183 acres (74 ha) ½m above Runnymede Bridge on River Thames, between Windsor and Staines, S of A308, Surrey   [176:TQ007720]

These historic meads on the banks of the Thames are the site of the signing of the Magna Carta, the great charter of English liberties, by King John in June 1215. A network of footpaths links the Magna Carta memorial with the memorials to John F. Kennedy and the Royal Air Force on neighbouring land. Further paths lead through the meadows and agricultural land, up the wooded slopes of Cooper's Hill, to Langham Pond and along the river.

A wide range of plants grow in the rich swards of the meadows and pastures, such as pepper saxifrage, cowslip, common knapweed, great burnet, betony, sneezewort and devil's bit scabious. There are mature oaks in the old boundary banks on Cooper's Hill, some fine old hornbeams and huge wild cherry trees.

Langham's Pond includes fen, wet grassland and open water habitats, and is notable for the variety of invertebrates, with many damselflies, dragonflies and water beetles. Aquatic and fen plants include frogbit, fine-leaved water dropwort and flowering rush. Brown-eared, pipistrelle and noctule bats can be seen feeding over the ponds in the evenings, and the wetland habitats attract many birds such as redshank, mallard, coot, lapwing, pied wagtail, and sedge and reed warblers.

ACCESS: Network of footpaths; Thames National Trail along river; station at Egham.

PARKING: Riverside car park (seasonal).

FACILITIES: Tea-room (seasonal); WCs; information board; boat trips; fishing (daily permits available from Warden).

ST CATHERINE'S

270 acres (109 ha) 2m W of Niton, off A3055, Isle of Wight
[196:SZ495755]

St Catherine's Point, the most southerly point of the island, is surrounded by the agricultural land of Knowles Farm, a geological SSSI. The strange, tumbled landscape, the western extremity of the Isle of Wight undercliff, extends from St Catherine's to Bonchurch, and is the result of the blue lias clay slumping under the weight of the chalk and sandstone above.

A variety of unusual plants thrive on the point, occupying the wide range of habitats from landslip and cliffs to grassland and scrub. Of special note are milk vetch, tufted centaury, subterranean clover and hoary stock. There are also many rare lichens. The invertebrate fauna includes species which are on the northern edge of their European range. There are a number of rare beetles, weevils, bees, wasps and ants, and a renowned colony of the glanville fritillary butterfly, an Isle of Wight specialist which is virtually restricted to National Trust property.

The ridge of St Catherine's Down, a mile inland from the point, rises in a steep west-facing escarpment of greensand to the chalk knoll of St Catherine's Hill, with the fine fourteenth-century lanterned lighthouse (in the care of English Heritage), originally part of an oratory and possibly the oldest in the country apart from the

Pharos at Dover. From the summit there are spectacular views of the rest of the island. At the other end of the down is the Hoy Monument (not owned by the Trust), erected in memory of a visit by Tsar Nicholas I in 1814.

ACCESS: Open access to St Catherine's Hill and Down (not accessible from Knowles Farm); network of footpaths on St Catherine's Down.

PARKING: Car parks at St Catherine's Hill and Windy Gap.

FACILITIES: Viewpoint on St Catherine's Hill.

SCOTNEY CASTLE ESTATE

770 acres (312 ha) 1m S of Lamberhurst, on E of A21, 8m SE of Tunbridge Wells, Kent   [188:TQ688353]

This romantic ruin of a fourteenth-century moated castle, surrounded by charming gardens and parkland, lies on the steep slopes of the River Bewl. The remains of the old manor are hidden among the ancient woodlands and old parkland trees, within the High Weald AONB. Various features of medieval life in the park and woodland have been identified, such as banks, ditches, lynchets (the strips between two pieces of ploughed land), and ridge and furrow farming. There are some quarries, and the sites of possible old iron workings.

The mature trees within the parkland and remnant woodland pasture, the ancient and more recently planted woodlands, and coppices of sweet chestnut all provide a network of valuable wildlife habitats. Old trees support several scarce lichens, making the estate of considerable importance for lichens within the region. Insects associated with dead wood are also of particular interest.

An area of pasture woodland is partly enclosed by old boundaries. Ponds in some old marl pits have now been colonised by wetland plants and hold good populations of dragonflies and damselflies, including the rare brilliant emerald dragonfly. The River Bewl, which crosses the property, and the River Teise to the north, flow through areas of unimproved meadows rich in flowers. Brown long-eared bats roost in the old buildings.

ACCESS: Castle and garden open seasonally; several public footpaths cross estate; 2 circular walks from car park (5m or ¾m); local station at Wadhurst and bus service from Tunbridge Wells.

PARKING: Car park at castle.

FACILITIES: WCs open as garden; information board and map in car park near entrance to garden; benches at scenic points along circular walks.

SELBORNE HILL

250 acres (101 ha) 4m S of Alton, W of B3006, Hampshire
[186:SU735333]

Encompassing some fine examples of beech 'hanger' woodlands on the chalk escarpments of east Hampshire, and designated an AONB and SSSI, these fragments of ancient landscape around Selborne are of great ecological importance. The observations of the Rev. Gilbert White, pastor and naturalist, published in *The Natural History and Antiquities of Selborne* in 1788, are an invaluable record, with lists and locations of individual scarce plants, of the ancient hangers, the valleys of the Short and Long Lythes, the historic wood pasture, chalk grassland and mixed woodland of Selborne Hill and Common. His famous zig-zag path to the top of the beech hanger on Selborne Hill is still in use.

Although the storms of 1987 and 1990 severely damaged the mature trees, new vistas have been opened up, with glades encouraging the regeneration of the natural vegetation.

The well-drained soils on the chalk substrate, ideal for beech with some maple and ash along the lower slopes, also support a distinct range of flowers such as woodruff, yellow archangel, wood spurge, wood anemone and bird's nest orchid. Above the hangers, mixed woodlands of oak and ash grow on the clay plateau of Selborne Hill, with wood sorrel, yellow archangel, broad buckler fern and enchanter's nightshade. The woods harbour many rare invertebrates and molluscs associated with dead wood and pollards, including the ash black slug, which is characteristic of ancient woodland sites, and five species of Ctenophora cranefly (large, spectacular creatures with feathered antennae). Beech pollards stand on old wood pasture, grazed until the mid-nineteenth century.

The woodland glades provide feeding grounds for many butterflies, including the silver-washed fritillary, green and purple hairstreaks and the occasional white admiral and purple emperor. Nightingale regularly breeds.

ACCESS: Via Selborne village; network of paths.

PARKING: Car park.

FACILITIES: Shops, museum, pubs and tea-room in village; WCs (including disabled) in car park; leaflets and guidebooks.

THE SEVEN SISTERS: CROWLINK AND BIRLING GAP

708 acres (286½ ha) 5m W of Eastbourne, S of Friston, via East Dean to Beachy Head road linking A259 and B2103, East Sussex
[199:TV545974 and 554960]

Beachy Head stands at the eastern end of these famous cliffs, known as the Seven Sisters, one of the longest stretches of undeveloped coastline between Southampton and Hastings, and a Marine Conservation Area. Best appreciated from a distance, the varied landscape includes chalk hills, dry valleys, brilliant-white chalk facings and grasslands rich in wild flowers and butterflies. Much of the land was cultivated during the Second World War, and so supports a rather limited flora dominated by the vigorous torr grass.

The grassland towards the cliffline has the richest variety of flowers, with round-headed campion, field fleawort, bastard toadflax, chalk milkwort and autumn lady's tresses. Butterflies include adonis blue and dark-green fritillary. The gorse scrub provides ideal shelter for wheatear, stonechat, whitethroat, goldfinch and yellowhammer, and in the summer skylark and meadow pipit sing overhead. In places there are small areas of chalk heath near the edge of the clifftops, which support plants associated with both limestone and more acid soils. The narrow strip of foreshore is of particular interest for its marine wildlife.

Every effort is being made to sympathetically protect and manage this impressive part of the East Sussex Heritage Coast, which falls within the Sussex Downs SSSI.

Birling Gap has a series of buildings (including coastguard cottages and a hotel), currently being refurbished.

Of archaeological interest are the Beaker camp settlement and Iron Age earthwork at Belle Tout, covering much of the hilltop to the east of Birling Gap, and three Bronze Age round barrows at Baily's Hill. There are numerous other sites of cultivation terraces, tumuli and an obelisk in the area.

ACCESS: Footpaths and bridleways; South Down Way along coast; stations at Eastbourne and Seaford.

PARKING: Car parks on road to Crowlink, south of Friston Church and at Birling Gap.

FACILITIES: Refreshments at Birling Gap; WCs (including disabled); information boards at Crowlink and Birling Gap; access for disabled from Crowlink car park to Flagstaff Point (only in dry weather).

SHOREHAM GAP AND SOUTHWICK HILL

596 acres (241 ha) 2m NE of Shoreham, West Sussex   [198:TQ2407]

Overlooking Brighton and Shoreham, this ancient chalk downland landscape is located on the dip slope of the South Downs, and part of an AONB. A large dry combe cuts the rise, and there is just visible evidence of a prehistoric field system.

The Brighton by-pass has been diverted through a tunnel under the hill, to avoid damaging the landscape.

Areas of ancient unimproved chalk grassland contain good downland plants such as horseshoe and kidney vetches, rock-rose and dropwort. Butterflies such as small blue and chalkhill blue occur.

ACCESS: Network of footpaths; South Downs Way.

PARKING: Car park near South Downs Way at Upper Beeding and Kingstone lane.

FACILITIES: Local facilities.

THE SLINDON ESTATE

3520 acres (1425 ha) 6m N of Bognor Regis, on A29, West Sussex
[197:SU9608]

This property consists of a large expanse of sweeping downland dissected by dry valleys, with hanging beech woods on the scarp and old wood pasture on the dip slopes, much of which was destroyed in the storms of 1987 and 1990. The estate includes Bignor and Coldharbour hills, and Glatting Beacon, from which there are spectacular views of the South Downs and the coastline. The famous Bignor Roman villa is nearby.

Other points of historical interest include a neolithic causewayed enclosure at Barkhale, some Bronze Age round barrows, two cross-ridge dykes, the medieval deer bank surrounding Slindon Park and a folly overlooking Court Hill Farm.

Much of the original downland on the more gentle slopes has been intensively farmed under arable cultivation in recent years, but large areas have now been put back to permanent pasture. There is an area of more acid grassy heath and scrub on the plateau above the scarp.

Encompassing most of the village of Slindon with its flint and brick cottages, the estate is also crossed by the largest remaining section of Stane Street, a Roman road. There is evidence of the pitched chalk and flint surface with ditches on either side.

In Slindon Beech Wood is a preserved shingle beach, showing that the sea level was once 130 feet higher than it is today. The old Slindon Park on the northern part of the estate still has the impressive bank and ditch of its medieval park pale.

Several beech and oak woods are on ancient woodland and wood pasture sites, including the fine beech woods on the steep scarp slope, and the beech and oak woods of Slindon Park. The storm-damaged woods are beginning to regenerate, with saplings and woodland plants flourishing in the lighter glades caused by the storms; ash and yew are also common. Typical ground plants of the beech woods include bluebell, dog's mercury, wild garlic, wood anemone, wood sedge, greater butterfly orchid, butcher's broom, nettle-leaved bellflower, twayblade and over sixty-five species of moss and liverwort. White admiral and silver-washed fritillary butterflies occur.

The grassland supports stemless thistle, small scabious, rock-rose, cowslip, and early purple and common spotted orchids.

The North Wood plantation is leased to the Forestry Commission.

ACCESS: Network of footpaths and bridleways; South Downs Way; Slindon Park open daily; stations at Barnham and Bognor Regis.

PARKING: Car parks at Dukes Road and Park Lane, Slindon and Bignor Hill.

FACILITIES: Information board at Bignor Hill car park and Gumber Bothy (camping barn).

STOCKBRIDGE DOWN

223 acres (90 ha) 12m E of Salisbury, Hampshire [185:SU379349]

This ancient chalk downland, designated an AONB and SSSI, has a long history of common grazing rights, although it has not been grazed for fifty years. These historic manorial customs are still maintained by the Trust, Lord of the Manor since 1946, which is now grazing its own flocks of sheep in order to maintain the rich grassland and to control the further invasion of scrub. A major scrub-reduction programme is currently in operation.

Distinctive plants of the chalk grassland include cowslip, thyme, harebell, horseshoe vetch, greater knapweed, yarrow, agrimony and violet. There are many downland butterfly species, including chalkhill blue, and some scarce moths. The scrub of hawthorn, blackthorn, dogwood, privet and juniper provides valuable nesting sites for birds such as blackcap, yellowhammer, nightingale, and garden and willow warblers.

Of historical interest are some Bronze Age barrows, and the very important Iron Age camp of Woolbury Ring at the north-east corner of the property.

ACCESS: Network of footpaths.

PARKING: 2 car parks.

FACILITIES: Information boards in main car park; limited access for disabled.

STONEHENGE DOWN

1438 acres (582 ha) 1–3m W of Amesbury, at junction of A303 and A360, Wiltshire [184:SU1212]

The famous and well-chronicled circle of ritual standing stones, owned by the State and under the guardianship of English Heritage, is the focal point of the surrounding open downland. A substantial part is owned by the Trust and forms part of a designated World Heritage Site. Over a period of time, the Trust intends to return arable fields to pasture, as a more appropriate setting for the many prehistoric remains.

The area is an internationally important prehistoric landscape, containing monuments such as the Cursus and the Stonehenge Avenue, neolithic long barrows and large numbers of Bronze Age barrows – many in distinct groups.

At present just over half of the estate under cultivation, there are some relics of chalk grassland in the enclosures around the barrows which support a variety of wild flowers such as clustered bellfower, rock-rose, small scabious, stemless thistle and cowslip. The seventy acres of nineteenth-century woodland plantations provide useful habitats for resident birds, including the sparrowhawk, a local speciality.

ACCESS: 8 miles of permitted paths; bus service from Salisbury to Stonehenge.

PARKING: Car park.

FACILITIES: English Heritage shop; refreshments; WCs (including disabled); archaeological walks leaflet available from shop and NT shop in Salisbury; 12 information panels.

STOURHEAD

2645 acres (1070 ha) at Stourton, off B3092, 3m NW of Mere on A303, Wiltshire [183:ST7735]

Situated below the escarpment of the Wessex chalk plateau, Stour-head is famed for its fine house and classic eighteenth-century parkland and garden, with many beautiful features including lakes, bridges and temples.

Although much of the planting dates from the eighteenth century, there are some remnants of the medieval 'Forest of Selwood' and wood pasture, part of the old manorial estate, which are particularly important for the diversity of their plants, birds, invertebrates and lichens. Woodcock, green and greater spotted woodpeckers, jay, nuthatch, tree creeper and chiff-chaff are common.

The lakes and ponds, lying on a natural springline, create valuable wetland habitats, attracting birds such as great crested grebe, coot, kingfisher, tufted duck and mute swan. The upper pond is good for dragonflies.

The formal landscape, an AONB, merges with the wooded ridges and valleys, many with ancient woodland sites and rich in wildlife. Overlooking the estate, White Sheet Down and Hill (now in part a nature reserve, SSSI and the site of a neolithic causewayed camp, Bronze Age barrows and Iron Age hill fort) are important tracts of chalk grassland which harbour many notable snails, butterflies and grasshoppers. The southern and south-western slopes have the most interesting flowers, with cowslip, clustered bellflower, thyme, ox-eye daisy and several orchid species. Butterflies include marbled white, and chalkhill and adonis blues.

The hedges, although boundaries of historical importance, have suffered from the effects of modern agriculture or neglect. Recently, however, several have been replanted and there is a definite improvement in local attitudes to their maintenance.

Other points of interest are an Iron Age hill fort in Park Hill Woods, some Celtic and medieval field patterns with strip lynchets and pillow mounds, and Pen Pits, small quarries once used for grindstones and whetstones.

ACCESS: House open seasonally; garden open all year during daylight hours; local stations at Gillingham and Bruton and bus service from Gillingham.

PARKING: Car park.

FACILITIES: NT shop; inn and restaurant; WCs (including disabled); garden accessible to wheelchairs and path round lake (very steep in places); Wiltshire Trust for Nature Conservation leaflet and general leaflet; guidebook available at house; base camp.

TOYS HILL

368 acres (149 ha) 5m SW of Sevenoaks, 2½m S of Brasted, 1m W of Ide Hill, Kent   [188:TQ465517]

Former heathland and wood pasture, and part of the historic commons of Brasted Chart, Toys Hill is one of the most important tracts of ancient woodland in Kent. Standing on the greensand ridge south of the North Downs, within an AONB, the woodlands are a prominent feature in the landscape.

The Trust is now seeking to re-create aspects of the former historic landscape, where peasants grazed pigs and cattle, beech and oak trees were pollarded to provide firewood and food for grazing stock, and charcoal was produced for the Wealden iron industry and for hop-drying. The old banks and sunken tracks which can be seen thoughout the woods resulted from these activities.

Only a few of the old beech pollards survived the storm of 1987. Birch is regenerating strongly throughout the damaged areas, although beech seedlings are locally numerous. Holly, rowan and Scots pine are also frequent in places. The plateau supports one of the largest native stands of sessile oak in the Weald, and there is an interesting transition to pedunculate oak downslope. A large area of Scords Wood is designated a 'non-intervention area', where natural regeneration can gradually come through the devastated native beech woodland. Ash and wych elm woodland occurs along the undamaged lower slopes.

The woods hold valuable pockets of lowland heath, which the Trust is endeavouring to conserve and enlarge by pony grazing. Many woodland birds are found and fungi are plentiful, including poisonous species such as death cap and apricot yellow chanterelle. There are some rich unimproved meadows outside the woodland.

ACCESS: Circular walk linking Emmets Garden, Ide Hill and Chartwell; green and red waymarked trails; circular bridleway.

PARKING: Car park.

FACILITIES: Leaflet; guide for Chartwell (the home of Sir Winston Churchill); information panels; viewpoints; non-intervention zone for scientific monitoring; picnic area; base camp; circular route for wheelchairs.

VENTNOR

570 acres (231 ha) on SE coast of Isle of Wight, off A3055 or B3327
[196:SZ 570782]

The southernmost chalk downs in the country, designated an AONB and SSSI, this property lies inland from the town of Ventnor. The crest of St Boniface, the highest point on the Isle of Wight, rises to 787 feet. St Boniface Down, the first Trust acquisition on the island, commands impressive views across to the mainland and is notable as one of the richest chalk grassland in Britain. Adding to this interest, on the acid soils on the top of Luccombe Down is one of only two remaining areas of heathland on the island.

The Trust is currently involved in a programme of heathland restoration, using New Forest ponies for grazing. The downland is being managed by cattle-grazing, and by a continuous programme of clearing the invasive scrub, particularly the alien holm oak. Heathland plants include bell heather, ling, dwarf gorse and bilberry. The grassland supports a very wide range of plant species such as horseshoe vetch, rock-rose, autumn gentian, slender centaury, common broomrape and a variety of orchids. The property is also very important entomologically, with an interesting colony of adonis blue butterfly.

Woodlands such as the semi-natural Luccombe Copse include mature field maples and evidence of some old coppice stools.

Luccombe Down is the site of a Civil Aviation Authority radar station, which was originally one of the first radar stations established to defend the English Channel. There are also eight Bronze Age burial mounds. Luccombe Farm, (the buildings are not owned by the Trust), is made up of a traditional pattern of meadows, downland, beach and cliffs.

ACCESS: Off Down Lane in Upper Ventnor, E off Newport road; network of footpaths.

PARKING: Car park off private road from Ventnor Dairy.

FACILITIES: Local facilities and information in Ventnor.

WEST WIGHT: HEADON WARREN, THE NEEDLES AND TENNYSON DOWN

459 acres (186 ha) SW of Totland, off B3322, Isle of Wight
[196:SZ310851]

The Needles headland, at the western extremity of the chalk back-bone of the Isle of Wight, is part of the impressive Heritage Coast west of Brightstone. Between the Needles and Tennyson Down (named after the Poet Laureate who lived at Farringford in the 1870s) is West High Down, and these properties, with Afton, Compton and Brook downs, form a distinctive ridge of chalk downland from which there are spectacular views of the island and across to the mainland.

The ridge originally extended across Christchurch Bay to Dorset, where the chalk of Ballard Down can be seen in the distance. The ancient grassland has changed little over the centuries, and forms one of the most important downland sites in Britain. There are many archaeological remains along the prehistoric ridgeway. Alum Bay (not owned by the Trust) is a popular tourist spot renowned for its multi-coloured sands, and backed by steep sandstone cliffs. The clifftop is dominated by heathland and the scrub of Headon Warren where the occasional Dartford warbler can be seen.

Some of the richest chalk grassland in Britain can be found on the West Wight ridge, with a remarkable variety of plants and insects, including several maritime chalk species. The important heathland site supports bell heather, ling and dwarf gorse, and on the land-slipped undercliffs there is a variety of habitats in the small cliffs, scrub and wet flushes.

On Tennyson Down there is an area of chalk heath where chalk plants coexist with acid-loving species such as heather. Cormorant, shag, guillemot, fulmar and razorbill nest along the cliffs.

Of historical interest on Headon Warren and the chalk downs are a number of notable Bronze Age and neolithic burial mounds and enclosures. On the Needles headland is the Old Battery, a Palmer-stonian fort built in the 1860s with impressive views of the Needles and Christchurch Bay; the New Battery was built in 1891. There is also a rocket-testing site, built in 1960.

ACCESS: Downland accessible from Alum Bay, High Down car park and Freshwater Bay; Isle of Wight coastal path; Tennyson Way; waymarked paths; network of footpaths across downs; Battery open seasonally.

PARKING: NT car parks at Afton, Brook, Mottistone and High downs; parking at Needles Pleasure Park in Alum Bay.

FACILITIES: Tea-room in coastguard look-out at Battery; WCS and small kiosk at the Needles; guidebook to the Needles Battery; information boards in main car parks; bus service to Alum Bay.

WEST WITTERING: EAST HEAD

110 acres (45 ha) E of entrance to Chichester Harbour, via A286 and B2179, West Sussex   [197:SU766990]

This narrow spit of sand and shingle beach is located at the mouth of Chichester Harbour, an important natural tidal inlet. Designated an SSSI, East Head and Chichester Harbour form one of the most important sites in western Europe for populations of overwintering waders and wildfowl.

Along the shingle, occasional little tern and ringed plover can be seen, and breeding sites are cordoned off to protect the colonies. The large numbers of wintering waders and wildfowl include sanderling, shelduck, Brent goose, wigeon, pochard, teal, mallard, goldeneye, merganser, redshank, curlew, grey plover, and bar-headed and black-tailed godwits.

The shape and position of the sandy promontory has fluctuated over the years, as has the build-up of saltmarsh communities sheltered by the spit. The protection that East Head gives to the tidal inlet is also important in sheltering the harbour, and for the development of the series of estuarine creeks, mudflats, saltmarshes and reed beds.

Erosion of the dunes has caused great instability, which could lead to more sand 'blow-outs' and to the eventual breach of the spit by the sea; an appeal has therefore been launched for money to repair such breaches. Visitors are asked to keep to the paths to avoid further erosion of the dunes.

Over a hundred species of flowering plants are found among the coastal dune habitats around East Head, including thrift, sea heath, sea bindweed, golden samphire and evening primrose. On the sand and shingle sea holly, salt wort, sea heath, sea rocket and yellow-horned poppy can be seen, with a rich assemblage of plants such as glasswort, sea lavender and sea spurrey in the saltmarsh. East Head is entomologically very rich, especially for moths, mining bees and digger wasps.

ACCESS: By foot only; station at Chichester.

PARKING: Car parks (not NT).

FACILITIES: Leaflet.

THE WEY AND GODALMING NAVIGATIONS

20m of navigation and towpaths from Godalming to the River Thames at Weybridge, through Guildford, Surrey

[176:TQ073655 to 186:SU997489]

This stretch of navigation or canalised river is a historic link from Surrey to the main thoroughfare of the Thames and the 2000-mile inland waterway network. Pleasure craft have now replaced the horse-drawn barges which used to negotiate the sixteen locks from Godalming to the Thames. Today it is an important 'wildlife corridor' in a heavily populated area. On the banks of the waterway are pollarded willows, and the tranquil backwaters support a great abundance of waterside flora and fauna. There is also a disused railway line which is now a pleasant walking diversion bordering meadows owned by the Trust, some of which are SSSIS.

The river was opened for navigation in 1653, connecting London to Guildford, and was extended to Godalming in 1760. It is no longer used by commercial traffic, but a small area of Dapdune Wharf in Guildford, where the wooden barges were built, is open to the public and has some interesting displays. The Worsfold Gates at Send still have the original hand sluice paddles.

ACCESS: Open access to towpath from all bridges; boat access from Thames at Weybridge, or slipways at Stoke Lock or Pyrford

Marina; stations close to navigation at Addleston, Byfleet, New Haw, Guildford, Farncombe and Godalming.

PARKING: Several car parks.

FACILITIES: Leaflet and maps; free mooring for visitors; 4 boat hire centres; regular boat trips from Guildford and Godalming; navigation office at Dapdune Wharf.

NOTE: Navigational licences required for all craft (reduction for NT members).

THE WHITE CLIFFS OF DOVER: ST MARGARET'S BAY, BOCKHILL FARM, LANGDON CLIFFS, GREAT FARTHINGLOE

323 acres (131 ha) between Capel-le-Ferne and NE Dover, Kent
[179:TR370451, 366437, 370455, 335422 and 290393]

This string of properties along the famous Dover chalk cliffline is situated where the North Downs meet the English Channel. Arable farmland, seaside tourism and industrial development around Dover, in particular around the mouth of the Channel Tunnel, have given greater importance to the Trust's role in protecting these clifftops, chalk grasslands and stretches of white rock.

The remaining fragments of ancient grassland on the clifftops support an exceptionally rich flora, including burnt-tip, pyramidal, bee and fragrant orchids, meadow clary, ivy-leaved broomrape, chalk milkwort, knapweed, ox-eye daisy and rock-rose. Fulmar, kittiwake, house martin and peregrine inhabit the cliffs, and flocks of migrant birds use them as a point of arrival or departure for their journeys. The shrubby thickets are also important staging posts for migrant warblers, thrushes and finches in spring and autumn. The chalk is famed for its collection of fossils such as echidnoids. Butterflies are plentiful, including chalkhill and adonis blues.

St Margaret's Bay includes a number of properties of clifftop grassland and farmland. To the east, Kingsdown Leas covers a mile of clifftop, and Bockhill Farm, 275 acres of farmland abutting the clifftop, is crossed by numerous footpaths. South Foreland Point, a small area of downland with a nineteenth-century lighthouse, lies to the east of Langdon Cliffs and Langdon Hole, properties with particularly valuable grasslands which attract many orchids. Great Farthingloe, to the west of Dover, covers a mile of exposed clifftop with flower-rich grasslands backed by farmland. Many of these clifftop grasslands are neglected and in need of sensitive grazing.

The area is peppered with wartime relics (fortification and heavy-gun sites, and a subterranean radar complex), and the Trust land surrounds the nationally important granite obelisk of the Dover Patrol Memorial.

ACCESS: System of maintained paths along coast and across farmland; the Saxon Shore Way coastal path; statutory path waymarked by the Countryside Commission.

PARKING: Car park on seaward side of memorial; car park at Langdon Cliffs.

FACILITIES: Café and kiosk; WCs at Langdon Cliffs; information board and map near Memorial; viewpoints from Langdon Cliffs over Port of Dover; wheelchair access on paths from car park and roads, and to viewpoints on the Leas and Bockhill; no horse riding or mountain biking on any part of property.

WICKHAM MANOR FARM

394 acres (160 ha) 1m SW of Winchelsea, 2m W of Rye, 9m E of Hastings on A259, East Sussex [189:TQ898165]

The Trust owns much of the ancient village of Winchelsea, plus part of the Royal Military Canal which was built at the beginning of the nineteenth century as a defensive measure against the perceived threat of invasion by Napoleon.

A mile to the south-west of the village, on the road to Pett, is Wickham Manor Farm, a working Sussex farm. This property is of great nature conservation interest, and commands extensive views across open arable farmland towards the sea. A large variety of birds can be seen, including kestrel, green woodpecker and mistle thrush. Pett Level and Pewis Marsh provide an ideal habitat for the native marsh frog, and mute swan can be found on the canal.

The broadleaved woodland of Wickham Farm contains English elm, sweet chestnut, ash and sycamore, and has a marvellous ground flora of red campion, yellow archangel and cowslip. There is a rookery in the southern end. The much-altered fifteenth-century farmhouse (not open to the public) once belonged to William Penn, the founder of Pennsylvania in 1672.

ACCESS: Pedestrians only on footpath across farm and leading to village; access to canal footpath at Appledore; station at Winchelsea.

PARKING: Limited roadside parking in Winchelsea.

FACILITIES: Tea-rooms, shops and WCs in Winchelsea.

WITLEY AND MILFORD COMMONS

377 acres (153 ha) 5m W of Godalming, 1m SW of Milford, Surrey
[186:SU9240]

Designated a nature reserve, Witley and Milford commons are good examples of Surrey heathland and scrub, with woodland fringes. Like most Surrey heaths, the commons were central to the local communities until early this century, when they were used for grazing, turf-cutting and other enterprises.

The Trust is reclaiming heathland from pine woodland and bracken, managing different areas for different species, and rotationally managing the scrub at Milford to encourage breeding birds. The varying water-table levels lead to areas of both wet and dry heath, with heather, bell heather and bilberry in the drier parts, and in wet places common cotton-grass and mosses. Nightjar, nightingale, siskin and many warblers are among the birds to be found, and the bushes of dwarf gorse are an important food source for a number of scarce insects. Heathland butterflies such as green hairstreak and silver-studded blue occur, and purple emperor can be found in the woodland.

The birch, oak and pine woods provide some shelter and habitat variety, although some areas are being cleared in the programme of heath reclamation. Reptiles such as common lizard and adder can be seen, as well as roe deer on the common.

Of historical interest are some Bronze Age burial mounds, and iron workings from the sixteenth and seventeenth centuries. The commons were used as army camps during both World Wars.

ACCESS: Footpaths.

PARKING: 3 car parks.

FACILITIES: Information and exhibition centre; leaflet; WCS; way-marked nature trails (yellow routes accessible to wheelchairs in dry weather); dogs permitted on leads.

WOOLBEDING

1102 acres (446 ha) 2m NW of Midhurst, West Sussex   [197:SU8724]

This large estate, part of the Sussex Downs AONB, encompasses an Anglo-Saxon settlement with farmland, woods, hedges and commons of great conservation value. To the north near Redford, Woolbeding Common is registered commonland consisting of heathland and ancient wood pasture. Woolbeding Wood is a characteristic hanging wood above the River Rother, and a number of other woodlands containing a rich diversity of wildlife are thought to be on ancient sites. There are a few old pollarded trees.

Heather, cross-leaved heath, bell heather, dwarf gorse, gorse, bristle bent, bilberry, bracken and purple moor grass can be seen on the open expanses of heath, which are being enlarged by clearance of the birch wood and dense bracken.

In spring and summer nightjar can be heard, and other birds include redstart, lesser spotted woodpecker, wood warbler and tawny owl, with grey wagtail and kingfisher along the river banks. The open heath is important for bees and wasps, including colonies of the potter wasp, a cult insect which makes a nest out of mud in the shape of an earthen pot.

ACCESS: Access to commons and part of woodlands only; restricted to rights of way over farmland.

PARKING: 3 small informal car parks.

FACILITIES: Guided walks (usually when heather in flower, or on request).

Wales and the Welsh Borders

WALES · AVON · GLOUCESTERSHIRE
HEREFORD & WORCESTER

The National Trust owns and protects some impressive and beautiful expanses of the Welsh countryside, ranging from the dramatic glacial landscape of Snowdonia to the spectacular Pembrokeshire coastline. The variety of habitats within the Snowdonia National Park – moorland, grassland, woodland, lakes and streams – attracts unique associations of plants. This historic landscape also contains numerous archaeological remains, with upland farms and vernacular buildings scattered over the hillsides; ancient oak woodlands and relics of a once thriving mining industry also line the valleys. To the north-west, the Anglesey coastline and Llyn Peninsula include complex rock formations supporting a variety of habitats and botanical interest. Anglesey is an eroded platform – an island with an intricate coastline of low cliffs alternating with coves, pebble beaches and secluded villages, much of it designated as Heritage Coast. Inland, marine heaths conceal an ancient landscape with numerous Bronze Age burial mounds scattered across the island.

To the east, the mountains of Snowdonia descend to the fertile lowlands of Clwyd. Towards the central part of Wales, in the remote, hilly landscape of central Powys, the Trust owns an extensive estate of remote upland grass and heather moorland, including Abergwesyn Common in the Cambrian Mountains. From here it is possible to look across to the red sandstone mountains of the Brecon Beacons National Park, on the border with Gwent. The uplands lead down to a landscape of small farms, pockets of broadleaved woodlands and rivers: the Cothi Valley and wooded hillsides of the Dolaucothi Estate are particularly beautiful.

Further south, the spectacular Ceredigion coast and contorted coastline of Pembrokeshire provide a stronghold for sea birds; an ancient landscape on the headlands has preserved defensive hill forts and Celtic farming systems. Inland, the remote heathlands and commons of Pembrokeshire offer a contrast to the popular coast. Glamorgan, considered to be the industrial heart of South Wales, also contains some beautiful countryside. Of particular interest is the varied Gower Peninsula with its prominent grey limestone cliffs (notably Pennard Cliffs and Three Cliffs Bay), estuarine habitats, sand dunes, rocky headlands and commons.

Hereford & Worcester is characterised by pastoral lowland of oak woods and traditional farmed pastures. The Malvern Hills form a distinctive narrow ridge running north-south and rising above the pastoral landscape of the Severn Plain. From here the Cotswolds – a landscape characterised by the warm-coloured local stone and rolling hills – stretch across the plain into Gloucestershire.

ABERGLASLYN

965 acres (390½ ha) 12m SE of Caernarfon, on A4085, extending S for 1½m from Beddgelert, Gwynedd [115:SH600468]

This famous Snowdonia beauty spot includes the lower end of the spectacular Aberglaslyn Pass, the racing waters of the River Glaslyn (popular for salmon fishing), the steep wooded slopes above the pass and an expanse of mountainous land. There are good views from Pont Aberglaslyn, the stone bridge at the narrowest point of the gorge.

Heath, grasslands and mires create a range of wildlife habitats.

The heath is unusual as it contains several species usually found at lower altitudes, such as western gorse, grayling butterfly, bloody-nose beetle and stonechat. It also has some excellent expanses of bell heather. The mires include local plants such as the insectivorous oblong-leaved sundew and white-beaked sedge, while the gorge itself is important for its mosses on riverside rocks.

The woods at Aberglaslyn include some small areas of old oak-wood and some more recent plantations. Rhododendron is invading the wood and the sides of the gorge. When established, it completely shades out the native flora, so much time and expense have to be devoted to its control.

The property also includes some rushy fields on the previous estuary of the Afon Glaslyn, once a navigable waterway which was reclaimed at the beginning of the nineteenth century. The remains of the old harbour by the deep pool which gives the river its name are now several miles from the sea. Dotted throughout the landscape is evidence of previous settlements ranging from Bronze Age cairns and early Iron Age huts to latter-day upland shepherds' shelters and the cableways, pits and stopes which are the remains of a copper-mining industry.

In the village of Beddgelert is an ancient cottage named Llywelyn Cottage, once a public house known as Ty Isaf and now a National Trust shop. It is possible to set off from here on a network of paths which lead to the grave of Gelert, according to local legend the brave dog of Prince Llywelyn. The land around this monument, running down to the river, was bought with grants from the Portmeirion Foundation in memory of Clough Williams-Ellis, and the Countryside Commission, in 1987. Continuing past the grave, the path joins the route of the old Welsh Highland Railway, which closed in 1937. A series of spectacular tunnels lead through to Nantmor.

ACCESS: Network of walks through the pass and to Gelert's grave; Festiniog Railway runs between Porthmadog and Festiniog (seasonal).

PARKING: Car parks at Beddgelert and Nantmor.

FACILITIES: WCs at Beddgelert and Nantmor; leaflet for Aberglaslyn; track from Beddgelert for adventurous accompanied wheelchair users; no camping.

ABERGWESYN COMMON

16,500 acres (6678 ha) in the Cambrian Mountains, W of Llandrindod Wells, extending from Irfon Gorge to the Wye Valley, Powys
[147:SN8359 to 9861]

This extensive and remote moorland in central Wales has escaped the blanket afforestation of much of the surrounding countryside. Drygan Fawr and Gorllwyn are the highest peaks along the central ridge with the western and northern slopes of the plateau cut by deep river valleys.

This large upland area exhibits some of the problems of managing upland commons, with heavy sheep–grazing, burning and spread of bracken. Nevertheless, there are some very valuable habitats here. The summit plateaux support upland heath and blanket bog with an important community of breeding birds which include dunlin, golden plover and red grouse. The slopes, where not too bracken-infested, have dry heath of heather and gorse, rich flushed grasslands and small areas of alder and other semi-natural woodland. The area is feeding territory for the rare mid–Wales speciality, red kite.

At least fifty prehistoric cairns are scattered across the moors, re-built in the nineteenth century into beehive structures as markers for commoners, and evidence of the ancient use of these wild open spaces. Other features of historic interest are the standing stones, stone alignments and old drove roads which cross the property.

ACCESS: Main access points north of A483; easy access from Abergwesyn and Llanwrtyd Wells; network of footpaths accross plateau.

PARKING: Informal parking.

FACILITIES: Local facilities.

BISHOPSTON VALLEY

153 acres (62 ha) on the Gower Peninsula, 6m SW of Swansea via A4067 and B4436, West Glamorgan
[159:SS575894]

This deeply incised and sheltered valley has one of the best and most extensive areas of ancient woodland on the Gower, with a great variety of trees such as ash, oak, small-leaved lime, holly, field maple and wild service tree; hazel, spindle and dogwood occur as shrubs. There is a rich ground flora, including soft shield fern, columbine, tutsan, wood anemone and wood spurge. Coppicing has been re-introduced by the Trust.

The underlying geology is carboniferous limestone, and here it displays karst features such as swallow holes, pot holes, dry valleys, collapsed caverns and limestone screes.

Apart from ancient woodland, this valley has an excellent diversity of habitat, with wet meadows, herb-rich limestone grassland, bracken, scrub and stream (above ground in part of the valley) where nesting dipper can be seen.

An Iron Age promontory fort, obscured by trees and shrubs, is perched on the east side of the valley, and derelict quarries and lime kilns also offer clues to the past.

ACCESS: Footpath through valley.

PARKING: Small parking area by church at Kittle.

FACILITIES: Leaflet.

BRAICH-Y-PWLL

122 acres (49 ha), at tip of Llyn Peninsula near Aberdaron; 18m S of Pwllheli via B4413, Gwynedd [123:SH140254]

This wild and beautiful extremity of the Llyn Peninsula is the point from where the first pilgrims set off during the Middle Ages to Bardsey Island. The ruins of St Mary's church, once used by these medieval pilgrims, and remains of medieval field patterns with ridge and furrow can still be seen. In the spring and summer numerous birds such as fulmar, cormorant, greater and lesser black-backed gulls, herring gull, kittiwake, razorbill, guillemot, kestrel, raven and, notably, the rare chough nest on the most inaccessible ledges of the high cliffs, which are made up of ancient precambrian rocks. Grey seal breed in the caves and coves.

A variety of plants, such as golden samphire and sea spleenwort, grow among the cliffs, and there are some important maritime lichens on the rocks. On the clifftops stonechat, wheatear, whitethroat, linnet and meadow pipit can be seen.

Ecologically, the highlight of this part of the Llyn Peninsula is the superb expanse of coastal heath, one of the best examples in Europe. Bell heather, heather and western gorse are the dominant species, clipped short and waved in places by the prevailing winds, and the bell heather and gorse create spectacular colour in July and August. This short heath provides the all-important summer feeding habitat for the rare chough. Heavy grazing and heather burning on commonland has led to loss of heath, and its replacement by gorse or acid grassland and bracken, but there are still excellent strands on Trust land.

The farmland behind the cliff zone, where the chough feed in winter, has areas of ancient field patterns bounded by earth walls or stone hedges known as clawdds.

ACCESS: Network of footpaths.

PARKING: Car park.

FACILITIES: Facilities at Aberdaron.

THE BRECON BEACONS

8150 acres (3298 ha) 5m S of Brecon, E of A470, Powys   [160:SO2101]

This impressive landscape of glacial valleys cutting into an escarpment of old red sandstone rocks is dominated by the flat-topped summits of Penyfan and Corn Ddu, the highest points in southern Britain. To the east Cribyn, although lower, makes an equally dramatic skyline.

The upper slopes of this common are heavily grazed by sheep and horses, resulting in a uniform grassland which includes matt and purple moor grasses, but the flora becomes more interesting on the steep north-facing slopes where sheep cannot venture. Here, plants such as purple saxifrage are a reminder of the last Ice Age. The wide-open tracts also provide a habitat for many upland birds including raven, buzzard, ring ouzel and red grouse. In places, remnants of heathland and blanket bog add to the diversity of habitats.

Run-off from the upper slopes channels down rocky gullies, through bracken-covered lower slopes, to form tumbling streams which flow through the oak and hazel woods of the valley floor.

Piles of moss and lichen-covered rocks beside deep depressions in the Beacons mark the sites of old quarries, the source of stone for sheep pens and miles of drystone walls. Older tracks, still in use today, mark the Roman and Norman routes across the escarpment, and high on the summits of Penyfan and Corn Ddu lie burial mounds dating from the Bronze Age.

On a clear day, a walk to the summits will afford spectacular views as far as the Devon coast, Herefordshire and Plynlimon.

ACCESS: Unrestricted rights of way over commonland.

PARKING: Local authority car parks.

FACILITIES: Facilities at Brecon.

BROCKHAMPTON

1680 acres (680 ha) 1½m E of Bromyard, N of A44, off B4224, Hereford & Worcester [149:SO682546]

This extensive estate consists of gently undulating wooded slopes and parkland. The slopes are cut by small valley streams or 'dingles' with wooded banks, probably ancient woodland sites. Wild service trees are common and the woods include a typical flora of sweet woodruff, wood spurge, dog's mercury, yellow archangel and enchanter's nightshade. Woodpecker, pied flycatcher, redstart and great tit can be seen. The younger plantations of conifers and beech attract willow warbler and chiff-chaff in the spring.

A number of mature oaks harbouring rare lichens have survived from the original woodland, although some unusual conifers such as redwood, pine and cedar have been planted for ornamentation in the parkland. Birds of prey include buzzard, sparrowhawk and kestrel. The house outbuildings are a nationally important roost for the rare lesser horseshoe bat, which hunts over the park and lake.

ACCESS: Paths, bridleways and way-marked walks through estate.

PARKING: Informal car park by chapel in top park; small car park at medieval hall in Lower Brockhampton; parking for woodland walks in Bringsty lay-by beside A44 opposite Bringsty Forge.

FACILITIES: Leaflet; information on walks by chapel in top park; way-marked parkland and woodland walks.

BRYN BRAS

234 acres (95 ha) S of Ponterwyd on A44(T), 12m E of Aberystwyth, Dyfed
[135:SN745800]

This isolated stock farm above the spectacular Rheidol Gorge in a remote region of central Wales is situated on an upland ridge with crags, screes, dry and wet heath rich in mosses and lichens, and upland grassland. Upland birds such as raven, buzzard, whinchat and wheatear can be seen, as well as the rare red kite.

Common plants of the heath on the north and west-facing slopes include heather, bilberry, bell heather and crowberry, while shrubby thickets of western gorse occur on the warmer slopes. Mires and flushes, found in hollows, support three species of club moss, now increasingly rare in the heavily grazed uplands. Green hairstreak and pearl-bordered fritillary butterflies are present.

The oak woodland of the Rheidol Gorge is part of a nationally important woodland site, notable for its ungrazed heathy ground layer, tall herb ledges, moss communities on wet rocks and oakwood invertebrates and birds.

ACCESS: Footpaths crossing property; access from Ysbyty Cynfyn via Parson's Bridge; Vale of Rheidol Railway runs from Aberystwyth to Devil's Bridge (seasonal).

PARKING: Limited roadside parking; nature trail from Devil's Bridge.

FACILITIES: Local facilities.

THE CARNEDDAU ESTATE

17,385 acres (7036 ha) 8m SE of Bangor, both sides of A5, near Capel Curig, Gwynedd
[115:SH6760]

This large estate includes some of the finest scenery in the Snowdonia National Park. There are numerous lakes, including Llyn Idwal, at 1223 feet above sea level, which is part of the Cwm Idwal National Nature Reserve. The estate lies both sides of the A5, which runs through the Nant Ffrancon and Nant y Benglog valleys, surrounded by the rugged peaks of the Carneddau and Glyderau massifs. Among the peaks, which rise to over 3000 feet above sea level, are Carnedd Llewelyn, Tryfan, the two Glyder peaks (Bach and Mawr) and Carnedd Dafydd.

Typical upland features abound, such as drystone walls, ancient sheepfolds and isolated farmhouses, many of which have been farmed by the same families for generations. Clues to even earlier habitation is evident in the numerous archaeological remains, such as mountain-top cairns, stone circles, standing stones and ancient hilltop forts.

Indications of past glacial activity such as hanging cwms, stone-strips and glacial striations can be seen. Geology, climate and management dictate the diversity of vegetation in this complex area. The main Carneddau ridge is the largest area of montane grassland in Britain south of the Cairngorms. Bogs and mires are rich in mosses, insectivorous plants such as sundew and butterwort, rare sedges and other damp-loving plants. The heavily grazed mineral soils support acres of acid grassland, but some upland heath survives where grazing pressure is not too great. The steep, base-rich cliffs, inaccessible to sheep, support an almost unique Arctic-Alpine flora, including rare saxifrages and the well-known but rarely seen Snowdon lily, found in Britain only on a few sites in Snowdonia.

There are many footpaths, some of which are showing signs of numerous visitors with large erosion scars, on which sensitive remedial work has to be undertaken.

ACCESS: Network of footpaths.

PARKING: Car parks along A5 between Capel Curig and Bethesda.

FACILITIES: Tea-room at Ogwen Cottage; WCS.

CEMAES

51 acres (21 ha) on E side of Cemaes Bay, 8m W of Amlwich on A5025, Anglesey, Gwynedd   [114:SH3794]

The Camaes Estate includes a stretch of the northern Anglesey coast with two rocky headlands, bays, cliffland and a harbour wall and promenade to the north of Cemaes. Characteristic landscape features include small fields bounded by walls and old lime kilns used to make slaked lime for top dressing fields, and a small area of saltmarsh to the north of Cemaes, an unusual habitat along this particular stretch of coast. To the north an old church dedicated to St Patrick has links with local legends and folklore. The Wylfa Nuclear Power Station looms above the shingle bay.

Popular with geologists because of the range of rocks and structures revealed in the cliffs, Camaes has a classic cliff section through the ancient precambrian 'Mona Complex' rocks, contorted lavas, limestones and grits, baked and compressed at least 1000 million years ago.

There is also much of wildlife interest. At Llanbadrig Point exposures of ancient rocks are covered with rare and unusual lichens. Rock samphire, kidney vetch, thrift, sea spleenwort, saxifrages and sea campion fill the crevices of the rocks. A small disused cliff quarry, now colonised by heath and grassland, attracts a number of butterflies including wall brown, grayling and gatekeeper, while the regular mounds of yellow meadow ant nests indicate the antiquity of many of the clifftop grasslands. Thickets of scrub create valuable habitats for typical clifftop birds such as stonechat, whitethroat and dunnock, and although the cliffs are too low for nesting sea birds, common tern, herring gull, cormorant, redshank and oystercatcher can be seen.

ACCESS: Open access to cliff; coastal footpath.

PARKING: Small car park; car park at St Patrick's church.

FACILITIES: Facilities at Cemaes.

COED CAE FALI

*472 acres (191 ha) off A487(T), 7m E of Porthmadog, E of
Penrhyndeudraeth, Gwynedd*   [115:SH635403 and 124:SH635403]

Overlooking the Dwyryd Estuary in the Vale of Ffestiniog, this property on a steep valley side within the Snowdonia National Park consists of a mix of ancient oak woodland with more recently planted beech and conifers such as larch and Norway spruce. It was bought by the Trust recently with the express purpose of restoring the semi-natural oak woodland, of which there are many nationally important examples in the Ffestiniog area.

The extensive replanting has shaded the woodland floor, much reducing the wildlife interest and entirely changing the character of the wood; beech and conifers are now being selectively removed. The invasive rhododendron, a problem throughout Snowdonia if not controlled, prevents new tree growth and shades the woodland flora, which includes wood sage, hard fern, cow-wheat and common polypody. A rich community of mosses can also be seen on the woodland floor, while bilberry, ling, cross-leaved heath and bell heather grow in the more open areas of the wood. Birds nesting in the woodlands include pied flycatcher, redstart, wood warbler and tree pipit – the four classic upland oakwood birds.

There is evidence throughout the woods of traditional methods of woodland management, such as hazel and oak coppice stools, and old walls and barns are a reminder of a time when woodland clearings were farmed.

ACCESS: Footpaths; Ffestiniog Railway runs between Porthmadog and Blaenau Ffestiniog (seasonal).

PARKING: Parking in lay-by off A487.

FACILITIES: Nature trails.

THE COLBY ESTATE

973 acres (394 ha) immediately NW of Amroth, Dyfed [158:SN155080]

The Colby Estate, a National Park and SSSI, adjoins Carmarthen Bay either side of Amroth, a little holiday village on the Pembrokeshire border. Reaching $1\frac{1}{2}$ miles inland to a ridge of carboniferous limestone, it surrounds and protects a beautiful wooded valley which runs north from the sea and forks at Colby Lodge. Farmland, cliffs and coastal pastures, steep wooded valleys with fast-running streams, abandoned fields regenerating to oak and ash woods, overgrown quarries and mine workings provide important habitats for a rich variety of animals and birds.

Overlying the Pembrokeshire coalfield, the estate was extensively mined for its anthracite until the middle of the nineteenth century. It takes its name from John Colby, an industrial entrepreneur of the early nineteenth century, who built Colby Lodge. Along the footpaths and in the woods, the evocative remains of the industry lie scattered beneath the peace and tranquillity of the present landscape.

ACCESS: Footpaths; Colby Woodland Garden open seasonally; local station at Kilgetty and bus service from Tenby.

PARKING: Car park.

FACILITIES: NT shop and refreshments at Woodland Garden; WCS; part of Woodland Garden accessible to wheelchairs.

CREGENNAN

820 acres (332 ha) 1m E of Arthog, A493 up steep winding road or Cadair Idris road from Dolgellau, Gwynedd [124:SH6614]

The Cadair Idris massif, in the south-western quarter of the Snowdonia National Park, is an impressive mountainous landscape with a wide range of nationally important upland habitats (lakes, crags, heath, mires, scree and open grassland) and classic features of a glaciated mountain terrain. Cregennan lies to the north-west of the summit with views of the massif and across the Mawddach Estuary to Barmouth Bay. Dinas Oleu, an area of cliffland above Barmouth, was the first property to be acquired by the Trust.

The clear waters of the two lakes, known jointly as Llynnau Cregennan, are fed by streams running off the mountains, creating a network of wetland habitats. A combination of mosses (including club mosses), sedges, heather, cross-leaved heath, bilberry, crowberry and lichens make up these valuable habitats; Cregennan Bog, in particular, is covered with *Sphagnum* moss and bog myrtle.

The ungrazed islands on the lakes contain examples of the vegetation that could grow without grazing pressure, such as vigorous tall heathland plants. There are also some significant areas of bushy dry heath around the lake, with bilberry, cross-leaved heath, mosses, grasses and lichens, and peregrine, raven and buzzard are a common sight overhead. A small area of woodland, dominated by ash, forms a landmark and there is also an interesting area of upland hazel scrub. The crags and rock crevices support important wildlife communities, inaccessible to sheep grazing, with mossy and starry saxifrages, Wilson's filmy fern, roseroot and beech fern.

Recent archaeological surveys have uncovered a succession of significant remains scattered over the landscape, dating back to a prehistoric age, including standing stones, rectangular huts and ring cairns, evidence of a continuous pattern of settlement in what appears to be a wild and inhospitable terrain. A network of drystone walls and vernacular farm buildings dotted throughout the valleys reveal more recent efforts to make a living from farming in these mountains.

ACCESS: Minor gated metalled road; footpaths around northern edge of lake; car access through property.

PARKING: Car park at Lynnau Cregennan.

FACILITIES: WCs at Llynnau Cregennan; youth hostel at Aber-Gywant.

CROFT AMBREY AND CASTLE

1385 acres (561 ha) 6m NW of Leominster, via B4361 from Leominster or B4362 from A49 Ludlow to Leominster road, Hereford & Worcester
[137:SO455655]

This historic landscape records centuries of working the land, battles, changes and fashions from prehistoric time through the medieval and Tudor periods to the nineteenth century. The hill is dominated by a spectacular Iron Age hill fort, with a triple ring of banks and ditches, offering stunning views across to the Welsh borders. Other earthworks remain from Iron Age and Roman building, and there are some pillow mounds or artificial rabbit warrens.

The extensive and varied estate of Croft Castle encompasses ancient pasture woodland and formal parkland, avenues of lime and sweet chestnut trees. Oak, ash and beech are among the mature trees, some of which are thought to be up to 350 years old. Ancient pollards are important for dead wood insects, molluscs and lichens, and the pasture woodland, used for centuries for grazing, fuel and cut wood, probably occupies an ancient site. A major new plan to reinstate pasture woodland is now being activated, in liaison with the Forestry Commission.

Fallow and muntjac deer can be seen in the woods of oak, ash, hornbeam, sweet chestnut, beech, hawthorn and elder, along with birds such as tree creeper, pied flycatcher and lesser spotted woodpecker. The uncommon hawfinch, with its strong protruding beak, feeds on the seeds of hornbeam.

Hares, grey and red squirrels, fallow deer and weasels are found throughout the estate. The scarce Natter's bat lives in the old buildings, relying on the surrounding varied habitats for its food. Buzzard are often seen overhead. Several species of butterflies, including the silver-washed fritillary, feed on the grasslands, and in the woodland rides and glades. Other scarce fritillaries are found on the hillside and on the bracken slopes.

ACCESS: Castle open seasonally; footpaths through estate; station at Leominster and local bus service from Birmingham and Hereford.

PARKING: Car park at Croft Castle (seasonal).

FACILITIES: refreshments available at Berrignton Hall ($5\frac{1}{2}$m); wheelchair access to parts of grounds; leaflet; information board in car park; picnics in parkland; dogs allowed on leads.

DINAS FAWR, DINAS BACH AND CARREG FARM

184 acres (75 ha) 3m NW of Aberdaron, Gwynedd   [123:SH156285]

A continuation of the magnificent Llyn Peninsula coastline with its bevelled profile of headlands, islands and bays, this property commands spectacular views along the coast and on a clear day across to Ireland. The two tiny islands and the adjoining cliffs of Dinas Fawr and Dinas Bach are overlooked by Carreg Farm. The absence of woodland is notable on this very exposed wind-clipped landscape, although streams, flushes and ungrazed ledges provide valuable protection from grazing, leading to rich areas for plants and insects.

Grey seals are common along the coastline, as well as a variety of sea birds, but there are no significant colonies. The uncommon chough will be seen feeding in the area.

The cliffs and rocky outcrops are covered with maritime lichens, some of importance for their rarity, and the coastal grassland, heavily grazed, is floristically rich in places. Spring squill, kidney vetch, thyme, rock spurrey, thrift, primrose, burnet saxifrage and restharrow are some of the many flowers to be seen.

ACCESS: Footpath; access to islands at low water only.

PARKING: Car parks at Porthor and Carreg.

FACILITIES: Local facilities.

DINAS HEAD

9½ acres (4 ha) 7m NE of Fishguard, off A487(T), Dyfed [157:SN010404]

With dramatic views across Cardigan Bay, this prominent headland provides an important nesting site for sea birds, including guillemot, razorbill, fulmar and gulls, especially on Needle Rock. The rare chough and raven may also be seen here, and grey and Atlantic seals swim off the headland, which is linked to the 'mainland' by a valley – a glacial meltwater channel, now filled with thick peat deposits.

Interesting maritime grassland, open rock communities and extensive heathland occur on the cliffs, although there are large areas of less notable coarse grassland and bracken. Thrift clearwing moth and small blue butterfly are among the interesting invertebrates.

ACCESS: Circular walk around headland; permissive path across farmland.

PARKING: Car parks to W and E.

FACILITIES: Facilities at Pwll Gwaelod; WCs; leaflet from Dyfed Wildlife Trust.

DINEFWR ESTATE

240 acres (97 ha) off A40(T), entrance at Llandeilo, Dyfed
[159:SN615225]

Dinefwr Park has had a significant involvement with the early medieval history of Wales; the old Dinefwr Castle which overlooks the Tywi Valley was the capital of Deheubarth, one of the three ancient kingdoms of Wales. Newton House (or New Castle) has been the ancestral home of the modern Dynevor family since around 1500. The old castle is now a ruin, owned by the Dyfed Wildlife Trust and managed by Cadw.

The surrounding parkland is also a medieval feature and includes parks enclosed from the wildwood for deer and for wild white cattle. Descendants of the cattle were at Dinefwr for at least 700 years, until 1980. The park still contains descendants of the wildwood trees, and is a very important site for species of lichen and insect which are confined to sites with an unbroken continuity of ancient trees.

The park and adjacent farmland were later landscaped, in the eighteenth century, when much tree-planting was carried out.

As well as the park, valuable features at Dinefwr include the banks of the River Tywi, its flood pastures, old ox-bows (abandoned river meanders), woodlands and rock outcrops. The ox-bows have a rich aquatic flora which includes scarce pondweeds, floating marshwort, nodding bur-marigold and greater bladderwort. The flood plain and ox-bows are part of a site of international importance for wintering birds, including ten per cent of the British population of white-fronted geese (downstream), and teal, wigeon, shoveler, curlew, lapwing and other waders.

ACCESS: Via minor roads; station at Llandeilo.

PARKING: Small car park.

FACILITIES: Parkland walks.

THE DOLAUCOTHI ESTATE

2522 acres (1021 ha) between Llanwrda and Lampeter at Pumpsaint, off A482, Dyfed   [146:SN6640]

In the remote Cothi Valley, gold has been mined from these wooded slopes since Roman times. The gold mines are the main focus for a visit, but the estate is large and encompasses eleven tenanted farms and part of Pumpsaint village.

Oak and alder woods are rich in woodland plants. Llandre Carr, an alder woodland, is of note for its abundance of mosses and lichens, and pockets of old sessile oak woodland provide important cover for numerous breeding birds. The majestic red kite, a rare bird of prey, may also be seen over the woods.

ACCESS: Walks around mines and woodlands; local station at Llanwrda.

PARKING: Car park near mines.

FACILITIES: Visitor centre open seasonally; leaflets; booklets; trails; volunteer base camp.

THE DOLMELYNLLYN ESTATE

1350 acres (546 ha) 5m NW of Dolgellau, W of A470, Gwynedd
[124:SH7222]

This extensive and varied estate on the slopes of Y Garn in the Rhinog Mountains, within the Snowdonia National Park, includes parkland, two farms and two sheep walks. Wooded fringes, hay meadows and pastures lie along the River Mawddach, where royal fern and globe flower can be found in places.

Oak woodlands on the steep lower slopes include Coed Berthlwyd and Ganllwyd, the latter a National Nature Reserve of great interest for its mosses and liverworts. Woodland plants include hay-scented buckler fern, lemon-scented fern, Wilson's filmy fern and the mountain male fern, while birds in the woods include breeding nuthatch and buzzard. The local lichen, lungwort, occurs on well-lit trees at woodland edges, along the tracks and in the park, indicating a long continuity of woodland cover in this area and an unpolluted, humid atmosphere.

Cefn Coch and Berthlwyd gold mines, dating from the nineteenth century, are among the many relics of the mining history of the area. Small drystone enclosures, field barns and abandoned farmsteads make up the landscape of the lower hill slopes, while upland shelters or 'hafods' can be seen on higher ground. Many of the fields have unimproved grasslands, rich flushes and mires, and an abundance of the diminutive ivy-leaved bellflower is a feature.

The Rhinogau heather moors of Derlwyn and Y Llethr to the east are of interest, with excellent expanses of cross-leaved heath, bell heather, bilberry, cowberry, crowberry and a very varied 'understory' of mosses and lichens beneath the dwarf shrubs, as well as ungrazed crags with tall herb ledges and small mountain lakes and pools.

ACCESS: Well-used footpaths through wood.

PARKING: Car park at nature reserve; Forestry Commission car park on opposite side of river.

FACILITIES: WCs; leaflets; information panel; old mine site open to the public; fishing with permits.

DOVER'S HILL

184 acres (74½ ha) north of B4035 between Chipping Campden and Weston-sub-Edge, Gloucestershire [151:SP137397]

This natural limestone amphitheatre (part of the Cotswold AONB) lies on the edge of the Cotswold escarpment, with impressive views across the Vale of Evesham. It is the site of the annual 'Cotswold Olympick Games', a tradition dating back to the seventeenth century, on the Spring Bank Holiday weekend.

There are numerous steep walks up the slope, passing through pasture, scrub, old pollarded trees, springs and woodland. In a number of places the limestone has fallen away, leaving an unusual landslip scenery.

Lynches Wood is an ancient woodland with bluebell, dog violet and wood sorrel. Tawny owl, greater spotted woodpecker, tree creeper and blackcap are among the many birds to be found, and the large old ash, oak and field maple pollards support many specialist insects. The scrub of hawthorn, ash and sallow is ideal for white-throat, garden warbler and yellow-hammer. Meadow saxifrage, a local rarity, can be found in the grassland along with a large number of snails which rely on the calcium content of the soil.

ACCESS: Footpath to viewpoint; woodland trail; station at Moreton-in-Marsh.

PARKING: Large car park.

FACILITIES: Leaflet; information board in car park; woodland trail through Lynches Wood; disabled access to topograph at viewpoint.

FAILAND

363 acres (147 ha) 4m W of Bristol, S of A363, E of Lower Failand, overlooking River Severn, Avon [172:ST518739]

Situated within an area of small valleys with intervening hills, this rural landscape is characterised by small fields, orchards, sunken lanes, streams and small deciduous woodlands. Despite being so close to Bristol, the area has a wide range of wildlife, and visitors can enjoy some classic walks.

Summer House Wood is one of five main woodlands on the estate and contains some interesting plants, including ragged robin and lady's smock in marshy hollows beside the streams, and rushes, water forget-me-not, marsh pennywort, gipsywort and butterbur on the wooded banks. Another wood, dominated by alder, has a rich flora of marsh marigold, golden saxifrage and rushes. The hedgebanks include plants characteristic of the woodland edges, with herb robert, clematis, hawthorn, blackthorn, red campion and woundwort.

ACCESS: Footpaths.

PARKING: Limited parking.

FACILITIES: Local facilities.

GAMALLT

300 acres (122 ha) 3m NE of Ffestiniog, Gwynedd [124:SH7444]

This remote moorland is overlain by a thick layer of peat, and much valued for its well-developed dry heathland, upland lakes and an extensive 'blanket' bog which includes dwarf shrubs of heather, crowberry, cowberry, cotton grass and luxuriant carpets of *Sphagnum* moss. Heather flowers are an important food source for specialist upland invertebrates which include moths and bees, while the lakes, low in nutrients (oligotrophic), provide an important habitat for a number of rare water beetles. Common sandpiper, ring ousel, wheatear and meadow pipit are present, and Gamallt also supports an important upland breeding bird community.

Many notable archaeological remains are scattered across the moor, including a large Iron Age settlement with huts and enclosures. A Roman road known as Sarn Helen crosses the property.

ACCESS: On foot only, by track one mile from Ffestiniog on Bala road; Ffestiniog Railway runs between Porthmadog and Blaenau Ffestiniog (seasonal).

PARKING: Informal parking.

FACILITIES: Local facilities.

GLAN FAENOL

314 acres (127 ha) 3m SW of Bangor, 7m N of Caernarfon off A487, Gwynedd   [114 and 115:SH530695]

Bordering the Menai Strait between the mainland and Anglesey, this property includes an area of woodland and improved farmland associated with Vaynol Hall, the remains of one of the largest estates in North Wales. Views to the mountains of Snowdonia and across this beautiful, rocky, wooded, tidal strait (now an important marine nature reserve) have been depicted in a famous mural by Rex Whistler at Plas Newydd.

The parkland around the Hall has small pockets of natural deciduous woodland which are important for wildlife, and the Trust is gradually converting the conifer plantations to broadleaved woodlands and the arable land to pasture. A number of follies and estate buildings exist, with a round tower built to rival the column on Anglesey and a family mausoleum. Old lime workings are now colonised by a covert of ash, elm, birch, holly, hazel and dog's mercury, and the estate wall around the park is also of historic interest.

ACCESS: Footpaths; station at Bangor.

PARKING: Small car park.

FACILITIES: Local facilities.

GOOD HOPE

97 acres (39 ha) E of Strumble Head, 3m NW of Fishguard, on the Pembrokeshire coast, Dyfed   [157:SM912407]

Lying on the rugged coastline east of Strumble Head, this traditional farmed landscape includes narrow fields, historical field boundaries ('Pembrokeshire banks') and vernacular farm buildings.

The farmland consists of a patchwork of dry and wet pasture, scrub, rushes, gorse and bracken. Adder's tongue fern, a plant typical of old damp unimproved pastures, exists within a number of fields with many orchids, yellow bartsia, ragged robin, wild angelica, marsh bedstraw and lesser spearwort. The hedgebanks, an important feature of the landscape, add to the ecological interest of the property. Overgrown willow, blackthorn and bramble attract many birds such as willow warbler, chiff-chaff, grasshopper warbler, whitethroat and wren. An old green lane divides the farm into two.

The unfarmed clifftop includes areas of coastal maritime grassland and heath rich in plants such as heather, thrift, kidney vetch, ox-eye daisy and sea campion, which attract many insects. The rare chough, a speciality of coastal grasslands and heaths in Pembrokeshire and the Llyn Peninsula, can also be seen regularly.

ACCESS: Pembrokeshire coastal path; footpath through farmland.

PARKING: Car park at Strumble Head ($1\frac{1}{2}$m to W); no parking on property.

FACILITIES: Leaflet.

HARESFIELD BEACON, STANDISH WOOD, STOCKEND WOOD AND MAITLAND WOOD

361 acres (146 ha) 2–3m NW of Stroud, between A419 and A46, Gloucestershire   [162:SO820089 and 840087]

This series of properties, lying in the heart of the Cotswolds, has features typical of the scarp landscape: beech woodlands, limestone grassland, drystone walls and many archaeological remains. There are some disused quarries and old earthworks, with a dyke, a neolithic chambered long barrow and two round barrows on nearby Randwick Hill. A number of the woodlands are located on ancient sites, with evidence of historic land use, although some have been cleared and replanted.

Haresfield Beacon, designated a geological SSSI, is the site of a prehistoric hill fort, and gives impressive views across the Severn Estuary to the Welsh Hills. Remnants of old woodland pasture flank the hill.

Standish Wood, on the slopes of the escarpment, comprises several different woodlands containing a number of unusual plants associated with southern Britain. Among the stands of beech, ash, oak, birch and whitebeam grow bluebell, dog's mercury, wood anemone, sweet woodruff, wood spurge, and hart's tongue and hard shield ferns.

Stockend and Maitland woods, on the shallower slopes, are thought to be part of an old pasture woodland and show signs of a traditional pastoral way of life. There is evidence of old coppicing, with some beech coppice stools. These woods contain an interesting flora which includes spurge laurel, wood melick and hart's tongue fern.

Woodland birds include blackcap, chiff–chaff and greater spotted woodpecker, and the limestone grassland, with its wide range of plants, supports many butterflies such as the brown argus, common blue and small copper.

The ridges are easily reached on foot from a number of neighbouring Cotswold villages; Pitchcombe, Painswick and Sheepscombe are particularly attractive and well worth visiting.

ACCESS: Footpaths cross the woodlands; the Cotswold Way follows the scarp line; stations at Stroud and Stonehouse.

PARKING: One car park at Standish Wood; casual parking at other properties.

FACILITIES: Information board in car park; topograph on Haresfield Beacon; camping area off Cotswold Way; Slimbridge Wildlife Trust on opposite side of M5 (about 10m from Stonehouse).

HENRHYD FALLS AND GRAIGLLECH WOODS

188 acres (76 ha) N of Coelbren junction, midway between A4067 and A4109, Powys [160:SN850119]

Situated on the southern edge of the Brecon Beacons National Park, this area contains a complicated series of river capture and rejuvenation at the head of the Neath and Tawe rivers which has produced narrow, steep-sided gorges and waterfalls. One such gorge and waterfall can be seen here on the Nant Llech, a tributary of the Tawe. This impressive beauty spot is crossed by the course of the nineteenth-century Brecon Forest Tramroad, an early railway used to transport minerals.

The 'dingles', or woods on either side of the gorge, are rich in wildlife. Evidence of past woodland management is visible in the form of old coppice stools, and the woods to the north, dominated by ash and hazel, also contain remains of coppicing. To the south there is little coppicing, and the trees include wych elm and small-leaved lime. The remains of a Roman fort (not owned by the Trust) among the woods add further historic interest.

Rocks around the waterfalls are covered in mosses, ferns and liverworts, and on ledges tall herbs such as tutsan, meadowsweet, common valerian and lady's mantle occur. Many other more local plants are present in the Nant Llech valley as a whole.

ACCESS: Footpath to gorge.

PARKING: Car park N of gorge through Coelbren, off minor road.

FACILITIES: Local facilities.

NOTE: Care must be taken to avoid landslips.

KETE

168 acres (68 ha), 8m SW of Haverfordwest, off B4327, Dyfed [157:SM800045]

This property stands on the south arm of St Bride's Bay on the Dale Peninsula, and has good views across to the islands of Skomer and

Skokholm. The cliff areas support rich maritime grassland, grass-heath and open communities, and a small stream with a rich associated flora. The maritime grassland is particularly well developed on the small promontories and south-facing cliff slopes, with a wide variety of plants, animals and invertebrates present, the latter including two local species of beetle. Similar species-rich maritime grass-heath is present locally, and contains a number of plants of the rare prostrate form of broom with the associated broom beetle. Maritime open communities are widely developed and form valuable breeding habitats for mining bees and wasps. The narrow stream gully has a rich associated flora with the local royal fern.

This is a poor cliff section for breeding sea birds, with only a few herring gull nesting on the property. There is some ornithological interest, however, in species such as raven and stonechat, and the cliff grasslands are of value as a feeding area for chough.

There is much of historical interest, including platforms used for chipping flints, a distinct Iron Age promontory hill fort at Little Castle Point, and the remains of a camp used during the Second World War.

ACCESS: Footpaths across Kete to cliffs; permissive path from car park to join coastal path.

PARKING: Car park at Kete.

FACILITIES: Amenity island at car park; views of islands.

LAWRENNY

71 acres (29 ha) 16m SE of Haverfordwest, W of A4075 to Lawrenny on Pembrokeshire coast, Dyfed   [157 and 158:SN017068]

This ancient oakwood stands on the east bank of the Daugleddau Estuary between its two branches, Garron Pil and the Cresswell River. The estuary is of importance for its wildfowl and waders, and is of marine biological interest because of the change in plants and animals upstream as the saltwater merges with fresh.

The coppiced sessile oak woodland supports a rich association of beetles, mosses, lichens, woodland plants and the wild service tree, all indicators of the antiquity of the site.

ACCESS: Permitted footpaths on NT property.

PARKING: Car park at Lawrenny Quay.

FACILITIES: Facilities at nearby Lawrenny Quay.

LITTLE MILFORD

72 acres (29 ha), 3m S of Haverfordwest, Dyfed [158 and 157:SM967118]

Situated on the west bank of the tidal mouth of the Cleddau River, a branch of the Daugleddau Estuary, this wooded property fringes an important estuarine bird sanctuary with impressive wintering populations of wildfowl and waders, including greenshank, redshank, dunlin and ringed plover.

The wooded slopes of conifer and broadleaved trees include pockets of oak coppice with a rich woodland flora and fauna. Woodland plants include great woodrush, moschatel, common cow wheat and the local hay-scented buckler fern, here near the northern edge of its distributional range in Britain. Breeding birds include pied flycatcher.

The estuarine and alluvial flats are fringed by a small area of ungrazed saltmarsh, and a reed-bed.

ACCESS: Network of footpaths and 2 bridleways cross property.

PARKING: Small car park near entrance to property off main Haverfordwest to Freystrop road.

FACILITIES: Local facilities.

LLANRHIDIAN MARSH AND WHITFORD BURROWS

1271 acres (514 ha) on N and NW coast of Gower Peninsula, from village of Crofty, 6m W of Swansea off minor roads to Cheriton from B4295, West Glamorgan [159:SS490932]

These properties are outstanding both for their landscape beauty and for their wildlife. Llanrhidian Marsh is one of the best examples of a saltmarsh in Britain, and Whitford Burrows one of the best dune systems.

Llanrhidian Marsh is a high saltmarsh, only inundated by very high tides, which has been built up into the Burry Inlet far out in front of the old fossil limestone cliffline, a very distinct feature backing the marshes. It is commonland, heavily grazed by sheep and ponies, and provides an interesting contrast with the ungrazed marshes nearby, which have a very different saltmarsh flora. The site is of international importance for its huge populations of wintering wildlife (over 14,500) and waders (over 38,000), including oystercatcher, knot, turnstone, pintail, curlew, golden plover, grey plover, teal, shelduck, shoveler, dunlin, sanderling and redshank. This was the first Trust property to be acquired under the Enterprise Neptune appeal.

Whitford Burrows is a very extensive dune system. Although partly planted with pines to stabilise the dunes (a practice now known to reduce significantly the interest of sand dunes, mobile and fresh sand being essential for their natural functioning) the Burrows have an excellent series of dune habitats. These include embryo (new) dunes, yellow dunes with marram grass, stable dune grassland, superb damp hollows or slacks, and very interesting dune-to-saltmarsh transitions. The flora is exceptional, and includes many rare and local species, including early marsh orchid, fen orchid, early sand-grass, golden dock and dune gentian.

ACCESS: Via minor roads.

PARKING: Informal parking.

FACILITIES: Information from Countryside Council for Wales at Oxwich Reserve Centre, Oxwich.

LONGHOUSE COASTLINE NEAR ABERCASTLE

203 acres (82 ha) 14m NE of St David's, just NE of Trevine off A487, Dyfed [157:SM853337]

This property includes an impressive rocky headland with small off-shore islands, sea stacks, sheer cliffs, unimproved clifftops and farmland. Traditional hedgebanks rich in wild flowers surround some of the small fields, and herb-rich coastal grasslands, cliff ledges and scrub encircle the farmland.

The headlands include some important grasslands and rock crevices which support spring squill, kidney vetch, tormentil, pink thrift, rock spurrey, sea campion, sheep's bit and many other species. Of historic interest is a promontory hill fort which can be seen at Castell Coch.

ACCESS: Coast path; circular walk.

PARKING: Limited parking at Abercastle and Trevine (care must be taken to avoid blocking gates and lanes).

FACILITIES: Facilities at Trevine; WCs at Abercastle; leaflet.

LYDSTEP HEADLAND

54 acres (22 ha) 4m SW of Tenby on A4139, 3m E of Manorbier, Dyfed
[158:SS090976]

This impressive coastal promontory overlooks the island of Caldey and protects Lydstep Haven. It is made up of carboniferous limestone which forms high cliffs, deep inlets and caves.

The cliffs are important for sea birds such as fulmar, razorbill and guillemot which nest on the rock ledges, and the uncommon chough, a red-billed member of the crow family, can be seen quite frequently.

Clifftop grasslands are a mass of colour with cowslip, spring squill, wild thyme, ox-eye daisy, autumn gentian and the occasional green-winged orchid. A disused limestone quarry, once used by monks and possibly to export limestone in ships across the Bristol Channel to Devon and Somerset, is now being colonised by lime-loving plants.

ACCESS: On foot via public footpath from Lydstep village; Pembrokeshire Coast Path crosses property; stations at Manorbier, Penally and Tenby.

PARKING: Car park on headland.

FACILITIES: Nature trail leaflet.

MARLOES SANDS AND DEER PARK

524 acres (212 ha) SW of Haverfordwest, off B4327, Dyfed

[157:SM770085]

The most westerly section of the Dale-Marloes Peninsula is surrounded by a dramatic coastline with complex geological structures and a sweep of sands to the south. The rocks include unusual volcanic lavas, and a good example of the junction between the Silurian and Devonian geological periods. The name Deer Park refers to an enclosing wall built during the eighteenth and nineteenth centuries, although there is no evidence that deer were ever introduced.

On the south coast between Gateholm and the Deer Park, herb-rich unimproved grasslands, heath, scrub and lichens of national importance cover the rocks. The heath includes prostrate broom, a rare coastal plant.

Marloes Mere, leased to the Dyfed Wildlife Trust, is an extensive bog dominated by rushes with many other plants such as common cotton grass and ragged robin, and a rich habitat for birds.

Wintering wildfowl and waders include wigeon, shoveler, pintail, whimbrel, curlew and lapwing. Gateholm Island and promontory, the site of an ancient fort, lies to the north of Marloes Sands. Gateholm and Midland islands, together with the Deer Park, were bought with Enterprise Neptune funds in 1981.

On the north coast scrub and coarse grassland provide good feeding and nesting sites for stonechat, whitethroat, dunnock, linnet, yellowhammer and wren. The patches of heath, which are pruned and 'waved' by the strong salt-laden winds, attract insects feeding on heather, such as the oak eggar moth and heather beetle. The Trust has reintroduced grazing to the Deer Park to maintain short grassland and heath habitats, very important for chough which breed on the cliff ledges and feed on the cliff tops.

ACCESS: Public access to Marloes Sands and Martins Haven beach; long-distance path along coastline.

PARKING: Large car parks N of Runwayskiln and Martins Haven.

FACILITIES: WCs at Marloe village; leaflet for Deer Park; interpretive centre at Martins Haven, Lockley Lodge, run by the Dyfed Wildlife Trust; youth hostel.

MAY HILL AND MAY HILL COMMON

131 acres (53 ha) 9m W of Gloucester, towards Ross-on-Wye, N of A40,
Gloucestershire [162:SO695215]

This isolated conical hill with spectacular views over the Severn plain is designated an AONB. Formerly heathland, the hill was cultivated during the Second World War for barley and potatoes but has now reverted to a typical upland vegetation of coarse grass, gorse scrub, bracken and heather.

Pockets of wet flushes support mosses and damp-loving plants such as marsh pennywort, bog stitchwort, round-leaved crowfoot and bog pimpernel, and a number of ponds (a diminishing habitat in the county) add to the diversity of the wildlife with great crested newt, damselfly and pond skater.

A network of paths leads up the hill through attractive woodland to an SSSI on the summit, which is covered in gorse, bilberry and heather. Tree pipit and yellowhammer are common among the gorse and heather, and butterflies include the small copper and green-veined white.

ACCESS: Open access to Common; 2 footpaths; network of paths through woods.

PARKING: Small parking areas; no parking on road.

FACILITIES: Local facilities.

MINCHINHAMPTON AND RODBOROUGH COMMONS

580½ acres (235 ha) between Stroud and Nailsworth, E of A46 and SW of
A419, Gloucestershire [162:SO850038 and 850010]

Stretches of Jurassic limestone grassland occupy the plateau above the steep Cotswold escarpment (an AONB). Broken by patches of woodland and scrub, and containing a number of ancient earthworks and archaeological remains, the commons (designated an SSSI) are still grazed by cattle, horses and sheep by local graziers exercising their historic rights as commoners. The area is also popular for walking, jogging, golf and kite-flying. The Bulwarks, an Iron Age hill fort above the village of Amberley, commands splendid views across the Cotswold landscape to the Welsh Hills.

Both commons are recognised for the importance of their wild-life, and among the many flowers and grasses are the common rock-rose, eyebright, cowslip, pyramidal and common spotted orchids, stemless thistle and bird's foot trefoil. Butterflies include chalkhill and small blues, dark-green fritillary and Duke of Burgundy, and juniper bushes on the steep slopes also attract a number of interesting insects. Dog's mercury and bluebell flourish in the ash, oak and beech woodland remnants.

Rodborough Common, with its small coombes and spurs, con-tains a number of specific habitats which support a wide range of plants and associated invertebrates. Although the commons form one of the richest grassland systems in the country, the flora at Rod-borough is suffering from a decline in grazing, and species such as the rare pasque flower have declined considerably, while rank tor grass has increased phenomenally. The growing number of visitors is causing problems, particularly at Minchinhampton.

ACCESS: Open access; network of footpaths and minor roads across commons.

PARKING: Parking areas on edge of commons and on Rodborough Common.

FACILITIES: Information boards; leaflets.

MWNT

98 acres (40 ha) 4m NE of Cardigan, off A487, Dyfed
[145:SN1952 and SD4195]

This charming and safe family beach in a sheltered bay, bounded on the north by the dramatic headland of Foel y Mwnt, is a geological SSSI and part of the Ceredigion Heritage Coast. The maritime flora is more varied than is typical here, and includes spring squill, hard rush and fifty species of lichen (in contrast to the average of fifteen for this part of the coastline). In spring the headland has a glorious carpet of pink thrift.

Birds of prey hover over the surrounding agricultural pasture-land, and gulls, tern and fulmar occupy the precipitous cliffs. Grey Atlantic seal and bottle-nosed dolphin frequent the waters of the bay.

The bay is the site of a battle in 1155, when an invasion of Flemings was repelled by the native Welsh. The church of the Holy Cross was built in the thirteenth or fourteenth century on the site of an old Celtic saint's cell, on the pilgrimage route to Bardsey.

Imported lime, used to sweeten the acid soil of this west-coast seaboard, was burnt in the old kiln.

ACCESS: Steps down to beach.

PARKING: Large car park, free to members.

FACILITIES: WCs and refreshments (seasonal).

NOTE: Care should be taken near the treacherous cliff edges. Dogs are not allowed on the beach during the summer.

MYNACHDY, CLEGIR MAWR AND CEMLYN

884 acres (358 ha) 2m W of Cemaes Bay, off side roads from A5025 on N coast of Anglesey, Gwynedd [114:SH325933, 315913 and 295920]

This varied stretch of coast from Cemaes to Clegir on the north side of Anglesey is designated a Heritage Coast because of the unspoilt beauty of its small shingle beaches, rocky inlets, grassy headlands, islands, inshore water, farmed landscape and the numerous remains of an industrial and maritime past.

The landscape consists of drumlins, or small rounded rocky hillocks formed in the last Ice Age, often surrounded by narrow bands of arable land, pasture or, in some of the hollows, by bog and fen. Grassy and heathy headlands have a rich flora, with spring squill, kidney vetch, harebell, thyme, knapweed, devil's bit scabious, restharrow, bloody crane's bill and bird's foot trefoil.

Cemlyn, a lagoon created by the impounding of brackish water, attracts winter populations of wildfowl and a tern colony of Arctic and common terns during April to July; it is managed as a nature reserve by the North Wales Wildlife Trust.

Mynachdy, a recent acquisition, includes a fine stretch of the north-west corner of Anglesey with many coves, and views to Holyhead Bay. Old settlement sites and the remains of derelict copper mines can also be seen here.

Clegir Mawr and Cemlyn consist of gently undulating farmland with typical drystone walls surrounding small fields, rocky sea cliffs, headlands and shingle beaches. The beaches are colonised by pioneer plants such as sea kale, sea radish and sea holly, while the cliffs, encrusted with unusual lichens, thrift, rocky spurrey and sea campion, include some spectacular folds and ancient volcanic intrusions. They also provide important nesting sites for chough, raven, jackdaw and peregrine. The rocks here are amongst the oldest in Britain, some 1000 million years old, and are of great geological interest. Earthworks and a twelfth-century church are of historic interest at Cemlyn.

ACCESS: Way-marked path along the coast; network of paths linking with coast.

PARKING: Small car parks at Fydlyn and Hen Felin.

FACILITIES: Leaflets; information boards.

MYNYDD ANELOG

116 acres (47 ha) 2m NW of Aberdaron, Gwynedd   [123:SH150275]

This area of ancient commonland, with the remains of prehistoric hut circles, stands on one of the higher hills of the Llyn Peninsula, with precipitous cliffs commanding spectacular views across to Ireland, the Snowdonia mountain range, Anglesey and south to St David's Head.

Like that at Braich-y-Pwll, the coastal heath is one of the best examples of its kind in Europe, and the three dwarf shrubs – heather, bell heather and western gorse – grow well where grazing is not too heavy and burning not too frequent. It provides crucial summer feeding-ground for the rare chough, a red-billed member of the crow family which is now found in Britain only on the Llyn, Anglesey, in Pembrokeshire and in part of the western coast of Scotland. Like those on Anglesey, the Llyn rocks are ancient precambrian metamorphosed lavas and sediments of great geological interest.

The clifftop moorland is scattered with rock boulders and out-crops, providing an ideal point to view the small-scale, traditional farms of the peninsula, the unimproved coarse grassland and heather enclosed by walls, fences and stonebanks, ancient commons and scrubby pockets of woodland.

ACCESS: Footpath from Whistling Sands beach.

PARKING: Car parks at Carreg and Porthor.

FACILITIES: Local facilities.

PENARFYNDD AND PORTH YSGO

245 acres (99 ha) 5m E of Aberdaron, access by minor roads, Gwynedd
[123:SH217265 and 208266]

On the south side of the peninsula, Porth Ysgo, a sandy beach sur-rounded by cliffs, looks towards Bardsey Island and Seagull Island. In marked contrast to the steep, exposed cliffs of much of the Llyn, this site has soft, unstable cliffs which are low-lying, sheltered and scrubby. Penarfyndd is higher and has steep bracken-covered cliffs; there is also a mudflow here which supports some interesting grass-land and heath. Breeding birds include fulmar, cormorant, shag, kittiwake, razorbill and guillemot.

The dark, volcanic intrusions exposed on the beach are covered with maritime lichens, and the surrounding clifftops are fringed with a herb-rich grassland, typically found around the relatively ungrazed parts of the peninsula. The underlying rocks strongly in-fluence the plants; the more base-rich soils support finer grasses, with madder, rock sea lavender, thyme, sea campion and many species unusual to the Llyn coast.

The heather, gorse and bracken along the clifftop attract small birds such as stonechat, linnet and yellowhammer, while chough feeds on the shorter grassland and gorse.

ACCESS: Footpaths.

PARKING: 2 small car parks.

FACILITIES: Local facilities.

PENBRYN

*124 acres (50 ha) N of A487, midway between Cardigan and New Quay,
Dyfed*   [145:SN295519]

This gently sloping sandy beach, an SSSI and part of the Ceredigion
Heritage Coast, is approached via the picturesque Hoffnant Valley
from the Trust's car park at Llanborth Farm.

There are steep cliffs to the south-west, and more unusual rock
formations at the north-east end. Notable local plants include Portland and wood spurges and rocky stonecrop. The predominantly
sycamore and ash woodland of the valley supports important fern
communities and is rich in insect life.

The coastal scrub holds a good population of small birds including grasshopper warbler and whitethroat, although there is little or
no sea-bird interest. Bottle-nosed dolphin are sometimes spotted
from the beach.

The valley is referred to locally as Cwm Lladron or Robbers'
Valley, and is said to have been much used by smugglers, while the
Corbalani Stone, reputedly marking the grave of an early Celtic
chieftain, has been loosely associated with the Arthurian legend.

ACCESS: Footpath down the Hoffnant Valley.

PARKING: Car park, free to members.

FACILITIES: Shop, café and WCs open seasonally at Llanborth Farm.

NOTE: Dogs not allowed on the beach during summer.

PENNARD CLIFFS AND
THREE CLIFFS BAY

*248 acres (100 ha) 7m SW of Swansea, extending E of Pwll-du Head to
Southgate on Gower Peninsula, West Glamorgan*   [159:SS534875]

This impressive carboniferous limestone coastline is of great importance for its fossil-rich rocks and variety of archaeological remains.
Minchin Hole, a geological SSSI, is an unusual cave cut into the calcareous rocks, and archaeologists and palaeontologists have found
evidence of mammal bones and early man on this site.

High Pennard, one of the higher points along the cliffline, is capped with a prehistoric defensive hill fort, and Three Cliffs Bay contains a megalithic burial chamber, a pillow mound, a medieval tower and church at Penmaen, and some old lime kilns. A derelict limestone quarry, from which stone was exported to Devon, is also of historic interest.

Steep cliffs, broad sands and a meandering stream make up Three Cliffs Bay. A small sand-dune system and area of saltmarsh, used by many field study groups, add to the wildlife interest of the area, with a number of characteristic plants such as sea spurge, sea holly, eel grass, glasswort and sea plantain. The intertidal zone is of marine interest, and the wide sandbanks on the stream provide an ideal feeding ground for waders and wildfowl. A rich diversity of plants along the clifftop reflects the underlying calcareous soils. Where the grassland has escaped agricultural improvement, a greater variety of flowers exists, with wild thyme, kidney vetch, violets, bird's foot trefoil, rock-rose and small scabious, and these attract a number of associated butterflies such as the dark-green fritillary, small blue, brown argus and grayling.

Heather occurs where the soil has been leached and is more acidic, and blackthorn scrub also occurs on the clifftop, attracting many small birds such as stonechat, linnet and whinchat. Fulmar, kittiwake, cormorant and guillemot nest on the cliffs.

ACCESS: Via minor roads; access to Three Cliffs Bay from Pennard Burrows or via Great Tor.

PARKING: Car park at Southgate; car park at Nott Hill and Penmaen (limited space).

FACILITIES: Village shop; WCs; leaflets available from car park attendant at Southgate; part of guided walk programme; no disabled access.

PLAS-YN-RHIW ESTATE

416 acres (168 ha) near Pwllheli, access via minor roads off B4413, Gwynedd [123:SH207265 and 235295]

The former home of the three Keating sisters, the manor of Plas-yn-Rhiw is surrounded by a comparatively well-wooded estate overlooking the long sweeping curved beach of Porth Neigwl. The house retains features of many building periods from the Middle Ages to Tudor and Georgian times. The sisters bought the property in 1939 and subsequently donated it to the Trust 'to save a unique area of natural beauty in memory of their parents'.

In one of the few woodlands on the peninsula, oak, elm and sycamore create a damp, shaded environment for a wealth of ferns, and a mixture of scrub and grassland attracts a number of birds such as stonechat, whinchat and linnet.

Mynydd-y-Graig, the site of an ancient hill fort and some megalithic remains, is of historic interest and the subject of further archaeological studies.

ACCESS: Via minor roads; Plas-yn-Rhiw house open seasonally; station at Pwllheli and local bus service from Pwllheli and Aberdaron, alight at Botwnnog.

PARKING: Car park.

FACILITIES: NT shop; WCs (including disabled); information centre; picnic area; path through woods suitable for wheelchairs.

RAINBOW WOOD FARM

424 acres (172 ha) on Claverton Down, 1m SE of Bath, Avon
[172:ST777630]

This farmed and wooded landscape on the flat hilltop of Claverton Down is owned by the Trust, the Mallett family and the City of Bath, with the intention of protecting the open skyline above the historic city from development. Celtic field patterns of banks and lynchets can be detected in the surrounding fields, particularly on and around the golf course on Bathampton Down (not owned by the Trust). Limestone walls, hedgerows, scattered trees, pastures and woodland blocks make up this pastoral scene, while steep slopes overlook the incised valley of the River Avon.

The underlying limestone leads to a great diversity of plants and associated wildlife. Trees on the estate include pedunculate oak, beech, hawthorn, holly, cherry, hornbeam and yew, with woodland plants such as ramson, hart's tongue fern, wood melick, dog's mercury and bluebells. Badger paths dissect some of the woods, and tawny owl, nuthatch, jay, willow warbler and green woodpecker can be seen.

Some of the meadows are rich in flowers, with salad burnet, dwarf thistle, ox-eye daisy, fairy flax, self-heal, cowslip and lady's bedstraw attracting butterflies such as meadow brown and common blue. The field boundaries of hedges and drystone walls are also havens for wildlife.

ACCESS: Footpaths and permitted ways; station at Bath.

PARKING: Roadside parking nearby.

FACILITIES: Footpath leaflet.

RHOSSILI DOWN AND BEACH

531 acres (215 ha) 15m W of Swansea, at end of Gower Peninsula, West Glamorgan [159:ss420900]

The impressive sweep of Rhossili Bay is backed by a raised beach forming a rectangular platform known locally as the Warren.

Rising above the platform, Rhossili Down (a large whaleback ridge of grass, heath and boggy hollows) commands good views across the Bristol Channel, the Gower Peninsula and towards Pembrokeshire. The expanses of shrubby heath support a number of insects including some uncommon butterflies, with small pockets of scrub attracting many migrant birds. To the north, a boulder field is of particular interest for its lichens, and some important mires and wet heaths on the lower eastern slopes are also of great conservation interest.

A range of archaeological features has survived in this important prehistoric landscape, with cairns and burial chambers, stone circles and early field boundaries.

ACCESS: From Rhossili village and from the N; well marked footpath.

PARKING: Car park at Rhossili.

FACILITIES: WCs; information centre at Rhossili.

ST DAVID'S HEAD

520 acres (210 ha) 4m NW of St David's, on B4583, Dyfed
[157:SM730285]

One of Wales's most famous headlands, this rugged coastline reveals renowned and excellent expanses of Ordovician volcanic intrusions, of great geological interest. Biologically, the headland is just as notable, with one of the largest expanses of coastal heath in Britain, continuing inland on to the rocky promontory of Carn Llidi. On the most exposed seaward slopes the heath consists of heather, bell heather and the rare hairy greenweed, and is wind-clipped and short. Maritime species such as kidney vetch, spring squill, thrift, sea plantain, sheep's bit and musk stork's bill occur in the heath and grasslands here, and in the rock crevices are orpine, sea spleenwort and wild chives.

Moving inland, western gorse becomes abundant with the other dwarf shrubs, and the heath is taller. Associated plants here include lousewort, heath bedstraw, heath-spotted orchid, heath milkwort and various sedges. There are wet areas with purple moor grass, bracken, bramble, common gorse scrub, pools and mires, the whole providing a superb expanse of semi-natural habitat.

The invertebrate fauna is very interesting, and includes both north-western and south-western specialities such as a rare pill woodlouse and the green hairy snail, with local heathland beetles, heather-feeding moths and other species. Nesting sea birds are scattered thinly all along the Trust's cliffs, but only the commoner species are represented. Jackdaw, raven, chough, peregrine, house martin and swift are more notable among the cliff-nesters, all probably present here or on Trust-owned cliffs in the St Bride's Bay area.

St David's Head and Carn Llidi are common land, but until recently grazing had effectively ceased. The Trust is endeavouring to restore grazing so that the valuable heath and wetland does not become rank and scrub-invaded as it would, away from the windy coastal fringe.

The property is exceptionally rich in archaeological remains with prehistoric enclosures, forts and burial chambers at Coetan Arthur and on Carn Llidi, and an old field system behind the sheltered beach of Porthmelgan. Warrior's Dyke is a defensive Iron Age bank built to isolate the headland and creating a coastal fortress.

ACCESS: Coast path and footpaths from youth hostel at Whitesands Bay and Upper Porthmawr.

PARKING: Car park.

FACILITIES: NT shop, WCs and visitor centre at St David's; WCs at Whitesands Bay.

SAND POINT AND MIDDLE HOPE

191 acres (77 ha) 2m N of Weston-super-Mare, on coast road from Kewstoke, Avon [182:ST335665]

This prominent limestone headland projects into the Bristol Channel north of the popular Victorian seaside resort of Weston-super-Mare. Cliffs rise above a rocky shoreline, with good views south across Sand Bay to the Somerset Levels and Wales. Geological exposures reveal a juxtaposition of limestone against ancient volcanic 'pillow' lavas, formed instantly when the lava solidified on contact with water.

On the south-facing slope of Sand Point, the limestone grassland is particularly rich in plants such as lesser centaury, green-winged orchid, St John's wort, thyme, eyebright and dwarf thistle. There are also some national rarities such as Somerset hair-grass. Associated butterflies include grayling and brown argus. The scrubby headland is an important landing point for migrant birds such as swallow, swift and martin in spring, and large numbers of thrush and finch in winter.

To the east, the cliffline dwindles to the low, rocky shore of Middle Hope (an SSSI notable for its geology and calcareous grassland), and an important saltmarsh beside the Banwell Estuary, which is leased to the Avon Wildlife Trust. Sand Bay and the Banwell Estuary, at the mouth of the Severn Estuary, are both important for overwintering waders and wildfowl, with ringed plover, dunlin, mallard, teal, curlew, lapwing, redshank and knot. The saltmarsh supports some delightful plants associated with this habitat, such as sea lavender, sea purslane, sea milkwort and thrift. The rocky cliffs are covered with some unusual lichens and typical cliff plants, with cushions of sea thrift and samphire.

Remnants of the prehistoric and medieval landscape are scattered across the headland, and the remains of Celtic field systems can still be seen. There is a truncated Bronze Age cairn, and a sixteenth-century castle mound surrounded by well-defined field banks and lynchets. The fields are enclosed by drystone walls. Woodspring Priory (Landmark Trust) has some attractive buildings from the fourteenth and fifteenth centuries, including the monastic barn which is owned by the National Trust. At Kewstoke is an ancient flight of long steps, known as Monks Steps, which lead to good viewpoints.

ACCESS: Free access; no public access to Woodspring Priory or barn from Sand Point or car park.

PARKING: Car park at Sand Point.

FACILITIES: Nearest shop ½m; WCs at Sand Point; leaflet; interpretation board in car park.

SHERBORNE PARK ESTATE

4144 acres (1677 ha) 3m E of Northleach, each side of A40, Gloucestershire
[163:SP162138]

This large agricultural estate on the Cotswold plateau (part of the Cotswold AONB and the Sherborne and Windrush conservation areas) contains large areas of former parkland and has good views across the Windrush Valley.

Within the estate is Lodge Park, a seventeenth-century deer-coursing lodge set within a park and currently being renovated by the Trust. The landscape is peppered with copses and coppiced woodland, some on ancient wooded sites. The remnants of a number of meadows along the river were once part of a more extensive system of flood meadows, an old practice which allowed the river water to flow over the grassland during the winter months, releasing its nutrients and warming the land.

A colony of the scarce Duke of Burgundy butterfly inhabits an area of unimproved rich limestone grassland, and mature trees in the parkland harbour some rare beetles and lichens associated with old-established woodland. The copses, woodlands and sheltered belts of trees provide invaluable habitats for birds. The rare lesser horseshoe bat roosts in the older buildings, and on the river are water vole and birds such as little grebe, sedge warbler, reed bunting and mute swan.

Lodge Park contains a fine neolithic chambered tomb, and other evidence of prehistoric life exists on the estate, though Bronze Age barrows have been ploughed down over the years and other settlement evidence lies in cultivated land. An unusual survival is Windrush Camp, a defended settlement of the later prehistoric period (not open to the public).

ACCESS: Confined to roads, bridleways and footpaths; way-marked routes.

PARKING: Car park at Ewepen barn N of A40.

FACILITIES: Leaflets; information boards in Ewepen barn; way-marked walks.

SKIRRID FAWR

205 acres (83 ha) 3m NE of Abergavenny, 1½m E of A465, Gwent
[161:SO330180]

This isolated hill of old red sandstone in the Black Mountains is largely covered with a coarse, tussocky grassland and there are also areas of heather and bilberry on the northern slopes.

The western slopes have two distinct semi-circular landslips, with a variety of plants such as parsley fern and green spleenwort growing in the crevices of the crags, contrasting with the unbroken slopes to the east.

Areas of woodland and scattered trees cover the western and southern slopes. In places the woods have a well-developed flora which includes hart's tongue fern, shining crane's bill, dog's mercury and a rich variety of mosses. Shrubs of hazel, holly and field maple occur within the woods. Woodland birds include woodcock, redstart, wood warbler and buzzard. The woodland, formerly managed by the Forestry Commission, is in the process of being converted from conifers to broadleaved species, and Pant Skirrid Wood is now also in Trust ownership.

Footpaths lead through the oak woods and scattered scrub on to the grassy summit, which commands impressive views of the Sugar Loaf, the Usk Valley and the Black Mountains.

ACCESS: Footpaths from road to south of property; other footpaths provide access from small by-roads to the north; station at Abergavenny.

PARKING: Lay-by parking.

FACILITIES: Local facilities.

THE STACKPOLE ESTATE

1992½ acres (806 ha) 4m S of Pembroke, Dyfed   [158:SR977963]

This extensive estate south of Pembroke is a coastal property of great contrast which includes eight miles of cliff, headlands, beaches and sand dunes, elongated lakes bordered by trees, sheltered bays and mature woodlands. The name Stackpole originates from the Norse *stac* for isolated rock and *pollr* for a small inlet, aptly describing Stackpole Quay.

Two of the most interesting areas biologically, Bosherston Lakes and Stackpole Warren, are managed as nature reserves by the Countryside Council for Wales. The lakes were created between 1790 and 1840 by damming three narrow limestone valleys, two of which were formerly tidal. They are calcareous marl lakes with extensive beds of white water lily and stonewort, and in parts exceptionally clear water from submerged springs. The dunes, which supported a rabbit warren for the Cawdor Estate in the sixteenth century, and probably earlier, have a range of communities including open sand and rock, and stable calcareous dune grassland. Another excellent dune system occurs at Broadhaven. Interesting plants include hutchinsia, blue fleabane, yellow horned poppy, black bog rush, knotted pearlwort and lesser centaury, and notable invertebrates include native cockroach, several local snails, bush crickets, rare beetles and bugs and brown argus butterfly.

The long stretch of limestone cliffs supports rich calcareous and maritime grasslands, and is important for sea birds such as guillemot, razorbill, puffin and kittiwake, as well as resident chough, a Pembrokeshire speciality.

ACCESS: Long-distance footpath along most of property; network of footpaths (access on footpaths only in nature reserve).

PARKING: Car parks at Stackpole Quay and Broadhaven Quay.

FACILITIES: Educational centre with material available; volunteer base camp; fishing on lakes (permit from NT).

SUGAR LOAF

2300 acres (931 ha) 5m NW of Abergavenny, Gwent   [161:SO2718]

This cone-shaped mountain has impressive views across the Bristol Channel, and to the Brecon Beacons, the Black Mountains and Herefordshire. The name refers to its shape which resembles the sugar loaves which were once sold locally.

A number of important archaeological features can be seen, including a boundary bank which encircles a former deer park linked to the Priory of Abergavenny, charcoal-burning sites and associated tracks, and pollarded trees which are evidence of the area's history of wood pasture.

The open moorland is covered with extensive areas of bracken, but also supports important upland heath. Parts are dominated by heather; other areas by bilberry, with cross-leaved heath, cowberry, common cow-wheat, hard fern and various grasses and mosses. There is a rich invertebrate fauna of heathland associates, and Sugar Loaf has a small breeding population of red grouse.

The woodland, dominated by oak, includes one of the most extensive tracts of ancient woodland in east Wales and forms a distinctive landscape feature for miles around. The now neglected coppice and mature trees include both sessile and pedunculate oak and beech. The latter is present as old pollards, indicating its probable native status here, which is interesting, since beech in this part of the country, and certainly in most of Wales, is planted rather than wild. Notable breeding woodland birds include pied flycatcher, redstart and wood warbler.

ACCESS: Access to car parks difficult (roads steep and narrow); network of permitted paths and rights of way; station at Abergavenny.

PARKING: 4 car parks (limited).

FACILITIES: Information panel in main car park.

TREGWYNT AND ABER MAWR BEACH

250 acres (101 ha) 17m NE of St David's, off A487, Dyfed
[157:SM883346]

The major feature of this property is the Aber Mawr Valley, which contains extensive development of semi-natural habitats, ranging from the shingle ridge at the mouth of the valley through tall, marshland vegetation and sallow carr into broadleaved woodland. The combination of this great diversity of habitats and the extent of the semi-natural habitat makes the valley of great general wildlife value. Common and widespread species are present in abundance, but only a few more interesting species have been recorded. The scarcity of rarer species probably reflects the recent origin of the present mosaic of habitats, and of many of the individual habitats themselves.

The valley is rich in birdlife, with typical woodland breeding species such as chiff-chaff, jay and buzzard; scrub birds such as linnet, whitethroat and garden warbler; and wetland birds such as sedge warbler and reed bunting. Badger are present and otter have been recorded.

In addition to the biological interest, the valley is also notable for its geomorphological and palaeo-geographical studies. Behind Aber Mawr beach there is a succession of deposits which provide much information about conditions here during the Ice Age. Sand martin nest in the low cliffs of Pen Deudraeth, and there is a submerged forest which is exposed at low tide.

Remains of a proposed nineteenth-century Irish sea port (a scheme put forward by the engineer Brunel) and a vernacular farmhouse are interesting historic features.

ACCESS: Long-distance coastal footpath; network of paths cross property.

PARKING: Limited informal parking (avoid blocking access).

FACILITIES: Leaflet.

UPPER AND LOWER TREGINNIS

360 acres (146 ha) 3m SW of St David's, Dyfed   [157:SM725240]

Coastal farms cover the south-west tip of St David's Peninsula, which commands spectacular views of Ramsey Sound and Island, St Bride's Bay, and (on a clear day) Snowdon and Ireland.

Traditional farm enclosures of small fields and hedgebanks cover the plateau. The unimproved coastal fringe consists of a variety of wildlife habitats, with grassland, heath and scrub masking many archaeological remains. The clifftop grasslands have patches of heather mixed with a profusion of wild flowers such as spring squill, thrift, sea campion, wild carrot, tormentil and hairy greenweed. The heath includes ling, bell heather, cross-leaved heath and gorse, which attract a number of moths, butterflies and other insects.

This property contains much of historic interest: a neolithic promontory fort, a chambered tomb, the Iron Age fort of Castell Heinif, old copper mine workings at Porthaflod, and quarries and lime kilns at Porth Clais.

The high, vertical cliffs around Lower Tregennis, made up of igneous rocks, overlook sheltered inlets. Seals are commonly seen.

ACCESS: Coastal footpath; way-marked permitted paths.

PARKING: Car parks at Porthclais and St Justinians.

FACILITIES: WCs at Porthclais; leaflets.

WHARLEY POINT

386 acres (156 ha) S of Llanstephan, off B4312 from Carmarthen, Dyfed
[159:SN340093]

Described in the work of Dylan Thomas, this gentle coastal promontory commands delightful views across the Taf and Tywi estuaries to Carmarthen Bay.

The cliffs of Wharley Point are scrubby, and this coast is sheltered enough to permit development of woodland as well. There are, however, open habitats of interest. Unimproved grassland occurs along the top of the cliff in the Lord's Park Farm area; interesting calcareous grassland occurs around some disused limestone quarries, and small areas of saltmarsh occur at the seaward mouths of valleys. The scrub includes many shrubs, such as blackthorn, hazel, hawthorn, gorse, privet, dogwood, holly and large ivy 'bushes', and the limestone grassland has the robust scrambling pea plant (everlasting pea), and calcicoles such as carline thistle, burnet saxifrage and ploughman's spikenard. Butterflies include common blue and brown argus. There are important oystercatcher nesting areas in protected corners of the shoreline, a cormorant roost, and buzzard, raven and peregrine can be seen.

Several notable features of historic interest are the line of bulwarks of an Iron Age hill fort, the twelfth-century Llanstephan Castle (not owned by the Trust) and St Anthony's Well, which supposedly has healing powers.

ACCESS: Footpath from car park near St Anthony's Well; circular path.

PARKING: Car park at Llanstephan.

FACILITIES: Beach and shops at Llanstephan.

YNYS BARRI AND BARRY ISLAND

200 acres (81 ha) 9m NE of St David's, Dyfed   [157:SM805320]

This dramatic and rugged coastline between Abereiddi and Porthgain has much of industrial and archaeological interest. Porthgain (not owned by the Trust), has a well-documented history and was for many years a small port servicing a busy industrial region which exported slate, decorative stone and bricks. The remains of brickworks still exist at Porthgain, and tramways, workings, cottages and drowned quarry workings at Abereiddi, now overgrown by encroaching plants, provide a glimpse of this formerly prosperous area.

The bevelled, much indented coastline with its varying aspects and degrees of exposure supports a range of different vegetation types. Most notably, the clifftop has good areas of maritime grassland and coastal heath, the latter with the local petty whin, and both with dark green fritillary. Areas of exposed slate are particularly important for invertebrates. Cliffs and derelict slate quarries are used by nesting birds such as wheatear, peregrine, chough, fulmar and shag, and grey seal can be seen offshore. Some of the remaining hedgebanks have a rich flora, with cowslip, stonecrop and campion. A man-made basin drowned by salt water, the Blue Lagoon, is of particular marine biological interest with a fauna of active (rather than sedentary) suspension feeders which can cope with the amount of silt produced in the absence of any current, and are not dependent on a current for food supply.

ACCESS: Coast path; path through Barry Island farm to cliffs.

PARKING: Car park at Abereiddi.

FACILITIES: WCs at Abereiddi; telephone at Porthgain; bathing and beach at Traethllyfn.

NOTE: Care should be taken when bathing, because of dangerous undercurrents at south-west corner of beach.

London, Thames Valley and the Chilterns

BEDFORDSHIRE · BERKSHIRE · BUCKINGHAMSHIRE OXFORDSHIRE · LONDON

Now considered to be part of the commuter belt around London and constantly threatened by sprawling development, more and more motorways and 'improved' agriculture, this region can still offer the visitor much unspoilt countryside: the grand beech woods along the Chiltern escarpment, the delights of the Thames, or views from the rounded hills of the chalk ridge across the fertile lowland landscape.

The landscape of Bedfordshire is influenced by the River Ouse with its dykes, fens, woodlands, meadows and heaths. At Whipsnade Downs the Trust has reintroduced sheep grazing on its chalk downland sites, and where the grassland remains unimproved the great diversity of plant and insect life continues.

In Berkshire the spectacular rolling landscape combines with a variety of habitats. At the Holies near Streatley, for example, an improved network of footpaths takes the visitor through grassland, heathland and woods to magnificent views of the Thames at the highest points. The Berkshire Downs are a continuation of the ancient landscape of the downlands, including parts of Oxfordshire, and contain evidence of ancient routes, sarsen stones and the famous figures carved in the white chalk.

Despite the loss of woodland and hedgerows with progressive agriculture practices, Buckinghamshire still retains its rural charm. The Ashridge Estate includes the main ridge of the Chiltern Hills from Ivinghoe Beacon to Berkhamsted. The rest of the estate is almost level, with many fine walks through woodland and open commons. Typical characteristics of the Chilterns include beech woods and springtime carpets of bluebells. On the Hughenden Estate, which lies in the Chilterns AONB, woodland areas give way to open downland and the rich diversity of habitats harbour a variety of wildlife interest.

Encapsulated in the urbanisation of Greater London, relics of Royal Forests and old parkland such as Morden Hall Park are evidence of historic land uses. The protection of these parklands provides much needed green space – 'an air-hole for labouring lungs' – within the city and also a valuable wildlife corridor to the surrounding countryside.

ASHDOWN PARK AND THE UFFINGTON WHITE HORSE

735 acres (297 ha) 2½m S of Ashbury, 3½m N of Lambourn, W of B4000, and 6m W of Wantage, 2m S of Uffington, S of B4507, Oxfordshire
[174:SU301869 and 282820]

Situated on the border of three counties among the rolling hills of the Berkshire Downs, these properties are of great archaeological interest.

Uffington White Horse, a famous landmark for miles around, probably dates from the Iron Age, and above it the down is capped by a hill fort of similar age, and other archaeological remains. At the foot of the hill is the 'Manger' where the horse is supposed to graze once a year.

The parkland around the charming seventeenth-century Ashdown House is surrounded by woodland and farmland, and includes a deer park, probably medieval, and a field of sarsen stones (large hard sandstone boulders remaining from a previous layer of bedrock, the rest long since having weathered away).

The nature conservation interest is centred on the sarsen stones, which support an impressive number of rare lichens. The old trees in the park hold other lichens, together with some mosses. The woodland has interesting plants such as herb Paris, yellow archangel and nettle-leaved bellflower. The Trust is endeavouring to enhance the chalk grassland slopes by sympathetic management.

ACCESS: Guided tours only to house; some woods restricted access; open access to Uffington Hill.

PARKING: Small car park near house.

FACILITIES: Access difficult for wheelchairs; dogs on leads in woodlands only.

THE ASHRIDGE ESTATE AND IVINGHOE BEACON

3980 acres (1611 ha) 3m N of Berkhamsted, at Northchurch, between A41 and B489, both sides of B4506, Hertfordshire and Buckinghamshire
[165:SP9812]

Stretching along the north-eastern edge of the Chiltern escarpment on the Hertfordshire and Buckinghamshire border from Berkhamsted to Ivinghoe Beacon, this huge estate includes a varied landscape of commons, heath, ancient semi-natural and secondary woodland, farmland and downland. Ashridge Commons and Woods, and Ivinghoe Hills, have been designated SSSIs.

This property is rich in archaeological remains. Bronze Age barrows exist around Ivinghoe Beacon and an impressive Bronze Age hill fort at the top of the Beacon. The landscape is characterised by a surprising number of enclosures and settlement sites, with lynchets, sunken droveways and occasional dykes.

The highlights of the estate are woodlands on the chalk scarp and combe; wooded commons with giant old pollards, most notably at Frithsden Beeches; lawns and rides of the medieval Ashridge Park; and downland and scrub at Ivinghoe Beacon.

In the woods bluebell, sanicle and sweet woodruff grow among the beech trees, with hornbeam and whitebeam also present. Woodland birds include redstart, nightingale, wood warbler, lesser spotted woodpeckers, tawny owl, firecrest, sparrowhawk, tree pipit and hawfinch. Fallow and muntjac deer can be seen.

Ashridge Commons hold pockets of relict heathland, an unusual habitat in the north Chilterns, and huge old beech pollards, which support a number of rare beetles and other specialist dead-wood invertebrates. The spectacular downland slopes at the northern end of the property are important for calcareous grassland flowers and insects, especially those associated with rough downland. The slopes suffered severely from the loss of grazing rabbits, affected by myxomatosis; they became badly infected with hawthorn scrub and choked with coarse upright brome grass. The Trust is gradually reducing the scrub volume and implementing a suitable grazing regime. The slopes hold one of the strongest colonies of the Duke of Burgundy fritillary butterfly in the country, many other scarce downland insects, and a range of downland flowers.

ACCESS: Network of footpaths; station at Berkhamsted.

PARKING: Several car parks, including Steps Hill for Ivinghoe Hills, and at Bridgewater Monument; special parking for disabled by information centre.

FACILITIES: Monument, shop, refreshment kiosk and information centre open seasonally; WCs (including disabled); leaflet; disabled facilities in Monument area, on Monument Drive and to information centre; batricars.

NOTE: Dogs must be kept on leads.

BRADENHAM

1111 acres (449½ ha) 4m NW of High Wycombe, 4½m S of Princes Risborough, E of A4010, Buckinghamshire [165:SU825970]

This is a large estate surrounding the manor and village of Bradenham in Buckinghamshire (the Trust owns many of the village houses), with farmland and woodland including Bradenham Woods, an extensive area of ancient beech wood which is considered among the best in the Chilterns, containing valuable evidence of medieval landscape and woodland management. There are also some old field enclosures. Park Wood is another area of characteristic beech woodland on an ancient site, and Grimm's Ditch, running through the north-east corner of the wood, is also of historical interest.

Although beech has been the predominant species on this property for many years, the woodlands are now being managed to encourage other trees typical to the Chilterns, with oak, whitebeam, wild cherry and ash.

The woodland floor is covered in flowers such as dog's mercury, primrose, sweet woodruff, wood anemone and bluebell. The ash-black slug, a scarce species of ancient forests, occurs.

There are some small but extremely valuable pockets of chalk grassland along the south-facing slope below the woodland edge. Some scarce plants grow here, including juniper and fragrant, bee and fly orchids. There is also a rich butterfly fauna, notably small blue and Duke of Burgundy. The Trust has recently taken several thin soil fields along the valley side out of cultivation and is allowing them to develop a natural sward. Early results are highly encouraging.

ACCESS: Network of footpaths; open access to main areas of woodland; paths through Coppice and Park Woods; stations at High Wycombe and Princes Risborough.

PARKING: Small car park next to youth hostel (not NT).

FACILITIES: Local facilities.

BUSCOT AND COLESHILL

7500 acres (3035 ha) on A417 Faringdon to Lechlade road, and B4019
Faringdon to Highworth road, Oxfordshire [163:SU239973 and 2594]

These two large properties are situated in the fertile Thames Valley on the eastern edge of the Cotswolds. They include the attractive villages of Buscot and Coleshill, with the surrounding woodland and farmland. The Cotswold stone cottages in Coleshill village, with the Home Farm buildings, are an integral part of a well-planned nineteenth-century model farm. Also of interest is the Great Coxwell tithe barn, and Buscot's deserted village to the west of Weir Field.

Old pollarded trees line the River Thames at Buscot, and there is a large lake with a heronry in the landscaped park. The River Cole runs through the Coleshill Estate. Along both the Cole and the Thames there are fragments of old hay meadows, once very extensive in the Thames Valley, where there are some small reed beds and marshes. Curlews and lapwings feed on the meadows, and the occasional kingfisher can be seen along the rivers.

On Badbury Hill, the highest point in the area, is an unexcavated Iron Age hill fort.

Evidence of traditional woodland management can be detected in a number of woods, although many of the old coppice stools of oak and ash were replaced by conifers at the turn of the century. There are good hedgerows throughout the estate which support a wide range of wildlife.

ACCESS: Footpaths; circular walks.

PARKING: Car parks at Badbury Hill and Buscot village.

FACILITIES: Local facilities; picnic site at Buscot Weir (popular); equestrian centre at Wickstead Farm.

COOMBE HILL AND LOW SCRUBS

213 acres (86 ha) 1½m W of Wendover, 3½m SE of Princes Risborough, S of B4010, Buckinghamshire   [165:SP849066]

This stretch of chalk downland, designated an SSSI, is the highest point in the Chilterns with views across the Vale of Aylesbury, the Berkshire Downs and the Cotswolds. On the summit stands a monument (not owned by the Trust) dedicated to the men who fell in the Boer War.

The Trust has recently introduced its own flock of sheep to control scrub invasion and to encourage the rich grass sward of the downland. The grassland on the steeper slopes contains many flowers typically found on chalk, with thyme, harebell, bird's foot trefoil, horseshoe vetch, rock rose, dropwort and wild strawberry, which are used by a variety of downland butterflies and insects. Shrubs include juniper (which supports the juniper shield bug), wild privet and whitebeam.

On the plateau is some important relic heathland, and in the wooded areas oak and beech predominate. (Many of these woods have been planted over the last few centuries, but evidence of coppicing and ancient pollards suggests a longer history of wood pasture commons in the area.)

To the east lies Low Scrubs, an area of wooded common once used for gathering firewood. Woodland plants include helleborine, yellow archangel, broad buckler fern and enchanter's nightshade.

ACCESS: Network of footpaths; Ridgeway and South Bucks Way long-distance footpaths; station at Princes Risborough.

PARKING: Car park at Coombe Hill, off Dunsmore road.

FACILITIES: Local facilities at Princes Risborough; limited disabled access to plateau area.

DUNSTABLE AND WHIPSNADE DOWNS

285 acres (115 ha) 2m S of Dunstable, 4m N of Ashridge, both sides of B4541, Bedfordshire   [165 and 166:TL000190]

Commanding good views of the surrounding countryside, Whipsnade and Dunstable downs are scarp-slope ancient grasslands, the result of centuries of grazing sheep. The downs form the second largest area of chalk grassland in the county, and, despite agricultural improvement of some of the original downland and the encroachment of hawthorn scrub, the steep slopes are rich in flowers and grasses with associated flora and fauna.

The areas of ancient grassland are fenced off for grazing to maintain their conservation interest, and common rights still exist on thirty-five acres of Whipsnade Green. Sheep's fescue, quaking grass, crested dog's tail, dwarf thistle, orchids, rock rose, horseshoe vetch, thyme, harebell and bird's foot trefoil are some of the many flowers and grasses to be seen, with some local downland butterflies including chalkhill blue.

ACCESS: Network of footpaths.

PARKING: Car park.

FACILITIES: Facilities at Whipsnade Zoo and in village.

FINCHAMPSTEAD RIDGES AND SIMON'S WOOD

60 acres (24 ha) ¾m W of Crowthorne station, 4m S of Wokingham S of
B3348, Berkshire   [175 and 186SU:808634]

Located on the south-facing slope of the Blackwater Valley, Finch-
ampstead Ridges (crossed on the north side by the London to Sil-
chester Roman road and the Roman ride known as the 'devil's
highway') include a fragment of the formerly extensive heaths of
Berkshire and Hampshire, which is now being positively managed
and extended. This area is a popular venue for walkers, and the
views are impressive from the ridge across the Thames basin to the
neighbouring counties of Hampshire and Surrey.

Simon's Wood has a mix of conifers and broadleaved trees, with
pine, birch and sweet chestnut. Siskin and spotted flycatcher are
regular migrants. Birch and pedunculate oak grow in places where
the heath has reverted to woodland.

The dry heath supports a wide range of invertebrates and lichens.
Sphagnum moss, cross-leaved heath, common cotton grass, purple
moor grass, marsh pennywort and heather occur in the wetter areas.
Two ponds, including Heath Pool, provide a habitat for good populations of dragonfly, including the four-spotted chaser, and emerald
and common azure damselflies.

ACCESS: Open access; walk to Heath Pool; footpaths; marked
bridleways; station at Crowthorne.

PARKING: Large car park at Simon's Wood; roadside parking.

FACILITIES: Ridge plateau accessible by wheelchair.

THE HUGHENDEN ESTATE

347 acres (140 ha) 1½m N of High Wycombe, W of A4128,
Buckinghamshire   [165:SU866955 and 855957]

Once owned by Benjamin Disraeli, Hughenden Manor is set in
the rolling, east-facing slopes of the River Wye and contains many

mementoes of the great statesman. Some of the trees in the park are relics of his planting schemes. The surrounding farmland and woodland, including Timbers, Woodcock, Flagmore and Hanging woods, are an AONB which contains much of wildlife interest.

A number of the estate woods, such as Great and Little Tinker woods, are known to be on ancient woodland sites, and have a rich ground flora of primrose, bluebell, wild garlic and dog's mercury. Birds include tawny owl, green, greater and lesser spotted woodpeckers, tree creeper and nuthatch. A bourne stream runs along the valley bottom.

The park, which originally extended to the outskirts of High Wycombe, is dotted with large mature trees.

ACCESS: Open access to park; garden and house open seasonally; network of public and permitted footpaths; station at High Wycombe and bus service from Aylesbury to High Wycombe.

PARKING: Car park at house; special parking for disabled.

FACILITIES: NT shop; WCs (including disabled) at house; dogs allowed on leads in park and car park only.

LARDON CHASE, THE HOLIES AND LOUGH DOWN

67 acres (27 ha) just N of Streatley, W of A417, Berkshire
[174:SU588809 and 588813]

This spur of downland lies to the west of Goring Gap, with good views overlooking the Thames Valley where the river divides the Chilterns from the North Wessex Downs. The slopes form one of the largest remaining areas of chalk grassland in the county and support a wide range of flowers and butterflies.

The area has a long history of ancient settlements and there are several Neolithic and Iron Age forts. It is crossed by the Ridgeway and other ancient routes used by the Romans.

The grassland is being managed by controlled grazing and by scrub clearance, to encourage the growth of chalk-loving plants such as autumn gentian, clustered bellflower, blue fleabane, vervain, common rock-rose, horseshoe vetch and a good population of orchids. There are some good chalk downland butterfly species, including chalkhill blue and grizzled and dingy skippers.

Mining bees and wasps, and wolf spiders, can be seen, and a variety of birds nest and feed on the shrubs, with green woodpecker visiting the grassland anthills.

The Holies is a grassy combe, which before acquisition by the Trust was used for motorbike scrambling and turf stripping. Now the natural recolonisation of the bare land by chalk-loving plant species is being carefully monitored.

ACCESS: Open access; footpath from youth hostel at Streatley.

PARKING: Small car park at West Lardon Chase.

FACILITIES: Local facilities in village.

MAIDENHEAD COMMONS AND COCK MARSH

843 acres (341 ha) N and W of Maidenhead, Berkshire
[175:SU850800 to 890870]

Bought by local residents and given to the Trust in 1934, these properties include commonland and greens to the south of the River Thames. The sites include a variety of habitats, with woodland, scrub thickets, grassland, downland ponds, riverside and meadows, and are ideal for walking.

Cock Marsh is one of the best lowland wetland sites owned by the Trust, and is of great importance for its flora and for breeding waders, although it is a habitat much at risk from drainage and the abstraction of water on the adjacent land. Some Bronze Age bowl barrows can be seen here.

Maidenhead Thicket, mentioned in historic documents dating back to the seventeenth century and the site of a prehistoric Celtic farm enclosure, contains an impressive display of wild flowers in the spring.

The pond system and calcareous marsh are exceptionally rich, supporting a long list of rare and local plants, including greater bladderwort, flowering rush, water violet, needle spike-rush and two very rare water peppers. There is also an impressive aquatic

185

invertebrate fauna, including scarce dragonflies such as the variable damselfly and numerous specialist flies such as soldier flies. All three species of newt occur, along with an assortment of wetland birds.

ACCESS: Network of footpaths and bridleways.

PARKING: Several small car parks at Cookham Moor, Winter's Hill and Maidenhead Thicket.

FACILITIES: Local facilities.

MORDEN HALL PARK

124 acres (50 ha) E of A24 Morden road and A297 Morden Hall road, London [176:TQ259687]

The former parkland surrounding Morden Hall, on the banks of the River Wandle, forms an oasis of countryside in the London conurbation. Once the site of a historic deer park, the undisturbed river banks, mature trees, grassland, woodland and fen now create a haven for wildlife.

The unimproved grassland in the park supports a great variety of wildlife, including plants such as yarrow, sorrel, common knapweed and ox-eye daisy, and sedges and water plantain flourish in the meadows and fens. Holly blue, meadow brown, small skipper and green-veined white butterflies can be seen. Dragonflies, grey wagtail and kingfisher are also found on the river, and nuthatch, greater spotted woodpecker and spotted flycatcher inhabit the shrub.

The river divides into a number of natural and man-made watercourses after passing the old Snuff Mill, which ceased working in 1928. The Mill is now an environmental education centre for London school children.

ACCESS: Open access during daylight hours; footpaths and riverside walkways; Morden underground station 500yds away and regular local bus service.

PARKING: Car park in walled garden.

FACILITIES: NT shop; café; new visitor facilities; information display; garden centre (not NT); disabled access to riverside walkways through garden centre.

PULPIT WOOD

65 acres (26 ha) ¼m NE of Princes Risborough, 2½m SW of Wendover, off A4010, Buckinghamshire [165:SW832048]

This is an important area of what could be referred to as 'ancient secondary woodland'. It was once open farmland, but reverted to woodland long ago, and in recent centuries has been managed as beech woodland. Glades of earlier grassland survive on the slopes, with old juniper bushes (important here and elsewhere in the Chilterns). Rich chalk grassland with mixed scrub occurs at the western end of the property. Part of the wood is managed as a nature reserve by the Berkshire, Buckinghamshire and Oxfordshire Naturalists' Trust. The earthworks of an Iron Age hill fort can still be seen.

Ash and oak commonly occur among the beech trees, with wild privet, blackthorn, yew, guelder rose and the wayfaring tree forming a scrubby edge which is an important habitat for many birds. The woodland ground flora is dominated by dog's mercury, but other plants include sanicle, enchanter's nightshade, wood sorrel and sweet woodruff.

ACCESS: Network of footpaths; Ridgeway long-distance footpath runs alongside the wood; station at Princes Risborough.

PARKING: Small car park.

FACILITIES: Local facilities.

SHARPENHOE: THE CLAPPERS AND ROBERT'S FARM

136 acres (55 ha) 6m N of Luton, between A6 (Barton-in-the-Clay) and M1 (Harlington), Bedfordshire [166:TL067300]

The steep slopes of Sharpenhoe Clappers have for many years been undisturbed open downland, providing sheep walks or grazing pastures for the local farming community, although recent changes in agricultural practices have led to the gradual encroachment of scrub.

Many wild flowers and herbs still flourish on the unploughed grassland, with thyme, horseshoe vetch, clustered bellfower, salad burnet and several species of orchids. Brown argus, chalkhill blue and green hairstreak butterflies occur.

One of the few beech woods in the county, the fairly dense trees of Clappers Wood, crowning the ridge of Sharpenhoe, support some scarce species of beetles, and the ground flora includes dog's mercury, wild garlic, anemones and wood sedge. Green woodpecker, which breed in the wood, can be seen feeding on the grassland anthills.

Of historical interest is the site of an Iron Age hill fort.

ACCESS: Open access; network of footpaths.

PARKING: Small car park.

FACILITIES: Local facilities; information board.

WATLINGTON HILL

112 acres (45 ha) 1m SE of Watlington, E of B480, Oxfordshire
[175:SU702935]

Rising to 700 feet above the beech woodlands of Watlington Park in the Chilterns, Watlington Hill consists of skeletal soil chalk downland, scrub and beech copses and has impressive views over the surrounding countryside.

Together with neighbouring Pyrton Hill, it is designated an SSSI and is an excellent site for invertebrates, with over thirty species of butterflies and numerous other chalk grassland insects, especially those associated with heavily rabbit-grazed short turf. Typical flowers include horseshoe and kidney vetches, rock-rose, squinancywort, orchids and autumn and Chiltern gentians.

The beechwoods in Watlington Park are thought to be of ancient origin, although the trees have been felled and replanted several times. Woodland plants include common cow wheat and spurge laurel.

The marginal scrub of wayfaring tree, dogwood, whitebeam, privet and juniper provides a good habitat for scrub-nesting birds. The southern slopes are covered in yew woodland, a rare feature in the Chilterns.

ACCESS: Open access; footpaths; Upper Icknield Way long-distance footpath (on prehistoric trade route).

PARKING: Small car park for both hill and woods off Watlington to North End road.

FACILITIES: Local facilities.

WEST WYCOMBE HILL

55 acres (22 ha) 2m W of High Wycombe, W of West Wycombe, S of A40, Buckinghamshire [175:SU828947]

Commanding grand views of West Wycombe Park, the River Wye and the surrounding countryside, the hill is crowned with a great golden ball on top of the church tower of St Lawrence, built for Sir Francis Dashwood, and infamous for its association with the eighteenth-century Hell Fire Club which was said to meet in the church and in a cave dug out of the hill.

Next to the church are a huge hexagonal mausoleum (not owned by the Trust) and the remains of an Iron Age hill fort. Nearby is the delightful village of West Wycombe which contains buildings of interest from medieval to Victorian times, many of which are owned by the Trust.

Chalk grassland, ancient woodland, scrub, old hazel coppice and mature trees planted as part of the grander landscape design of West Wycombe Park, add to the significance of this historic landscape.

The grassland supports many wild flowers and herbs, with lady's bedstraw, bird's foot trefoil, common rock-rose, wild basil, stemless thistle and hairy violet. Yew, blackthorn, juniper, whitebeam and wayfaring tree scrub merges into oak, ash and beech woods which contain evidence of traditional management in areas of old coppicing.

ACCESS: Open access; footpaths; West Wycombe Park open seasonally; station at High Wycombe.

PARKING: Car park.

FACILITIES: Local facilities.

Central England

CHESHIRE · DERBYSHIRE · SHROPSHIRE · STAFFORDSHIRE
THE MIDLANDS · MERSEYSIDE

Dominated by sprawling conurbations and a network of roads and motorways, development in this region has disrupted the former pattern of life where small market towns supported local communities of farm, quarry and industrial workers. However, the industrial remains of areas such as the Black Country, with their web of canals and disused railways, form valuable wildlife habitats.

The Midlands has some beautiful tracts of countryside: to the east, the industrial lands give way to the extensively farmed landscapes of East Anglia, while to the west, the dominant feature of Shropshire is its windswept hill country. Here notable landmarks include the famous wooded limestone ridge of Wenlock Edge and the heathery heights of the Long Mynd.

Over sixty square miles of the Peak District is owned by the National Trust. Lying at the southern tip of the Pennines, its rich and diverse landscape ranges from the high, wild moors of the Dark Peak to the limestone plateau and dramatic wooded gorges of Dovedale and the Manifold Valley.

Derbyshire is also rich in historic estates and parklands such as Hardwick and Calke, and Kedleston with its surrounding landscape designed by Robert Adam. To the south and west, the moorlands and limestone landscape extend into Staffordshire.

Cheshire still has a number of tranquil parklands with pockets of ancient woodland. Sandstone forms a number of ridges, with spectacular views across the Cheshire plain. Woodlands, once extensively covering the ridges, are now restricted to the valleys and slopes.

The estuaries of the Dee and Mersey, despite heavy industrialisation, still provide vital coastal habitats for birds, particularly overwintering waders and wildfowl. North of Merseyside, at Formby, miles of sand dunes sustain important dune plants, and in hollows where salt marshes are establishing, the rare natterjack toad finds a refuge.

ALDERLEY EDGE

227 acres (92 ha) both sides of B5087 Alderley to Macclesfield road, Cheshire [118:SJ860776]

The majority of this estate was acquired in 1948, and the area is designated an SSSI for both biological and geological interest. To the east, the sandstone escarpment or 'edge' forms a steep and wooded slope, the result of faulting within the underlying rocks several million years ago. Its close proximity to areas of extensive urban population, its predominately open space, woodlands, and the unsurpassed panorama over the Cheshire plain make it an attractive property to visit.

Enclosed grazing pastures and copse woodland lie to the west on the more gentle slope. The area was formerly a mixture of heathland and ancient woodland, and many trees in the mixed woodland have been planted over several centuries, with the ancient woodlands of Waterfall and Clockhouse woods dominated by oaks which harbour important populations of invertebrates. The woods to the north are mainly beech, with some birch, ash and Scots pine.

On the remnants of the former heathland can be found heather, purple moor grass, bilberry, holly and birch, with a diverse associated moth, butterfly and insect fauna. Birds seen in the area include red poll, woodcock, green, greater and lesser woodpeckers, and tawny and little owls.

The underlying rocks are rich in minerals, and the remains of old quarries, mine shafts and mineral workings (which can be a hazard for walkers) in the woodland are evidence that cobalt, lead and copper were once mined in the area. A mythological wizard, reputedly Merlin, supposedly guards the entrance to one of the caves, hence the nearby Wizard Inn. Some Bronze Age pottery and tools have been discovered, and the Armada Beacon has been used as a signalling point since 1578.

The nature conservation value of the estate lies primarily in the farmland, much of which is managed under an agricultural tenancy agreement.

ACCESS: Part open access; network of footpaths, including link to Hare Hill Estate (approximately 2m, and return by same route); access to agricultural land only along designated routes.

PARKING: Main car park off B5087, next to Wizard Inn.

FACILITIES: WCs (including disabled) in main car park; small information point in stables next to Wizard Inn; horse riding permitted over certain routes in good weather, most footpaths suitable for wheelchairs.

ATTINGHAM

3718 acres (1505 ha) 4m SE of Shrewsbury, N of A5, Shropshire
[126:SJ550099]

Originally part of a manorial estate, the parkland was designed in the late eighteenth century to complement the newly built and grand Hall. The famous landscape designer Humphry Repton modified an earlier layout by planting Scots pine, oak, elm and beech trees, which now stand as mature specimens throughout the estate and include some old beech pollards. (These trees are important for their associated colonies of insects and fungi.) A series of Repton's watercolours and his 'Red Book' have been used by the Trust as a guide in its efforts to restore the parkland.

The estate includes part of the Roman town of Viroconium, and covers the site of an Anglo-Saxon village. Small woods, hedgerows, ponds, an old canal and a disused railway line can be seen around the main parkland, but are not open to the public.

The former medieval deer park is now grazed by a herd of fallow deer. Despite agricultural improvements, a number of traditional farming features remain, and behind the grand landscape lie some valuable wildlife habitats. The Severn and Tern rivers have an interesting array of upland and lowland catchment qualities.

ACCESS: House open seasonally; grounds open daily during daylight hours; permitted paths; restricted footpath and bridlepath; stations at Shrewsbury and Telford Central.

PARKING: Car park.

FACILITIES: NT shop; tea-room; WCs (including disabled); electric scooter for use in grounds; leaflet; guide to suggested walks; information centre; Mile Walk; guided walks; Braille guide.

CALKE PARK

2172 acres (879 ha) 9m S of Derby, on A514 at Ticknall, Derbyshire
[128:SK3622]

Calke Park is a baroque mansion built on the site of a twelfth-century priory. The monks lived in a well-wooded landscape, since north of the house there were two woods and the wooded expanses of the Derby Hills. Remarkably, areas of this ancient wooded landscape survive today in what later became the Deer Park. The large numbers of very old oak, beech, ash and small-leaved lime trees, some of which date back to the fifteenth century, are one of the main glories of Calke Park, and provide a direct link with the primeval wildwood forest.

Consequently, Calke is one of the top ten sites in Britain, and Europe, for the specialist insect fauna associated with very old trees and woods which have never been cleared. There is also a chain of old ponds with curious names such as China House Pond (named after a summer house that once stood on the island in the pond) or Dogkennel Pond (named after the kennels which originally stood alongside it), and a large expanse of more recent eighteenth-century parkland, separated from the gardens by a sunken wall.

The outbuildings at the Abbey include stables, a brewhouse, bake-house, smithy, dovecote and threshing barns. The church of St Giles is also notable.

ACCESS: Permitted routes to estate; one-way system around park; park open daily during daylight hours; house open seasonally; timed tickets to house (very popular, may be a long wait); stations at Derby and Burton-on-Trent.

PARKING: Car park.

FACILITIES: NT shop and restaurant; WCs; information room; car-riage display in stable block; leaflets and educational material; play area; dogs on leads in park only.

DERWENT AND HOWDEN MOORS

6468 acres (2618 ha) 13m W of Sheffield, via A57 Sheffield to Manchester road, Derbyshire   [110:SK1994]

Rising eastwards and northwards from the famous Derwent and Ladybower reservoirs, these moors contain some of the finest and most extensive stretches of heather moorland in the country. With Kinder Scout and the Snake Pass they form a very large and nation-ally important SSSI, mainly for the expanses of blanket peat and upland heath. These have some nine species of dwarf shrub (heather and its allies), including the unusual bearberry, rare outside northern Scotland. Wet heath and bog have cranberry, crowberry, cow-berry, bilberry, cloudberry and cross-leaved heath, with cotton grasses and *Sphagnum* moss. The upland breeding birds are of great importance here, with red grouse, golden plover, dunlin, curlew, ring ouzel, peregrine, wheatear and even the unusual twite. The dramatic emperor, fox and oak eggar moths feed on the heather.

Cloughs or steep valleys cut into the sides of the high plateaux, have important relicts of woodland, with oak, birch, aspen and ferns such as beech fern. Small springs, flushes and mires are also of in-terest, and the unusual ivy-leaved bellflower can be found here.

The blanket bogs have been badly affected by air pollution in parts of the High Peak (as outlined in the entries for Kinder Scout and Snake Pass) but the Derwent Moors are generally in good condition. Nevertheless, the Trust is monitoring the vegetation, and has undertaken a programme of regenerating the relict woodlands, mainly by natural means, supplemented by some planting. These areas provide important habitats for many insects and birds; grey wagtail, dipper, dunlin, golden plover, snipe, curlew and ring ouzel can all be seen locally, with occasional sightings of short-eared owl, merlin, peregrine and hen harrier.

The area has some interesting archaeological remains, ranging from the mesolithic period through to the Bronze Age. Flint and chert artefacts found on the site suggest that prehistoric communities once used the area for hunting, and the barrow of Pike Low is a typical Bronze Age monument. Derwent has also been an important boundary marker throughout history – at one time part of the property formed the eastern boundary of the Royal Forest of the Peak.

ACCESS: Open access; network of footpaths and bridleways.

PARKING: Car parks around reservoirs (limited road access to upper part of valley at weekends).

FACILITIES: National Park/Severn Trent information centre and facilities south of Derwent Reservoir at Fairholmes; leaflets (including walks).

DOVEDALE

1354 acres (548 ha) 4–7m NW of Ashbourne, W of A515, Derbyshire
[119:SK1453]

Over thousands of years the River Dove has carved its way through this massive limestone plateau within the Trust's South Peak Estate, to create a deep, sinuous and spectacular gorge, long famous for its rock pinnacles, spires, arches and caves.

Dovedale is of great geological and physiographic interest for this striking karst scenery. It is also of great ecological interest for its limestone grasslands, crags and woodlands. There are some of the best calcareous ash woods in the country here, although only small parts of the extensive woody cover are ancient, now linked by much recent secondary growth. The Trust has cleared some of the secondary woodland, which has grown up since the early 1900s as a result of the decline in grazing, to reveal the dramatic rock features. The ancient 'cores' have many unusual plants, such as angular Solomon's seal, lily-of-the-valley, herb Paris and small and large-leaved limes.

The limestone grasslands support many Derbyshire specialities, and both northern and southern limestone species mixed together, for example Nottingham catchfly, limestone bedstraw, stemless thistle, dropwort and greater burnet saxifrage. The crags, with their thinner soils and lack of grazing, harbour many more unusual plants such as Hutchinsia. All these habitats have specialist associated invertebrates, including glow worm and northern brown argus. Grey wagtail and dipper can be seen along the river.

There is evidence that the gorge was inhabited from early prehistoric periods. Surviving from later periods are some Bronze Age barrows, old lime kilns and post-medieval farm buildings. The names of the crags, such as Jacob's Ladder, Reynard's Cave and Lion Head Rock, originated with Victorian tourists, as did the famous 'stepping stones'.

ACCESS: Footpath (accessible in parts by wheelchair).

PARKING: Car parks at Milldale and stepping stones end.

FACILITIES: Facilities and NT information barn at Milldale; WCs at both ends; leaflet available from Ilam Country Park.

DUNHAM MASSEY

3172 acres (1284 ha) 3m SW of Altrincham, off M56, Cheshire
[109:SJ735874]

Dunham Massey Hall stands amid 250 acres of parkland, which provides an ideal rural setting for the eighteenth-century mansion. It is also of increasing importance as a haven for wildlife, and a buffer against the threats of development and intensive agriculture which press up to its walls.

The estate consists of the Hall, garden, park and farmland, and was bequeathed to the Trust in 1976, but has been a popular recreational resort for the growing population of Manchester since the early nineteenth century. It is the medieval deer park (an sssi) that is of prime importance to social historians and conservationists, since it embodies elements of the original forest or 'wildwood'. The current pattern of trees and woods dates from the landscape plantings designed in the eighteenth century (it is one of the last remaining unaltered formal English parklands), but these trees are now sufficiently old to have adopted the fauna which has lived in old trees on the site since the last Ice Age. A herd of fallow deer is protected in secluded areas of the park.

The park also provides sites for hole-nesting birds, including all three species of woodpeckers. An area of unimproved pasture and wetland is important for its range of plants, and there are a number of ancient ponds and water-filled marl pits which add to the range of habitats. An area of coarse grassland is an important source of nectar for the deadwood fauna.

ACCESS: Open access, except to areas designated as deer sanctuary; park open all year; Hall and gardens open seasonally; local stations at Altrincham and Hale.

PARKING: Large car park at entrance to property.

FACILITIES: NT shop and restaurant in South Stables; WCs (including disabled) in North Stables; electric wheelchair and scooter for use in grounds; information and park leaflet; guided walks.

EDALE

2500 acres (1012 ha) N of Hope Valley, off A625, Derbyshire
[110:SK1285]

The Trust owns a number of typical upland farms in the popular Derbyshire gritstone landscape of the High Peak Estate, lying south of the Kinder Scout massif and encircling the impressive conical form of Mam Tor and the head of the Vale of Edale. The open fells and moorland merge with enclosed farmlands. A patchwork of gritstone walls surrounding improved pastures and the vernacular farm buildings dotted throughout the valley are an integral part of the character of the landscape.

Despite the majority of the meadows having been improved for agriculture, and thereby losing the variety of their flora, a number of herb-rich fields have survived, with plants such as adder's tongue fern, devil's bit scabious, betony, yellow rattle and great burnet. Wooded cloughs, small woods and wooded river banks form an important part of the property and add to the wildlife interest. The Trust is actively conserving the remaining meadows, increasing the number of small woodlands and underplanting existing woods.

Beyond the field boundaries, rank grasslands overlying peat have been heavily grazed and have lost some of their wildlife interest, requiring years of careful management to reverse the effects. Small streams, wet flushes and pockets of a former more extensive cover of heath, sedges, rushes, mosses, crowberry and cotton grass remain, and are being managed to enhance their wildlife value.

Prehistoric burial practices on the ridge top are indicated by surviving barrows such as the Lord's Seat, a Bronze Age burial mound.

ACCESS: Network of footpaths.

PARKING: Car park.

FACILITIES: National Park information centre at Fieldhead in Edale; leaflets; mountain rescue point; camping.

FORMBY

494 acres (200 ha) W of Formby, of A565(T), Merseyside [108:SD275080]

Part of the fourth largest dune system in Britain, this Merseyside nature reserve is made up of roughly equal proportions of dunes and sandflats. Home to the nationally rare natterjack toad, and designated an SSSI and Ramsar site, it is located between the Ribble and Mersey estuaries.

The reserve is constantly changing as natural forces mould the mobile dunes and foreshore, and pine woodlands were planted at the turn of the century in an attempt to stabilise the sand. Great efforts are now being made by the Trust to control the considerable erosion of the whole dune system by fencing and the planting of marram grass. Formerly, asparagus–farming dominated the fixed dunes as an important agricultural crop, but this is now in decline.

The dunes are sparsely covered with marram and sea-lyme grasses, and the national rarities of dune and green-flowered helleborines can be found. The more stable dunes inland support creeping willow, bee orchid, dewberry, sand sedge, sycamore and birch, as well as alder in the damper areas.

Many waders, gulls and visiting migrant birds feed on the shoreline, and in the woods kestrel, tree creeper, wood warbler and greater spotted woodpecker can be seen. A small red squirrel population is maintained.

The footprints of animals, mainly elk, which grazed the saltmarshes in the neolithic period, are sometimes exposed by tides on the beach. Formby is the site of the first lifeboat station in the country (operational between 1776 and 1918).

ACCESS: Open access all year; footpaths through woods and to beach; walk around squirrel reserve; coastal footpath from Crosby to Southport; local stations at Formby and Freshfield.

PARKING: Car park (free to members).

FACILITIES: Information panel; leaflets; picnic sites; wheelchair walk on boardwalk across dunes; wheelchair access to red squirrel reserve.

NOTE: No barbecues, fires or camping (to avoid fire risk).

HAMPS AND MANIFOLD VALLEYS

1091 acres (442 ha) E of Grindon, Derbyshire   [119:SK1056]

The valleys of the Hamps and Manifold rivers form part of the Trust's South Peak Estate and, like Dovedale, are distinctive for their limestone scenery, caves, rock cliffs, grasslands and woods.

The Manifold takes its name from the many deeply incised meanders which reflect the tortuous contours of the valley. The river meets its main tributary, the Hamps, at the great rock cliff of Beeston Tor, before flowing on down to Ilam. During the summer months both rivers follow subterranean courses to emerge four to five miles downstream at the 'boil holes' in Ilam Country Park (see page 201). In the base of the valley runs the remains of the Leek & Manifold Light Railway track, which is now a metalled footpath popular with cyclists.

Both valleys contain a rich mosaic of grazed limestone grassland, small areas of meadow, scrub and woodland. The grassland supports many plant species such as rock-rose, thyme, melancholy thistle, cowslip, lady's mantle and occasionally grass of Parnassus. The naturally regenerating ash woodlands which cover the slopes of the valleys are rich with shrubs such as mountain currant and guelder rose, and parts have plants such as small-leaved lime indicative of the ancient origin of the woods. Wood vetch grows along the old railway track. Birds include wheatear, redstart and pied flycatcher. The valley sides contain some of the finest calcareous grasslands in Britain, which support many butterfly food plants, attracting species such as dark-green fritillary and the rare small blue.

Grindon Moor consists of twenty-three acres of heather moorland, containing cross-leaved heath, bell heather, cotton grass and bilberry. There is a good variety of upland birds, including curlew, lapwing, snipe and meadow pipit. A north-facing rock outcrop on the northern side of Ecton Hill has excellent examples of anticlines and sinklines, of interest to geologists. The property also contains the site of an old horse whim next to the winding shaft of the Deep Ecton copper mine (now sealed).

Many acres of woodland have been taken out of agricultural tenancy and fenced out to be managed for their high conservation value. In addition to property owned by the Trust, a further 1250 acres of the Throwley and Castern estates are protected by covenants.

ACCESS: Free access to Wetton Hills; network of footpaths; Manifold Track.

PARKING: Car parks at Wetton Mill and Weags Bridge.

FACILITIES: Shop; café; small campsite and WCs at Wetton Mill; Manifold Track suitable for wheelchairs.

HARDWICK PARK

1990 acres (805 ha) 6½m NW of Mansfield, 9½m SE of Chesterfield on A617, Derbyshire [120:SK463638]

Hardwick Hall is a spectacular Elizabethan mansion built in the 1590s for Bess of Hardwick, a squire's daughter who became one of the richest landowners and most prodigious builders in England. The house is situated on a prominent limestone escarpment and surrounded by parkland which encloses remnants of a former medieval deer park, originally used by the manor for hunting. The ruins of Old Hardwick Hall, rebuilt by Bess shortly before embarking on her new hall, are under the guardianship of English Heritage.

Much of the surrounding estate is now a country park, with many paths and features of interest. There are two large ponds, Millers Pond and Great Pond, and five smaller ponds, built as fish ponds 400 years ago. Another chain of four ponds, the Carr Ponds, can be seen a little further afield in the eastern part of the estate. There is an old duck decoy, an ice-house, an old sandstone quarry and several acres of old, herb-rich grassland with unusual plants such as adder's tongue fern. The ponds are of particular interest for wildlife, with birds such as great crested grebe, and many aquatic and marginal plants including branched bur reed, water plantain, marsh bedstraw, mare's tail, great reed-mace and many less common species. On Great Pond is an interesting area of alder and willow carr and fen.

A herd of longhorn cattle and a flock of white-faced woodland sheep, both rare breeds, graze the parkland.

ACCESS: Country park open daily during daylight hours; house and gardens open seasonally.

PARKING: Car park.

FACILITIES; NT shop and restaurant; WCs (including disabled); leaflets; information centre with exhibition; fishing permits from information centre; station at Chesterfield and local bus service from Chesterfield.

ILAM

84 acres (34 ha) 4½m NW of Ashbourne, Derbyshire   [119:SK132507]

Ilam Country Park is situated in one of the most popular positions in the South Peak District, with magnificent views towards Thorpe Cloud and the entrance to Dovedale. From the terrace in front of the Hall, the garden and lawns slope down to the River Manifold and the village church. Within the park are 'boil holes', where the rivers

Manifold and Hamps resurface after travelling underground, one of the largest resurgences in the country. A path leads from the boil holes along Paradise Walk, which is maintained as a landscaped promenade feature of the park.

From here one can view the ancient Hinkley Wood, of great interest to ecologists for its populations of two rare trees, small- and large-leaved limes, and hybrids between them. Sadly, the wood was devastated by Dutch elm disease in the 1970s, and some ash planting has been undertaken in the large gaps, after very carefully removing the dead elms in order to leave the limes untouched.

The river provides another important wildlife habitat, with birds such as kingfisher, dipper and grey wagtail commonly sighted along its banks.

Of historic interest are the remains of an Anglo-Saxon cross, and well-preserved remains of medieval ridge and furrow surviving in an area of permanent pasture.

ACCESS: Free access; network of footpaths; bus service from Derby.

PARKING: Car park (free to members).

FACILITIES: NT shop, restaurant and tea-rooms; WCs; leaflet; information centre; education room for visiting groups; youth hostel; camping and caravan sites.

KEDLESTON PARK

819 acres (331½ ha) 3m NW of Derby off A52, Derbyshire
[128:SK312403]

Kedleston Park is a magnificent and classic eighteenth-century landscape. Robert Adam's masterpiece of Palladian architecture is set in extensive grazed parkland, with a serpentine lake spanned by an arched Adam bridge; but there are also remnants of earlier landscapes. The church dates from the twelfth century, the last survivor of the old village of Kedleston, which was moved in the early 1760s. The dense groves of old oaks in the north part of the park, beyond the lake, are also medieval, surviving from an old deer park which once extended beyond the Trust's boundary to the north-east. On the slopes behind and west of the house, lines of old trees can be seen, representing hedges which were once part of an enclosed farmland landscape. The lake was created by damming the Cutler Brook with six weirs.

Like Calke, the main wildlife interest of Kedleston is the invertebrate fauna associated with the ancient trees. The best area is in the northern part of the park, coinciding with the medieval park, but old trees elsewhere are also important, especially in the Longwalk woodlands along the southern edge of the property. The lakes have breeding water birds, although the huge flocks of Canada goose damage the quality of the habitat, and trample and enrich the lakeside grasslands. Areas of rough grassland and scrub, not attractive to the Canada geese, are also of value. Greater spotted woodpecker and nuthatch can be seen in the woods.

ACCESS: House and park open seasonally; network of footpaths; stations at Duffield and Derby.

PARKING: Car park.

FACILITIES: NT shop and restaurant; WCS (including disabled); schoolroom and teacher's pack.

KINDER SCOUT AND BLEAKLOW

3291 acres (1332 ha) N of the Vale of Edale, S of A628(T), Derbyshire
[110:SK0988]

The mass trespass of Kinder Scout in 1932 by the Ramblers' Association and the beginning of the Pennine Way long-distance route have put the magnificent massif of Kinder Scout among the most well-known and popular moorlands in the Peak District. Kinder Downfall is an impressive rock escarpment on the western edge of the plateau, in the shape of an amphitheatre.

A thick blanket of peat, two miles thick, once covered the plateau. Over the last 300 years this has eroded into 'hags' and 'groughs', revealing the stony expanses of the gritstone bedrock and protruding gritstone knolls. Sheep grazing has exacerbated the main agent of erosion, air pollution. The slopes below Kinder Downfall were fragile and eroding too, mainly due to grazing, and there was virtually no heather here when the Trust acquired Kinder Scout in

1983. Since then, together with the Peak District National Park and researchers from Manchester and Sheffield universities, the Trust has initiated innovative restoration measures, on both the peat plateau and the slopes below. Grazing levels have been dramatically reduced, and many methods of revegetating the bare peat plateau are being undertaken. The slopes now support good expanses of heather, and some plants are growing again on the eroded peat.

Kinder Scout has some fascinating historical associations. Before the Norman Conquest it was part of a Royal Forest, and in the Middle Ages much of the land was owned by the Church who used it to breed horses, then later sheep. Kinder links with the Vale of Edale via Jacob's Ladder, a historic packhorse route which has recently been resurfaced using traditional techniques. Other historic features include remains of boundaries of medieval hunting forests, Edale Cross and the remains of a shooting refectory and shooting cabin dating from the late nineteenth and early twentieth centuries.

ACCESS: Open access; network of paths and bridleways; Kinder Round Walk.

PARKING: Car parks at Edale and Bowden Bridge (1m east of Hayfield).

FACILITIES: NT information point in Edale; County Council information centre in Hayfield; South Head information shelter; leaflets.

KINVER EDGE

283 acres (114½ ha) 4m W of Stourbridge, 4m N of Kidderminster, 1½m W of A449, Staffordshire   [138:SO835830]

Kinver Edge is a prominent sandstone escarpment rising above the village of Kinver. Once all commonland, much of the area was taken into agriculture following enclosure in the eighteenth century, but has since reverted first to lowland heath and, more recently, to naturally regenerated birch, oak and pine woodland which encroaches on the heathland, although the Trust has now introduced a successful programme of control. Fragments of the historic Mercia Forest remain in the old woodlands.

The mixed woodlands include oak, birch, crab apple, hazel,

spindle, guelder rose and aspen, with birds such as green wood-pecker, wood warbler, tree pipit, sparrowhawk, redstart and wood-cock. On the heath can be found heather, bell heather, wavy hair grass and bilberry, attracting butterflies, moths, grasshoppers, mining bees and moths. The grassland includes a fascinating area of mobile sand with the rare dune grass *Corynephorus canescens*, and adders, slow worms and lizards inhabit the sandy slopes.

One of the earlier properties to be acquired by the Trust, it is noted for the unusual dwellings dug out of the sandstone, which were occupied as late as the 1960s by local workers, mainly from the foundries. A rock house has recently been restored for a site manager. There is also an Iron Age promontory fort.

ACCESS: Open access; footpaths.

PARKING: Car parks and parking along road.

FACILITIES: WCs; information boards; Kingsford Country Park nearby; limited wheelchair access.

THE LONG MYND

5850 acres (2367½ ha) 15m S of Shrewsbury, W of Church Stretton Valley and A49, Shropshire [137:SO430940]

With impressive views across to the Black Mountains and Cheshire, this great ridge, extending for ten miles, is one of several plateaux in the Shropshire Hills designated an AONB and SSSI.

The thin, acid upland soils support a cover of heather and fine, tussocky grassland on wild open moors which, with more sheltered incised valleys, are home to birds of prey, plants and insects of upland bogs, and a host of invertebrates in the streams which provide food for dipper and fish. Raven, buzzard and curlew are a common sight over the uplands, and other moorland birds include wheatear, ring ouzel, stonechat and red grouse. The woodlands in the lower valleys attract the pied flycatcher and tree pipit, and dipper and grey wagtail can be seen along the fast-flowing streams.

Bilberry grows among the heather, and moisture-loving plants such as the common spotted orchid, butterwort, round-leaved sundew, bog pimpernel and *Sphagnum* moss are found on the higher slopes around the springs and damp flushes. The fine, wiry moor-land grasses are speckled with tormentil and heath bedstraw.

A scatter of archaeological remains from the Bronze Age, Iron Age and medieval times is evidence of centuries of man's habitation on the plateau, and sites of interest include a hill fort and earthworks, prehistoric tumuli, Bodbury Ring and the Port Way track, an old drove road.

ACCESS: Open access; roads; footpaths and bridleways cross the ridge; station at Church Stretton and Shrewsbury–Ludlow bus service, alight Church Stretton.

PARKING: Car parks at Carding Mill Valley.

FACILITIES: Shop, restaurant and information centre at Carding Mill; WCs (including disabled); leaflet on walking routes; viewpoints for wheelchair users.

THE LONGSHAW ESTATE

1097 acres (444 ha) 7½m from Sheffield, 3m SE of Hathersage, beside A625 Sheffield to Hathersage road, Derbyshire [110 and 119:SK2480]

This typical Pennine millstone grit landscape consists of low-lying moorland, the wooded banks of Burbage Brook, birch, rowan and oak woodland, enclosed farmland and old quarries where millstones were worked (numerous finished and half-finished stones can still be seen). Once used for shooting, it is now partly run as a country park with a network of popular paths leading through the extensive estate down towards the village of Eyam, famous for its self-imposed isolation during the plague of 1665 (members of one of the families are buried at Riley Graves, now protected and managed by the Trust).

The woods of Padley Gorge are the most important areas of ancient oak woodland remaining in the Peak District. The trees and boulders on the woodland floor are covered with unusual lichens, and birds include pied flycatcher, sparrowhawk and tawny owl. For several years the woods have been fenced to exclude grazing stock, so that the ground layer of bilberry and other plant species is unusually luxuriant.

Other habitats on the estate include upland heath, open grazed woodland, bracken, acid grassland and meadows. The Fish Pond is a valuable habitat for dragonflies and other insects.

The estate is of great interest for its landuse history, with features ranging from the prehistoric period to medieval times. On Lawrence Field and Sheffield Plantation are enclosures dating from the Bronze Age but with evidence of re-use several centuries later. A network of ancient tracks, used for transporting lead, millstones, salt and corn cross the estate and paved packhorse tracks can also be traced. A guidestone, dated 1709, in the middle of the estate marks the place where four roads met, providing clues to an early eighteenth-century road network. Other evidence of local industry includes a number of quarries which produced millstones and grindstones for use in the Sheffield tool and cutlery industries.

ACCESS: Network of paths and trails; local station at Grindleford and bus service from Sheffield.

PARKING: Car park.

FACILITIES: NT shop, restaurant and information centre; WCs (including disabled); Longshaw walks and family leaflets available from information centre; riding permits available.

PARK HALL MOOR

1613 acres (653 ha) W of Kinder Downfall, E of A6242, Derbyshire
[110:SK035885]

Merging with the Kinder Scout massif in the High Peak Estate west of Kinder Downfall, Park Hall Moor is a large tract of heather moorland which falls away to the outskirts of Glossop. The view across to the Kinder escarpment is impressive, and the foreground is dominated by enclosed spurs dissected by cloughs or river valleys. The lower slopes of the moor are crossed by gritstone walls, old enclosures made to create more productive upland pastures.

Park Hall Moor has been a shooting moor since the early nineteenth century, and the shooting cabin and adjacent shooting butts are in regular use today. Other popular activities include rambling, and during the Kinder Scout mass trespass the demonstrators walked along Snake Path (which opened in 1897) to reach Kinder and enforce their claim for access to beauty spots.

There are good expanses of wet and dry heathland here. Bilberry, crowberry and cowberry are three species associated with the drier heath, and hare's tail and common cotton grasses, *Sphagnum* moss and sedges with the wet heath. Rowan and birch trees are scattered up the steep river valleys.

The whole of Park Hall Moor was incorporated in the Royal Forest of the Peak around the time of the Norman Conquest.

ACCESS: Network of footpaths; the Pennine Way.

PARKING: Roadside parking.

FACILITIES: Local facilities.

SHUGBOROUGH

899 acres (364 ha) 5½m SE of Stafford on A513, entrance at Milford, Staffordshire [127:SJ992225]

Set within the former Forest of Cannock, this estate, administered by Staffordshire County Council, is dominated by parkland, farm-land and plantation woodlands. A few relics of the old hunting forest still survive, such as Haywood and Great Haywood parks, and include old oak pollards of biological and historical importance which support a range of beetles found only on trees associated with primeval woods. A variety of birds such as pied flycatcher, wood-cock, lesser spotted woodpecker and wood warbler can be seen in small areas of oak and birch woodland, as well as the barn owl (a nationally declining species); there are interesting displays of fungi in the autumn.

Shugborough Park Farm is now a working agricultural museum, recreating nineteenth-century farm life with displays, demonstra-tions and livestock. Its close proximity to the River Trent and its fragile wetland habitats of marsh, fen and alder carr enhance the value of the wildlife of the area.

There are over four miles of river frontage, and the wetland sites harbour reed bunting, sedge warbler, moorhen and coot. Insects such as dragonflies and damselflies inhabit the reeds and sedges.

ACCESS: House, museum and farm open seasonally; park open daily; footpaths; station at Stafford and bus service form Stafford and Lichfield.

PARKING: Car park.

FACILITIES: NT shop and tea-room; WCs (including disabled); guided walks and trails; visitor centre with audio-visual display; play area; museum and farm accessible to wheelchairs.

SNAKE PASS AND HOPE WOODLANDS

16,600 acres (6718 ha) 10m E of Glossop, both sides of A57, Derbyshire
[110:SK100939]

Located between the two large moorland massifs of Kinder Scout and Bleaklow, Snake Pass and Hope 'Woodlands'(a misnomer since very little of the property is wooded) form part of 33,000–acre Trust property of the High Peak Estate, and include a substantial block of moorland, hidden valleys and woods surrounding the rivers of Ashop, Alport and Westend which run down to Ladybower Reservoir.

Crossed by the bleak and high road between Manchester and Sheffield, it is often blocked by snow in winter. As in other areas of the High Peak, the deep blanket peat of the moorland is bare and exposed in many places due to pollution damage over the past 300 years which has affected the growth of the protective layer of *Sphagnum* moss, cotton grass and other bog species. Excellent expanses of upland heath remain on the plateau, however.

The plateau is dissected by deeply incised valleys or cloughs where the soil is less peaty and acid, and here there are relict woodlands, grassland and bracken. Dependent on the high rainfall and the underlying blanket of peat, the moorland supports a mosaic of grassland, bogs, wet flushes, eroded peat hags as well as the expanses of heather moor. Hare's tail and common cotton grasses, purple moor grass, bilberry, cowberry, crowberry, bell heather, cross-leaved heath and ling provide habitat for a rich upland bird community which includes red grouse, golden plover, dunlin, curlew, wheatear, skylark and meadow pipit. Woodlands and rivers provide additional habitat and shelter for many birds such as goldcrest, nut-hatch, dipper and common sandpiper, and the inaccessible rock outcrops and pockets of natural oak woodland harbour a rich diversity of wildlife. The alternating bands of gritstone and shales are unstable in places, resulting in dramatic landslips.

The moors have been heavily grazed since the medieval period (Hope Woodlands have also been utilized as rough grazing for sheep since this period), although grazing pressure has been controlled by the Trust over the last ten years. The moorland is crossed by a Roman road (north of the Snake Inn), and the large ditch known as 'Devil's Dike' is thought to have been cut by the monks of Basingwerk in Cheshire as a boundary for their land. Also of interest are several vernacular gritstone buildings recently repaired by the Trust in Snake Pass, and some old drove roads and sheep folds.

ACCESS: Open access; network of footpaths; property includes sections of the Pennine Way.

PARKING: Car parks at Birchen Clough Bridge, north of Ladybower Reservoir.

FACILITIES: Local facilities; camping.

SPEKE

98 acres (40 ha) on N side of River Mersey, 8m SE of Liverpool, 1m S of A561, Merseyside [108:SJ419825]

Gardens, mixed woodland, small lakes and relics of a former heathland surround this magnificent timber-framed manor house on the outskirts of Liverpool. Walks laid out over the estate provide good views of the house from a distance, and at the southern end of the property a steep climb up a grassy bank will reveal the River Mersey, designated an SSSI and an important estuary for wildfowl.

Parts of the woodland were previously pasture woodland associated with the historic manorial estate, but most have been planted. The Clough is known to be an ancient woodland site, although it has been replanted with trees not native to this country. Other woods of interest are Speke Dams (oak and birch) and Stockton's Wood (a block of mixed woodland).

ACCESS: Open seasonally; walks through woods; no path to estuary; local stations at Garston and Hunt's Cross.

PARKING: Car park; special parking for disabled.

FACILITIES: NT shop and tea-room; WCs (including disabled); woodland path suitable for wheelchairs; leaflets; picnic area in orchard.

STYAL COUNTRY PARK

274 acres (111 ha) 1½m NW of Wilmslow, off B5166, Cheshire
[109:SJ835836]

Styal Country Park, one of the first in the country to be established, is set in the wooded valley of the River Bollin. The woods of ash, oak and wych elm, some on ancient woodland sites, have a history of industrial use, with the coppicing of the underwood for stakes and the production of charcoal, and the periodic removal of mature timber for building, creating a specific community of wild flowers, birds and other wildlife.

Arthur's Wood on the northern slopes of the river contains some giant redwoods, and in spring bluebells cover the ground in Willow Ground Wood. The river cuts down into a steep gorge, exposing a geologically interesting succession of rocks. Lesser woodpecker, woodcock and tawny owl can be seen, and dipper, grey wagtail and the occasional kingfisher feed along the riverside, which is rich with mosses, ferns and liverworts, attractive damselflies and dragonflies.

Much of the woodland was planted by the Greg family who founded Quarry Bank Mill in 1784, now a working museum of the cotton industry. Styal village, an old industrial complex at the centre of the property, was also built by the Gregs. It is one of the few remaining unaltered factory colonies of the Industrial Revolution, and contains housing for workers and apprentices, a school, shop and two chapels.

ACCESS: Country park open all year during daylight hours; circular walk from main car park; footpath across property (approximately 3m); walks through woods and along river; station at Styal.

PARKING: Large car park (free to members) at Quarry Bank Mill; local authority car park at Twinnies Bridge.

FACILITIES: NT shop and restaurant; WCs (including disabled); information boards with maps at all entrances to property; country park guide with details of walks available from car park kiosk, mill and estate office in village; guided walks; picnic areas; wheelchair route from car park at Twinnies Bridge (central and western woodlands are steep with several flights of stairs).

WENLOCK EDGE AND WILDERHOPE

786 acres (318 ha) between Ironbridge Gorge and Craven Arms, NE of A49, via B4371 crossing the ridge; Wilderhope 6m SW of Much Wenlock, 5½m E of Church Stretton, Shropshire
[127:SJ605002, 138:SO595988, 570965 and 545929]

Approached from the west, the famous narrow limestone escarpment of Wenlock Edge in Shropshire runs for fifteen miles from Craven Arms to Ironbridge. The limestone, of international repute as an example of old coral reef deposits, supports an array of richly flowered grassland and ancient woodland, making the area an important SSSI.

Throughout the woods and along the scarp is an area of industrial and agricultural activity, with evidence of quarrying and limestone workings. Lime kilns and coppice woodland used to produce charcoal for firing the burners are clearly seen. On the Wilderhope Estate are the remains of old ridge and furrow in a number of fields. The Trust has acquired recent plantings of conifers, which changed the character of the Edge; now the balance is being redressed by replacing the conifers with the broadleaved trees natural to the area.

Several woods on the scarp slope are on ancient woodland sites, rich with unusual flora and shrubs. Small- and large-leaved limes, ash, hazel, wych elm and field maple are some of the trees to be seen, and the woodland flora includes the nettled-leaved bellflower, spurge laurel, yellow archangel, soft-shield fern, early purple orchid, common dog violet, dog's mercury and woodruff. Along the rides or in newly coppiced areas the flowers grow in greater profusion and attract many butterflies. Badger and dormouse inhabit the woods, and woodcock, nuthatch and spotted flycatcher are among the woodland birds. Buzzard can be seen overhead.

The herb-rich grassland along the upper edge of the wooded scarp supports pyramidal orchid, common gromwell and basil thyme. The estate of Wilderhope, situated in the remote and pastoral countryside on the southern slope of Wenlock Edge, surrounds a splendid, unspoilt Elizabethan manor built of limestone and now leased to the Youth Hostel Association. The landscape of wooded stream valleys, herb-rich grasslands, ancient woodlands, copses and old hedgerows forms the setting for Mary Webb's Shropshire country novels of the early years of this century.

Ash, oak, spindle, spurge laurel and yew grow in the ancient woods. Stanway Coppice is notable for its variety of woodland plants such as great woodrush, wood sorrel and foxglove (in the wetter areas). Dog's mercury, broad buckler fern and wood melick are common along the wooded streamsides, and the remaining unimproved limestone grasslands support a wide range of flowers, including eyebright and salad burnet. The hedges along the old trackways are thick with hazel, dogwood, rose, elder and blackthorn, and a small area of alder carr in a damp flush is a refuge for golden saxifrage, mosses and sedges.

ACCESS: Footpaths and bridleways; Wilderhope Manor open seasonally; permitted routes in Wilderhope; Shropshire Way runs along Wenlock Edge; circular paths; station at Church Stretton.

PARKING: 2 car parks; lay-by parking; car park at Wilderhope Manor.

FACILITIES: Local facilities; leaflet describing routes; viewpoints; easy access route.

THE WINNATS AND MAM TOR

780 acres (316 ha) 2–3m W of Castleton, Derbyshire
[110:SK135826 and 126836]

Winnats Pass (the name is a corruption of 'wind-gates') is a deep and impressive gorge which cuts into the limestone escarpment south of Mam Tor. It contains many characteristic features of a limestone landscape, with imposing crags, steep grassy shoulders and cavern openings which disguise a network of caves and old workings of lead, Blue John spar and calcite mines, and form this classic karst scenery.

The pass leads out on to a plateau landscape of pastures enclosed by typical grey limestone walls to the west, and the popular walkers' and cavers' centre of Castleton to the east. Old pack-horse routes cross the area. The grassland is rich in many lime-loving plants, with rock-rose, small scabious, harebell, thyme and many species characteristic of the Derbyshire limestone. Shady rock crevices are colonised by woodland species such as wood sage and dog's mercury. On the northern slopes, taller herbs include meadowsweet, wild angelica and sweet cicely. The crags harbour many unusual plants that survive where grazing pressure is light.

Mam Tor, less than a mile to the north of the pass, is known as the 'shivering mountain' because of the frequent landslips of grit and shale on the south-eastern side. It is popular for windswept walks with panoramic views for miles around, towards Kinder Scout and to Lose Hill on the eastern edge of the ridge (also owned by the Trust). The old A625 below the Tor was closed many years ago after a substantial landslip severely disrupted the road, but this is now an impressive attraction for sightseers.

Few visitors realise that the grassy slopes of the summit conceal the remains of one of the best-preserved Bronze/Iron Age hill forts in the county. The Tor is also the site of two Bronze Age barrows. The (until recently) very heavily grazed acid grassland does not have the varied flora of the nearby limestone grasslands of Winnats Pass, but the steep gullies that have in the past escaped the pressure of grazing support ferns, mosses and woodland herbs. Pockets of oak and wych-elm woodland at the base of the slopes add to the diversity of wildlife interest.

ACCESS: Footpaths from west and from the ridge.

PARKING: Car parks in Castleton and below Mam Tor on old A625; no parking in Winnats Pass.

FACILITIES: Facilities in Castleton; National Park information centre; leaflet.

Eastern Counties

CAMBRIDGESHIRE · NORFOLK · SUFFOLK
ESSEX

In no other region has the transformation of the original landscape been so rapid. East Anglia has been an agricultural centre for centuries, but in the last forty years hedges have been removed and the fens and wetlands drained to form an intensively farmed agricultural landscape.

The Trust protects an extensive range of man-made and natural landscapes. Two great landscape architects have strong connections with East Anglia: 'Capability' Brown and Humphry Repton. Sheringham Park in north Norfolk was Repton's favourite work, and both Brown and Repton worked at Wimpole in Cambridgeshire.

Wicken Fen in Cambridgeshire is the product of centuries of human exploitation, but is now one of the last remaining relics of undrained fenland in East Anglia and the oldest wetland nature reserve in the country, supporting a unique collection of wildlife. As surrounding farmland has been drained, only constant efforts to preserve the perimeter bank and maintain the high water table ensure that the reserve retains its sponge-like character.

Hatfield Forest in Essex is another property with an interesting history of land use. It is the product of 900 years of well-documented and complex management, where today coppicing and pollarding are still carried out to maintain the historical features of the Forest.

The Essex marshes provide important overwintering for birds, and at Copt Hall and Northey Island the Trust is working to improve the habitat for Brent geese. Just to the north, on the Suffolk/Essex border, the Trust owns land at Flatford and Dedham where the traditional Constable countryside has been designated an ESA.

In north Suffolk one of the most important surviving examples of the Suffolk Sandlings heathland, which once ran the length of the county's coastline, is cared for by the Trust at Dunwich. Conservation work to maintain this diminishing habitat is particularly critical.

The north Norfolk coast, much of it now designated Heritage Coast, is an area of rare beauty but also under increasing pressure from tourism. Balancing the needs of conservation and public access is a continuous management dilemma, especially at Blakeney Point, which is an internationally important nature reserve, visited by thousands of holidaymakers every summer.

THE BLACKWATER ESTUARY: NORTHEY ISLAND, RAY ISLAND, COPT HALL

1000 acres (405 ha) off B1025 S of Colchester; Northey Island and Ray Island reached by causeways at low tide; Copt Hall 8m S of Colchester near Little Wigborough, Essex   [168:TL872058, 007150 and 980147]

The fingered pattern of drainage creeks, mudflats, bleak windswept saltmarshes and grazing lands, austere dykes and sea walls, tidal islands and fluctuating channels of water make up this estuarine coastline which is of international importance for its birds. The Trust owns a small part of the estuary, and part of its holding (Ray Island) is managed by the Essex Wildlife Trust. Seasonal birds of prey such as short-eared and long-eared owls patrol the marshes, and geese feed on them in winter. Erosion and the development of marinas still pose a threat to the saltmarshes and rough grasslands, while the views are dominated by Bradwell nuclear power station.

At Copt Hall, in a combination of farmed land and estuarine habitats, grass has been sown on formerly arable fields to attract waders and geese, new copses planted and a new green lane created. There are old salt workings thought to date from Roman times, and known as Red Hills.

On Ray Island, a long strip of alluvial mudflats and saltings near the causeway to Mersea Island, over 20,000 waders and wildfowl have been recorded, including Brent geese, shelduck, teal, golden-eye, dunlin, knot, curlew, grey plover and bar-tailed godwit.

Northey Island (the Trust property includes South House Farm on the mainland) is dissected by a maze of tidal creeks, with characteristic saltmarsh flora of sea plantain, sea lavender, sea spurrey and grasses. The many wading and overwintering birds include up to 5000 Brent geese mainly on specially managed farmland.

Somewhere around the island is the site of the celebrated Battle of Maldon in AD991, when the Anglo-Saxon Brihtnoth was defeated and killed by marauding Vikings.

ACCESS: To Northey Island by appointment only from the Warden; minor road to Ray Island just before Strood Causeway to Mersea Island; public access to Copt Hall, circular walk around farm (keep to way-marked path).

PARKING: Small car park at Copt Hall.

FACILITIES: Northey Island nature trail; Copt Hall information board; access for wheelchairs.

NOTE: Do not walk along the top of the easily damaged sea wall at Copt Hall, to avoid disturbance of wildfowl.

BLAKENEY FRESHES, SALTHOUSE BROAD AND GRAMBOROUGH HILL

146 acres (59 ha) N of Blakeney, 1½m NE of Cley and ½m NE of Salthouse on A149, Norfolk   [133:TG040447, 061448 and 086441]

The important grazing marshland of Blakeney Freshes in the Norfolk Broads is frequented by flocks of overwintering wildfowl and other birds, with Brent geese, wigeon, gadwall and shoveler. Snipe, oystercatcher, lapwing and yellow wagtail frequent the permanent pasture in summer, and bearded tit, reed bunting and reed warbler inhabit the reeds. The drainage ditches (now part of a renovation programme to control the water levels which attract large populations of breeding birds) are rich in insects and wetland plants.

Salthouse Broad (known locally as Arnold's Marsh) is of particular interest for the great variety of birds, and access to the lagoons is very limited to avoid undue disturbance. Next to the Cley marshes and managed by the Norfolk Naturalists' Trust, it adds an important expanse of open water and marsh to this valuable sanctuary for birds.

Gramborough Hill is another area of great importance for overwintering wildfowl and waders, standing next to a saltmarsh east of Cley and abutting the shingle bank. The damp meadow, a habitat now nationally in decline, is of interest for the variety of plants and as a feeding ground for birds. The remains of a Roman settlement exists on the hill.

The Freshes do not have public access, but can be viewed from the shingle bank.

ACCESS: All year (restricted in parts); coastal footpaths; station at Sheringham.

PARKING: Car parks.

FACILITIES: Board with information of bird sightings; birdwatchers' hides; access to Salthouse Broad for disabled.

BLAKENEY POINT

1184 acres (479 ha) between Wells and Sheringham, access by boat from Blakeney or Morston, both off A149, Norfolk [133:TG0046]

This spectacular example of a shingle spit forms a constantly changing hand-shaped promontory, with shifting channels and anchorages, seven miles in length off the north Norfolk coast. It holds a range of classic coastal habitats, with sand and pebble beach, saltmarsh and sand dunes. Common seals breed off the point of the spit, and can be seen at close range from the boats.

An internationally important site for research on vegetation, it is well-documented. The mudflats and saltmarsh support plants such as marsh samphire, sea lavender, sea aster and sea purslane, and on the sand dunes grow sea bindweed, common stork's bill, tree lupin and grasses. Sea campion, sea sandwort and yellow-horned poppy can be seen on the shingle.

Over 260 species of birds have been recorded, including some unusual migrants and large nesting colonies of common, Sandwich, Arctic and little terns. Ringed plover and oystercatcher are often seen.

ACCESS: From Cley Beach (3-mile walk) or by ferry from Morston and Blakeney; North Norfolk Railway (seasonal); station at Sheringham and local bus service from station.

PARKING: Several car parks.

FACILITIES: Shop; lifeboat house (open during season); information centre at Morston Quay; leaflets; display; birdwatchers' hides (one accessible by wheelchair); guided walks (groups by appointment); bathing (dangerous).

BLICKLING PARK

4768 acres (1930 ha) 1½m NW of Aylsham on A140, 15m N of Norwich, 10m S of Cromer each side of B1354, Norfolk [133:TG17280]

This beautiful parkland surrounding a Jacobean mansion was landscaped during the eighteenth century. Concealed within the grander design are remnants of the earlier medieval manor, with approximately 600 acres of woodland (some on sites of ancient and pasture woodland), 800 acres of permanent pasture, a long artificial lake, hedgerows, the River Bure and a disused railway line in the Norfolk countryside.

The estate covers a wide range of wildlife habitats from river meadows (in an ESA) to the woodlands. The lake provides a habitat for many species of wildlife, including some locally rare insects and birds such as tufted duck, great crested grebe and Egyptian and Canada geese, with kingfisher on the river. Lesser spotted woodpecker can also be seen.

ACCESS: House open seasonally; park open all year; network of circular walks; Weavers Way long-distance footpath; station at North Walsham.

PARKING: Several car parks; special parking for disabled.

FACILITIES: NT shop and restaurant; tea-room with ramp for wheelchairs; WCs (including disabled); leaflet with map; educational groups; plant centre in orchard; picnic area; coarse fishing in lake (permits available from warden).

BRANCASTER

2150 acres (870 ha) between Wells and Hunstanton, off A149, Norfolk
[132:TF800450]

Over four miles in length, this property includes an extensive area of saltmarsh, intertidal mud and sand flats, a wide beachline and high dunes stabilised by marram grass inland. It is the site of the Roman shore fort of Branodunum. The harbour and wharves of Brancaster are of historic interest. (The golf course, on former marshland, is not owned by the Trust.)

The rich variety of coastal habitats and its location opposite the Scolt Head Nature Reserve (leased by English Nature) contribute to the value of the area. The beachline is littered with the remains of marine life swept up with the tide, and a colony of little tern nests on the beach and shingle. Cord grass grows in the lower and younger saltmarsh, and sea arrowgrass, sea lavender and sea aster cover the upper marshes in a mosaic of pink flowers. The sand and mudflats attract hoards of Brent geese, shelduck, oystercatchers, redshank and black-headed gulls. Sedge warblers and bearded tits breed in the reed beds.

ACCESS: 4 access points to the marshes; boardwalk to beach.

PARKING: Golf club car park at Brancaster Beach.

FACILITIES: Information centre with access for wheelchairs; leaflets; bicycle hire at Brancaster Staithe Harbour; boat hire to Scolt Head Island at Brancaster Staithe (old boat wreckage a hazard); nature trail on Scolt Head Island.

DANBURY AND LINGWOOD COMMONS, BLAKE'S WOOD

321 acres (130 ha) 5m E of Chelmsford, S of A414, Essex
[167:TL7805 and 773068]

This nature reserve consists of woodland and commons on a sandy ridge between the Crouch and Blackwater estuaries. The two commons are fragments of the medieval manors of St Clere and Herons, and together they remain the second largest area of commonland in Essex after Epping Forest. The natural character of the land, combined with its exploitation by commoners for heather, grazing and woodcutting, has led to the development of a number of interesting wildlife habitats.

Danbury Common, the Backwarden part of which is managed by the Essex Wildlife Trust, has an open character with expanses of heath invaded by bracken, broom, gorse, scrub and woodland of oak and birch. Recent clearance of the encroaching scrub is helping to re-establish more of the former heathland habitat with its associated wildlife of heather, heath bedstraw, milkwort, tormentil and common lizard, adder, butterflies and moths.

To the north, Lingwood Common is more heavily wooded with birch and oak where grassy glades are rich in butterflies and moths. Neolithic flints have been found on Beacon Hill, its highest point overlooking Danbury village and the Chelmer Valley. Blake's Wood is an area of sweet chestnut and hornbeam coppice, typical of the south-east, and is renowned for its bluebells and wood anemones. Oak, birch and hazel, coppiced in the past, are also common.

The area has strong links with the military past, with an earthwork on Danbury Common dating back to the Napoleonic Wars. Smugglers operating out of the estuaries also used the common to graze their ponies.

ACCESS: Open access; footpaths and bridleways; station at Chelmsford.

PARKING: 4 main car parks.

FACILITIES: Leaflet; information boards; guided walks and talks.

DUNWICH HEATH AND MINSMERE BEACH

214 acres (86½ ha) 2m S of Dunwich on coast between Aldeburgh and Southwold, E of Yoxford, access signed on Westleton to Dunwich road, Suffolk [156:TM475683]

On the coast and next to the RSPB bird reserve of Minsmere, Dunwich Heath is an important remnant of the once extensive Sandlings Heaths, an area of sandy soil which used to cover this stretch of coastline. Now very important for conservation, it was used as a sheep walk in medieval times, and has since been grazed by sheep belonging to the Freemen of Dunwich. The heathland is covered in a blanket of heather, with heath bedstraw and three species of gorse (common, western and dwarf). Common lizard, grass snake, adder, glow worm, heather gossamer spider and heather beetle are some of the associated wildlife. Towards the sea, gnarled bell heather and clumps of gorse provide perches for stonechat and winchat. Nightjar breed here on two managed sites and many butterflies can be seen, such as common blue, meadow brown and small copper. Red deer graze on the heath.

To the south-west, the heather gives way to birchwood, and a programme of cutting back this invasive scrub is reversing the alarming decline of the heathland.

The badly eroded and unstable beach was once commonland to the thriving medieval town of Dunwich which gradually disappeared into the sea over the centuries as the cliffs were eroded. Later, the cliffs became the site of one of the first Second World War radar stations in England.

To the south lie the Minsmere reed beds, separated by the flooded Docurra's Ditch, itself an interesting wildlife habitat. To the west lies woodland and heathland, part of the RSPB reserve, and a similar area to the north in private ownership. Minsmere Beach and its sandy cliffs run the full length of the eastern boundary.

ACCESS: Network of footpaths; access to beach and coastal path.

PARKING: Car parks.

FACILITIES: NT shop and tea-room; WCS (including disabled); leaflets; information room; education base and officer; viewpoints; sea fishing on beach; picnic area; stair lift to information room and lookout; batricar; holiday flats.

FELBRIGG PARK

1697 acres (687 ha) 2m SW of Cromer off A148, Norfolk [133:TG197397]

Before the building of Felbrigg Hall in the seventeenth century, the park was a wild expanse of heathland exposed to the sea. The surrounding grounds were subsequently planted to screen the house from the open landscape of the north Norfolk coast. All that remains of the medieval village, which was burned to exterminate the plague, is a flint church within the estate. The village was then rebuilt approximately a mile north of the original site. Earthworks give evidence of a sixteenth-century park and manor, and also of note is the mound of a Bronze Age barrow.

Humphry Repton is thought to have been involved in the design of the parkland, for which the drawings and plans still exist. Some fine examples of ancient pollarded beech and oak trees are to be found in Felbrigg Great Wood, which was planted in the last few years of the seventeenth century. The owner, William Windham, was a keen tree-planter who set up his own nursery to supply the planting schemes, and a mosaic of woodland sites, including conifer plantations, is scattered across the estate.

The mixed woodland consists of oak, sweet chestnut, beech, pine, rowan, birch, holly and hazel, and in the parkland some of the mature trees date back to 1581. A wide range of fungi can be seen, particularly on the decaying beech. Woodland birds include great spotted woodpeckers, woodcock, tree creepers and nuthatches, and the herb-rich meadows support orchids and ragged robin.

ACCESS: House and park open seasonally; woodland and lakeside walks open all year; free entry to woods and parkland; Weavers' Way long-distance footpath and other paths cross the estate; stations at Cromer and Roughton Road.

PARKING: Car park at house.

FACILITIES: NT shop and restaurant; WCs (including disabled).

FLATFORD

64 acres (26 ha) on N bank of River Stour, 1m S of East Bergholt, Suffolk
[168:TM077332]

Located along the lower reaches of the River Stour in the Vale of Dedham, Flatford is a medley of classic timber-framed farmhouses and cottages now let to the Field Studies Council. Valley Farm, dating from the sixteenth century, is of particular note, and the famous seventeenth-century water-mill, the subject of John Constable's paintings, is now listed.

Judas Gap Marsh and Gibbonsgate Field and Pond, adjoining Willy Lott's Cottage, add to the charm and wildlife interest of the area with its series of wetland and valley habitats. Because many of the wetland sites are drained, and affected by high nutrient levels in the water which reduce the range of plant species, it has become important to protect the remaining habitats in this ESA, now also under heavy pressure from visitors during the summer.

Many insects, including damselflies and dragonflies, inhabit yellow flag on the ponds and marshes, and butterflies, moths and bees feed on purple loosestrife, water mint and water speedwell. Willows (some pollarded), reeds and bulrushes fringe the ponds.

ACCESS: Via one-way traffic system; footpath along river to Dedham, Brantham or Manningtree; local station at Manningtree.

PARKING: Car park at top of hill (walk down); special parking facilities for disabled.

FACILITIES: NT shop, information and display at Bridge Cottage (limited opening); tea garden; WCs; birdwatchers' hide on Gibbonsgate Pond; information panel on Gibbonsgate Field circular walk.

HATFIELD FOREST

1000 acres (405 ha) 3m E of Bishop's Stortford, access from a side road leading S from A120 at Takeley Street, Essex   [167:TL540200]

A unique British historic landscape, Hatfield was first mentioned in the Domesday Book. Having escaped the widespread grubbing out of woodland over the centuries, it remains as a vestige of the once enormous Forest of Essex. The medieval core remains, and provides a record of the forest's evolution, with deer and cattle grazing among the coppiced and pollarded woods and timber trees. Increasing pressure is being placed on the ancient woodland and its rich wildlife by changes in the surrounding landscape, such as the intensification of agriculture, building of roads, development of a golf course and the expansion of neighbouring Stansted Airport.

The forest is divided into sections separated by permanent woodbanks, with areas of grassland, glades, footpaths and wide grassy rides where flowers such as water figwort, common fleabane, meadowsweet, hedge woundwort and wood speedwell flourish. Four hundred species of plants have been recorded. The woods contains thirty-six native species of tree and shrub with many plants characteristic of their ancient origins, such as herb Paris, oxlip and purple helleborine. The old hornbeam coppices are of particular interest since this tree is common only in the south; its hard wood was used for firewood, tool handles, wheel rims and hubs. The forest is the site of the Doodle Oak, which may have stood for 800 years.

A lake, created as part of an eighteenth-century landscape in 1746, now has one of the largest fen areas in Essex, and provides a habitat for water birds such as the great crested grebe. Nightingales are among the many birds inhabiting the forest, with owls, great and lesser spotted woodpeckers, whitethroats and blackcaps. Fallow deer can still be seen in great numbers, and up to forty muntjac live in the woods.

Portinbury Hills are the remains of the earthwork of a late prehistoric settlement in Beggar's Hall Coppice, and there is an Iron Age hill fort underlying the rabbit warrens. Shell House, a rustic grotto, is worth visiting, and there is a medieval forest lodge (now tenanted) from which the affairs of the forest were conducted. A disused railway line runs to the north of the property.

ACCESS: Open access for pedestrians; seasonal vehicular access; footpaths along rides; station at Bishop's Stortford.

PARKING: Car park.

FACILITIES: Local facilities; refreshments; WCs (including disabled); leaflets; observation hide with wheelchair bay and ramp (keys obtainable for annual fee); riding for members of Hatfield Forest Riding

Association only; fishing by day permit during season; limited access for wheelchairs as some paths unsuitable and grass often wet.

ICKWORTH PARK

1792 acres (725 ha) at Horringer, 3m SW of Bury St Edmunds W of A143, Suffolk [155:TL8161]

The park of the grandiose early nineteenth-century house at Ickworth was certainly influenced and possibly planted by the great landscape designer 'Capability' Brown. Clumps of imposing, ancient oak pollards, some more than 400 years old with encrusted bark supporting valuable communities of lichens, fungi and beetles, are scattered throughout the estate which is thought to be a former medieval wooded pasture and deer park. Signs of the field systems of the old manor (thirteenth and fourteenth centuries) can still be seen.

The ancient woodlands are also of great interest, with mature oaks and hazel coppice dominating a rich ground flora of bluebells, lords and ladies, wood anemones and ferns. Other trees and shrubs include elm, ash, dogwood, spindle and hawthorn. Of particular note are Lownde Wood and Dairy Wood, which has old ditch and bank boundaries.

Remnants of the previous landscape, typical of the Suffolk countryside, can be detected in the hedgebanks, hedgerows and field trees. A chain of rich wetland habitats is created by the River Linnet, which runs through the estate, with the Fairy Lake, a series of ponds and a canal attracting numerous birds on the open water and reed fringes.

ACCESS: Open all year during daylight hours; footpaths; waymarked woodland and park walks; house open seasonally; station at Bury St Edmunds.

PARKING: Car park.

FACILITIES: NT shop and restaurant; WCs (including disabled); picnic area; children's playground; leaflets; guided walks.

MORSTON AND STIFFKEY MARSHES

1076 acres (435 ha) between Wells and Blakeney, access from A149, Norfolk   [132 and 133:TG010445 and 040447]

Morston Marsh is a maze of creeks, mudflats and long-established saltings lying opposite Blakeney Point on the coast, and continues into Stiffkey Marsh, which contains some of the oldest saltmarshes along this historic coastline of changing channels and anchorages.

Between the villages of Stiffkey and Blakeney, the saltings of Morston Marsh support communities of plants such as sea purslane and sea aster, and in July the marshes are purple with sea lavender. The nutrient-rich tidal creeks around both marshes attract many wading and overwintering birds such as redshank, Brent geese, shelduck, wigeon and teal. Clinker-built boats with seaweed-strewn mooring ropes add to the character of this important wildlife site.

Inland from Stiffkey the marsh supports many flowers and grasses, with a wide range of insects and butterflies.

ACCESS: All year round; coastal footpaths; track to Morston Quay; station at Sheringham.

PARKING: Car parks at both sites.

FACILITIES: Leaflet; viewing platform at Morston Boathouse (seasonal).

SHERINGHAM PARK

770 acres (312 ha) 5m NE of Holt, 2m SW of Sheringham, Norfolk
[133:TG135420]

This parkland is important as one of the most complete and best-preserved landscapes designed by Humphry Repton, who brought up his family in the area. He described it as his favourite project, and in his 'Red Book' are views of the landscape before and after his work. Wooded hills frame the park and act as an important backdrop to the parkland.

The extensive woodland cover includes some ancient sites and pasture woodland, and contains some impressive displays of rhododendron and azalea. The old oak and beech trees support interesting communities of lichens and beetles, and the pond provides ideal surroundings for great crested newts. A number of bats are attracted by the combination of old buildings and different wildlife habitats.

The estate extends to the coast and includes a section of the coastal path, where the cliffs contains some interesting geological deposits and provide nesting places for sea birds such as fulmars.

Of historical interest are Howe's Hill barrow, and some old sunken roadways. Also of interest is the folly, based on a suggested design in Repton's Red Book, and completed in 1976. The location of this landscape feature, on a small knoll, was carefully chosen so that it could be seen from the Hall.

ACCESS: Open all year round; way-marked walks; station at Sheringham.

PARKING: Car park; coaches to book.

FACILITIES: WCs (including disabled); leaflet; visitor information; boardwalk; gazebo/viewing tower overlooking park and coastline; two observation platforms overlooking azaleas and rhododendrons (May/June); raised boardwalk from car park; wheelchair and batri-car available.

THE SUFFOLK ESTUARIES: PIN MILL AND KYSON HILL

12 acres (5½ ha) 7m SE of Ipswich off B1456, S of Woodbridge
[169:TM206380 and 270477]

Characterised by the deeply indented outline of the Deben, Orwell and Stour estuaries, this vulnerable stretch of mudflats, saltmarsh, cliffs and lowland woodland is rich in plants and birdlife.

On the south side of the River Orwell, much used by barges and sailing boats, the Pin Mill property (featured in Arthur Ransome's *We Didn't Mean to Go to Sea*) consists of a pocket of saltmarsh grading through cliffs to woodland. Sections of the woods were severely damaged in recent gales, and it is hoped that some areas will be restored to open acid grass and heathland.

Kyson Hill (managed with the help of Suffolk Coastal District Council), has good views through wooded viewpoints over grazing meadows and the estuarine creeks of the River Deben.

ACCESS: For Kyson Hill, footpaths along estuaries, from Broom Hill and along River Deben, circular walks around properties; for Pin Mill, circular walk around property with access up steps from Pin Mill Road.

PARKING: Car park on road to Pin Mill; car park at Broom Hill for Kyson Hill.

FACILITIES: Local facilities; information board at Pin Mill car park.

WEST RUNTON

107 acres (43 ha) between Sheringham and Cromer, 1m S of West Runton station, off A149, Norfolk [133:TG177417]

This property consists of a stretch of heathland and secondary woodland on the Cromer–Holt ridge, commanding good views along the north Norfolk coast. Deep, dry valleys dissect the ridge from north to south.

Known locally as the Roman Camp, a low rectangular earthbank predates the Napoleonic Wars, and includes the highest point in Norfolk. There are also late Anglo-Saxon iron-working pits seen as circular hollows on the spurs of glacial ridges, excavated in 1964. In the past, bracken was pulled for bedding, and birch used for brush-making.

The woodlands support oak, ash, rowan, birch, sweet chestnut and beech. Birds include fieldfares and redwings, and adders and slow worms are also found. Since the introduction of myxomatosis and the reduction of the rabbit population, scrub has encroached on some of the heathland but the open areas are still managed for habitats of heather, underwing moth and tree pipit.

ACCESS: Free access all year; footpaths from Britons and Calves Well lanes; station at West Runton.

PARKING: Car park.

FACILITIES: Local facilities in West Runton; tea-rooms (not NT) opposite car park; information board.

WICKEN FEN

605 acres (245 ha) S of A1123, 4m E of Stretham via A10, 3m W of Soham via A142, Cambridgeshire [154:TL5570]

Since Roman times East Anglia's Great Fen, a vast peaty wetland largely overlying gault clay, has systematically been drained by an extensive pattern of channels, dykes and sluices. Wicken Fen, an extremely important remnant of this ancient landscape, is made up of a series of wetland habitats, protected from drying out by the careful control of water levels and maintained by traditional reed and sedge harvesting techniques.

The Fen is the Trust's (and indeed the country's) oldest nature reserve, with the first part acquired in 1899, and its range of habitats (reed beds, sedge fields, carr and water) is rich with birds, plants and insects, and remains an island of natural life in the surrounding agricultural landscape. The water teems with countless aquatic invertebrates, among which are eighteen species of damselflies and dragonflies. Butterflies such as the brimstone, comma, wall brown, ringlet and Essex skipper flit over the open fields. Wigeon, shoveler, mallard, teal and tufted duck spend the winter here, and in spring the display of courting great crested grebe can be seen on the water, while snipe and woodcock display overhead. Four species of owl, water rail, bearded tit, sparrowhawk and numerous warblers all breed, with many other species passing through on migration.

Ragged robin, yellow loosestrife, yellow flag, marsh pea, fen violet, milk parsley, comfrey and many other flowering plants and sedges line the ancient paths. Buckthorn, alder and guelder rose thrive in the damp ground, with birch, oak and ash dominating the developing woodland.

The area still shows signs of a long-established economy based on peat, reed and sedge-harvesting, and there are remains of old brick-pits and a wind pump. Of further interest is Fen Cottage, and the Wicken Lode, a man-made waterway which may be of Roman origin.

ACCESS: Open all year; Fen Cottage open seasonally or by appointment; station at Ely and local bus service.

PARKING: Car park near entrance; special parking for disabled.

FACILITIES: WCs (including disabled); William Thorpe building information room; school groups by appointment with Education Officer; birdwatchers' hides; boardwalk suitable for wheelchairs.

WIMPOLE PARK

350 acres (141½ ha) on N side of A603, 8m SW of Cambridge, 6m N of Royston, Cambridgeshire [154:TL336510]

Matching the grandeur of the eighteenth-century house, the surrounding parkland, set in the Cambridgeshire countryside, has been strongly influenced by a number of famous landscape designers such as 'Capability' Brown and Humphry Repton. Axial avenues of trees, lakes, ponds, clumps and belts of trees provide a glorious example of a landscaped park. Beneath this, however, exists a manorial estate with a former deer park where aerial photographs have revealed old field systems with evidence of ridge and furrow farming. An eighteenth-century folly gives commanding views over the park, Hall and farm.

Traces of deserted medieval settlements have been found, with a moated manor house. A Roman settlement on Ermine Street has recently been excavated.

A 1½-mile-long avenue of lime trees, Bridgeman's South Avenue (formerly elms), has recently been replanted. The mainly broadleaved woodland contains some interesting plants, and some of the mature parkland trees provide a habitat for unusual beetles. The parkland is managed by the Trust and grazed by rare breeds of farm animals, including Longhorn and White Park cattle.

ACCESS: Rights of way and a series of way-marked walks; Hall open seasonally; stations at Shepreth and Biggleswade.

PARKING: Car park at Hall.

FACILITIES: NT shop and restaurant; WCs (including disabled); guide for Hall; Braille guide; events programme; children's corner; Wimpole Home Farm with prize-winnimg rare breed farm animals; shire horse trailer rides to Home Farm.

North-West England

CUMBRIA · LANCASHIRE

The fame of the Lake District draws many to this compact region. In an area of thirty square miles are the highest mountains in England and the largest and deepest lakes. A dramatic and grand landscape of spectacular variety: fells, lakes, mountains, meadows, rivers, mires, tarns, ancient stone circles, drystone walls, farm communities and grand estates.

Generations have left their mark on the Lake District and historical evidence includes neolithic axe-factory sites, Iron Age hill forts, Roman forts and roads, monastic farming estates, Royal Forests, quarrying dating back to medieval times, and the small farming unit which has shaped the quintessential Lake District.

Within this cultural tapestry are areas of significant wildlife interest. The uplands with their communities of juniper scrub, mountain flora, mires and peat bogs; crags for nesting ravens and birds of prey; unimproved hay meadows; carrs, marshes and reed beds; lakes with their specialised animal and plant communities and broad-leaved woodland rich in mosses, lichens and ferns.

Each valley has its own character. Windermere, the central focus of the lakes, is the largest lake and the busiest, whilst Wasdale remains remote from the central core and hence maintains a sense of wilderness.

The Lakes have been used for recreational pursuits since the eighteenth century, and the balance of sustaining this outstanding landscape against the onslaught of so many visitors continues to cause much controversy. Whilst people arrive in droves there are still quiet places where those who don't want to join the throngs can enjoy the spirit of solitude. The National Trust, with the Lake District Special Planning Board, has designated Wastwater in Wasdale a quiet zone and strictly controlled the use of water-borne craft. At least one lake can be enjoyed for its sheer beauty.

Around the periphery of the Lake District are some unsung and yet delightful landscapes, such as the Cumbrian coastline, with its varied and internationally significant estuaries. The threat of tidal barrages still hangs over these fragile and fluctuating habitats that sustain migrating populations of waders and wildfowl. Morecambe Bay and Kent Sands are overlooked by Arnside and Silverdale – a series of limestone escarpments cloaked with ancient woodlands, limestone pavement and grassland where the Trust is fostering an organic farm.

Towards the south of Lancashire and the edge of Greater Manchester, the gritstone landscape of the North Pennines emerges, reflected in the characteristic gritstone walls, rough pasture of the moors, and enclosure patterns up the sides of the Pennine valleys.

ACORN BANK

187 acres (75½ ha) 6m E of Penrith, just N of Temple Sowerby, off A66, Cumbria [91:NY612281]

Situated on the north side of the Eden Valley in the foothills of the Pennines, this garden occupies a cool and exposed position with a comparatively high annual rainfall. The main cultivated area, however, is enclosed by warmth-retaining walls and has an unexpected and delightful tranquillity. The name Acorn Bank, first recorded in 1597, refers to the ancient oakwood which shades the descent from the walled garden to the Crowdundle Beck at the rear of the house, although the property was the site of a religious house of the Knights Templar in 1228. The house dates mainly from the seventeenth century, although parts of the sixteenth-century building survive. It is now leased to the Sue Ryder Foundation.

The walled garden is essentially an orchard, surrounded by mixed borders and bisected by a double avenue of yew hedges and cherry trees (the cherry avenue is of *Prunus cerasus* 'Rhexii', the small sour cherry, which produces its spectacular double flowers in mid-May).

In the Well Garden a circular pool and wishing well are overlooked by drystone terrace walls on which grow saxifrages and numerous other alpines. A host of bergenias and Japanese anemones can be seen in the borders by the house.

The Herb Garden is of particular note, and has been planted systematically with medicinal and culinary herbs. The present total of nearly 250 species is accommodated in three long borders which provide a variety of conditions.

ACCESS: Gardens open seasonally; admission to house by written application to Sue Ryder Foundation; woodland walk; stations at Langwathby and Penrith.

PARKING: Car parking within grounds.

FACILITIES: Small NT shop and plants for sale (open as garden); WCS (including disabled); baby changing facilities; wheelchair access to herb garden, herbaceous borders and greenhouse; leaflet.

BORROWDALE

10,700 acres (4330 ha) 3m S of Keswick, access from B5289 extending from S shore of Derwentwater to Honister Pass, Cumbria [89:NY2514]

It is hard to believe that this valley, now part of a National Park, was once a hive of industrial activity with iron-smelting, charcoal-burning and mining for copper and graphite. Scattered hamlets reflect the Nordic influence in their names, while stone walls and vernacular buildings chronicle centuries of farming. Today farmers struggle to make a living and visitors play an important role in sustaining the local community.

There is much of historical and literary interest in the area, including the late neolithic Castlerigg Stone Circle just east of Keswick, and the medieval pack-horse bridge at Ashness. It has long been a favourite haunt of writers and artists. Friar's Crag, at the Keswick end of the lake and one of the most famous viewpoints in the Lake District, is where John Ruskin awoke to aesthetic experience as a child, and St Herbert's Island, sanctuary of a hermit in the seventh century, was Beatrix Potter's 'Owl Island' in *The Tale of Squirrel Nutkin*.

Leading south from Derwentwater, Borrowdale is surrounded by rugged crags, inviting fells, old mine workings and wooded valleys with clear rivers. The fine sessile oak woodlands are of particular ecological interest, and the damp, western climate supports internationally important lichens, mosses and insects. An alder woodland and marsh along the shores of Derwentwater provides ideal nesting sites for wildfowl and waders. Brandelhow, on the west shore of Derwentwater, was the first large property to be bought by the Trust in 1902.

Borrowdale splits into three valleys, Watendlath, Stonethwaite and Seathwaite, each with its own distinctive character. The Trust's estate also includes the western half of Derwentwater and half the western shore with the fells behind, the eastern shore up to the watershed with Thirlmere, and the land around Seatoller up to the Honister Pass, with Seathwaite and Stonethwaite. There are a number of farms within the three valleys, managed by tenant farmers.

Many of the fields are edged with pollarded ash trees, some of which support rare lichens. Some of the fells support important expanses of upland heath, a habitat which has declined in England and Wales because of heavy grazing by sheep.

The gills or ravines in which streams cascade down from the fell tops are rich with woodland and mountain vegetation including alpine lady's mantle, mountain sorrel, columbine and starry saxifrage. Birch woodlands have colonised old quarry workings.

The upland heaths are important for moorland birds such as red grouse; peregrine and raven can be seen on the fells, with pied flycatcher, redstart and wood warbler in the oak woods.

ACCESS: By road (congestion in high season, particularly on road to Watendlath); access over Honister Pass; well-marked footpaths and bridleways.

PARKING: Numerous car parks and lay-bys; no parking on roadside.

FACILITIES: Footpaths; WCS; leaflet for Castlerigg Stone Circle from Lakeside Information Centre; information centres at Lakeside, Keswick (S) and Seatoller (S); mountain rescue post at Seathwaite; camping and caravan sites; youth hostels; boating and fishing facilities (for further information contact regional office); disabled access to Crow Park and Friar's Crag.

THE BUTTERMERE VALLEY

7250 acres (2934 ha) and covenants over 4650 acres (1882 ha) 9m S of Cockermouth, via B5289 from Cockermouth or Keswick, Cumbria
[89:NY175170]

The Buttermere Valley lies in precipitous lakeland scenery with few settlements, and encompasses three lakes, Crummock Water, Buttermere and Loweswater, all owned by the Trust. Buttermere was once linked to Crummock Water to the north-west, but flash-floods after the last Ice Age caused a band of alluvial deposits which now divides the two. Loweswater, north-west of Crummock Water, has several woods on its shores, while Buttermere is surrounded by Red Pike, Haystacks and Fleetwith Pike, which fall steeply down to the lakes and display the classic glacial features of corries, tarns, ridges and hanging valleys. (The Trust protects all the fells east of Buttermere and Crummock Water.)

The area is of great ecological interest, and the Buttermere Fells support the largest area of upland heath on Trust land in the Lake District, with rare plants such as the montane shrub bearberry. Buzzard, peregrine, raven and ring ouzel inhabit the fells.

Notable woodlands include Scales Wood (not owned by the Trust), above the apron of alluvial deposits between Buttermere and Crummock Water, which is nationally important for the rare lichens and mosses growing on the oak and ash trees. Lanthwaite Wood includes some old oak coppice and scrub oak, and glades support many interesting insects. Other broadleaved woods include Holme, Ghyll, Long How and Nether How.

The lakes are of particular interest for wildlife. Buttermere is low in nutrients, and supports a variety of rare Crustacea and fish, including char (an Ice Age relict fish), a deepwater trout which requires low temperatures. Loweswater's rich plant life provides good cover for great crested grebe and other water birds, including merganser, coot, mallard and goldeneye.

Among the sites of historical interest are a number of prehistoric settlements and evidence of fifteenth-century enclosures.

ACCESS: By road; limited access to Loweswater; network of footpaths.

PARKING: Car parks and lay-bys; no parking for coaches.

FACILITIES: Local facilities; mountain rescue point at Gatesgarth Farm; boating facilities (for further information contact regional office).

THE CONISTON VALLEY

5500 acres (2226 ha) 9m SE of Ambleside on A593, minor road to E of Coniston Water, 12m W of Windermere across ferry on B5285 through Hawkshead, Cumbria   [96 and 97:SD304964]

The best way to view Coniston Water and its surrounding panorama is from the steam yacht *Gondola*, restored by the Trust in the late 1970s, which since the mid-nineteenth century has regularly taken visitors down this glacial lake, past Peel Island at the southern end of the lake (the inspiration for Arthur Ransome's 'Wild Cat Island' in *Swallows and Amazons*). The 'Old Man of Coniston' can be seen rising up behind the village of Coniston and Coniston Old Hall on the eastern shore with Grizedale Forest and oak woodlands also to the east leading down to the lake.

At the head of Coniston Water (famous as the site of Donald Campbell's fatal attempt to beat the water-speed record in 1967), north-east of the village lies Tarn Hows, bought and sold on to the Trust by Beatrix Potter, a favourite place for excursions and with magnificent views of the mountains. It was landscaped to look like a Swiss lake in the nineteenth century. The shallow tarn has some important habitats, including a boggy area rich in wetland plants, with marsh cinquefoil, bogbean, common spotted orchid, sweet gale and hare's tail cotton grass. The slopes of Coniston Old Man (not Trust land) are scarred by old copper mines and slate quarries, and the remains of enclosures and bloomeries are evidence of a thirteenth-century monastic community. Tilberthwaite and Greenburn mines are now colonised by various species of birch.

The fells are covered in the ubiquitous upland grassland of mat grass, fescues and bents, with juniper on the screes and some fellsides. Characteristic oak woodlands, some of which are thought to date back to the last Ice Age, are of great ecological importance and support a wide range of mosses, lichens and invertebrates. Many pitsteads remain in the woods where charcoal was produced from coppicing. A scattering of ash, oak, rowan, hawthorn and Scots pine now covers the intake land of the fellsides, and in-bye fields in the valley bottom include some meadows rich in wild flowers.

ACCESS: Via minor roads; network of footpaths; open access to shore; steam yacht *Gondola* sails from Coniston Pier (timetable available locally); no wheelchairs on *Gondola* but guide dogs admitted; vehicle ferry across Windermere.

PARKING: Plentiful car parks.

FACILITIES: WCs at Coniston car park (north end of lake); caravan and camp sites.

DUNNERDALE

2323 acres (940 ha) reached by minor road between Little Langdale to Duddon Bridge, NW of Broughton-in-Furness, off A595, Cumbria
[89:NY246016 and 96:SD223968]

Running south-west from the central lakes, the remote and beautiful Duddon Valley is isolated from the heart of the Lake District by Wrynose Pass, lying between Langdale and Coniston fells. All the land on either side of the Pass road, west of the Three Shires Stone, is protected by the Trust.

In its upper reaches the river pours down the valley through resistant volcanic rocks with frequent rock pools, its course punctuated by forestry plantations. The valley widens out after High Wallowbarrow with farmsteads and enclosed wall pastures on either side, low craggy fells to the east and rich oak woodlands to the west.

The broadleaved Duddon Woods (coppiced in the past for charcoal) are of particular ecological interest, lush with mosses, ferns, lichens and invertebrates. Birds include wood warbler, blackcap, tree creeper, nuthatch and greater spotted woodpecker. Birds on the fells include raven, carrion crow, meadow pipit and wheatear, and buzzard are often seen above the valley hunting for small mammals.

Heavy grazing has reduced the heather cover and interest of the upland grasslands, but a few important areas remain. Bogs and mires, containing mosses and damp-loving plants fill the hollows among the fells. Patches of juniper scrub are of particular interest for wildlife, and Seathwaite Tarn (not owned by the Trust) provides valuable stretches of open water.

Of historical interest are cairns, cairn fields and standing stones from the Bronze and Iron ages, remains of Roman trade and military routes, and the remains of copper mining and quarrying (local names sometimes reflect past industries, as in Wallowbarrow Coppice and Kiln Bank).

The Trust's ownership is more patchy here than in other valleys: Baskell, Pikeside, Hazel Head, Wallowbarrow, Tongue House and Long House farms, and Cockley Beck and Blackhall Farms at the dale head.

ACCESS: Via narrow gated road; network of paths.

PARKING: Informal parking.

FACILITIES: Local facilities.

EAVES AND WATERSLACK WOODS

106 acres (43 ha) 4m NW of Carnforth, 1m N of Silverdale, Lancashire
[97:SD465758]

Overlooking Bank House Farm and Morecambe Bay, this wooded limestone escarpment is of great wildlife interest. Waterslack Wood, towards the east of the property, is known to be an ancient woodland site.

Although partly modified by later planting of conifers (which are not being replaced), the older wooded areas have a number of plants and insects indicating continuity of tree cover, such as herb Paris, small-leaved lime, wild service tree, lily-of-the-valley, dog's mercury, ramson and bluebell. Evidence of traditional woodland management is visible throughout the woods, with hazel coppice below the standard trees.

Elsewhere, dense thickets of self-sown yew and scrubby woodland disguise important areas of limestone pavement (a habitat that in other places has been much destroyed by removal for rockeries over recent years), and limestone grasslands, which were once grazing land. The Trust is now undertaking a sensitive programme of clearing trees and scrub to restore larger glades and open areas.

The limestone grasslands have some good anthills which provide food for green woodpecker, and associated plants include rockrose, quaking grass, spring cinquefoil and autumn gentian. Bloody crane's bill and hart's tongue fern grow on the limestone pavement. Butterflies, including high-brown fritillary, are abundant, and wild animals can often be seen in the woods, notably roe deer.

Of historical interest is the 'Pepper Pot', a Jubilee monument, and an old woodman's or fisherman's cottage.

ACCESS: By minor road; network of paths.

PARKING: Small car park.

FACILITIES: Facilities at Silverdale; leaflet; viewpoint; picnic site.

ENNERDALE

6000 acres (2428 ha), excluding Kinniside Common, approached from the W off minor roads from A5086 via Ennerdale Bridge, Cumbria
[89:NY093164]

The difficult access to Ennerdale protects it from over-visiting, and it remains one of the more secluded and quiet valleys. Great Gable, Pillar, Steeple, Haycock and Red Pike, some of the highest peaks in the Lake District, rise above Ennerdale Forest (Forestry Commission) which dominates the valley towards the east.

The Trust manages land around Ennerdale Water above the Forestry Commission land, as well as Kinniside Common, a bleak expanse of fell. As with Wastwater, the lake is of interest for its purity and low nutrient levels, and provides an important habitat for char, Crustacea and unusual plants. The poorly drained mire adjacent to the lake is rich in invertebrates and damp-loving plants.

The damp, western broadleaved woodlands, notably Side Wood, of sessile oak and upland birch abound in mosses, lichens and ferns, and on the crags, in the gills and on rock ledges are mountain plant communities which include saxifrages, alpine lady's mantle and heather. The region also contains an interesting expanse of heathland, illustrating the gradation in vegetation from lakeside margin through broadleaved woodland to heather moor. A huge re-walling project has recently been completed to separate this valuable heath from the overgrazed and grassy Kinniside Common.

Of historical interest are a neolithic settlement on Kinniside Common and medieval settlement patterns. There is a long history of bloomeries and iron-ore mining in the area.

ACCESS: No vehicle access beyond Bowness Knott car park; network of footpaths; circular walk round lake.

PARKING: Limited parking; Forestry Commission car parks; North-West Water car park.

FACILITIES: WCs at Bowness Knott car park; youth hostels; no camping.

ESKDALE

4235 acres (1714 ha) reached by minor road from A595, 2m N of Broad Oak to Hardknott Pass on the road to Little Langdale, Cumbria [89:NY3201]

A significant Roman military road follows this remote valley from Ravenglass to Ambleside, with the remains of the Hardknott Roman fort (not owned by the Trust) dominating the head of the valley. The varied terrain reflects the difference in the underlying rock structure, with the crags, screes and corries of the upper Esk of volcanic rocks, and the whale-back fells in the lower stretch of coarse-grained granite.

Before the establishment of the National Park, Eskdale and the Duddon Valley were part of a great controversy, with plans to plant large areas of fell with conifers; as a result it was agreed that in order to retain the open character of the landscape the central fells should not be planted. Drystone walls enclosing intake and in-bye fields are typical of the area; grey stone (volcanic rock) is more common but red-stone (sandstone) walls occur further down the valley. The river follows a sinuous course in places, bordered by old wooded banks and single holly trees creating characteristic features. Dipper and grey wagtail are typical of the birds to be seen along the river, and buzzard, peregrine and kestrel are common. The ravines have interesting relict woodland vegetation and plants that have escaped grazing by sheep (saxifrages, alpine lady's mantle, wood sage, heather and unusual ferns).

There are a number of herb-rich meadows with plants such as greater burnet, betony, knapweed, ox-eye daisy and a variety of grasses. On the fells, a number of valley mires and bogs support interesting mosses, grasses and sedges. The white downy heads of common cotton grass are quite distinct, and bog asphodel, sundew, butterwort, cross-leaved heath and marsh cinquefoil are also found.

The monasteries of Fountains and Furness held granges with extensive sheep walks in this area of the Lake District, and a medieval wall can still be seen at the valley head, defining the boundary of the monastic sheep farm. Also of historic interest is the Boot corn mill and the Woolpack Inn (neither are owned by the Trust) where the Fell Dales Sheepbreeders' Association (formed in 1864) holds its annual show on the last Saturday in September.

Eskdale retains evidence of the iron-ore mining industry, and visitors may enjoy a trip on the Ravenglass & Eskdale Railway, known locally as the 'Ratty', which started as an iron ore line in 1875.

The Trust owns all the land east of Penny Hill Farm (part of the Beatrix Potter bequest) to the Three Shires Stone, east of both Hardknott and Wrynose passes, arguably the most dramatic road in the Lake District.

ACCESS: Via narrow road from west; road from east over Hardknott and Wrynose Passes always impassable to caravans and to all vehicles in winter; network of footpaths, particularly around Boot; Ravenglass & Eskdale Railway (operates all year).

PARKING: Lay-by at Hardknott; informal parking.

FACILITIES: Local facilities.

GRASMERE

6677 acres (2702 ha), access off A591 and minor roads, Cumbria
[90:NY337077]

Approached from the north over Dunmail Raise, the picturesque landscape around Grasmere is an impressive sight, with heaps of glacial debris, drumlins and *roche moutonée* (a glaciated type of rock surface) littering the U-shaped valley of the River Rothay, which flows down to Lake Windermere.

To the west, the Trust protects Grasmere Common, descending to Loughrigg Fell and including Grasmere Lake, and to the east the estate extends up to Seat Sandal and Fairfield, then down to White Moss Common and the southern half of Rydal Water. Here, in a condensed version of other grander valleys, Wordsworth's village is surrounded by a varied landscape which includes a number of small lakes, areas of broadleaved and coniferous woodland, scree slopes and lichen-covered crags, drystone walls skirting the fells and bracken-covered commons crossed by many footpaths. There are historic pack-horse routes over the fells.

Grasmere and Rydal in particular are important for overwintering wildfowl, and goosander, red-breasted merganser, pochard, common sandpiper and grey wagtail can be seen. There are many different aquatic plants in Rydal Water, and the reed beds provide a good habitat for small nesting birds. A variety of rare snails and insects live among the tussocks of sedges and rushes, which form excellent stands of fen along the lake edges where there is no grazing.

The higher fells are covered predominantly by grassland and bracken, but with some fine stands of juniper, and the narrow ravines support relics of woodland with rowan, ash, birch and many mosses and ferns. The islands in Rydal Water (only Little Isle is owned by the Trust) have interesting examples of ungrazed ancient woodland, with small-leaved lime as well as later-introduced exotics.

ACCESS: Network of footpaths; open access to fells.

PARKING: Car parks in Grasmere and White Moss Common.

FACILITIES: WCs (including disabled) in Grasmere and White Moss

Common car park; information board at White Moss Common; no camping; boating and fishing facilities (further information from regional office).

THE LANGDALES

1060 acres (429 ha) W of Ambleside, from A593 and B5343 to Elterwater and Little Langdale, Cumbria [89:NY2906]

Dominated by the magnificent Langdale Pikes, Pike O'Bisco and Crinkle Crags, the two valleys of Great and Little Langdale have quite distinct qualities. Great Langdale, a sweeping, glaciated valley with steep, rugged sides and an ice-scoured wide, flat bottom, provides direct access to the surrounding fells. Little Langdale, a smaller valley with less dramatic landscape, is ideal walking country, a combination of rough fells, undulating valley floor, isolated tarns, meadows and a patchwork of woodlands.

The Trust's estate includes part of Great Langdale east of Millbeck and all the valley to the west, extending over to Little Langdale, south of Blea Tarn, together with the land around and including Little Langdale Tarn.

There is a wide variety of historical interest within this ancient landscape, with the 'Thing Mount' (the remains of a Viking parliamentary site), slate farmhouses with bank barns dating from the seventeenth and eighteenth centuries, and a thirteenth-century stone wall surrounding the head of Great Langdale.

The plants of the fell tops reflect the acid soils, heavy grazing pressure and underlying volcanic rocks. A thick mat of purple moor grass, wavy hair grass, mat grass and fescues covers most of the tops. Bogs and mires occupy damp hollows, with *Sphagnum* moss, common and hare's tail cotton grasses, butterwort, common sundew, and many sedges and rushes. Juniper scrub reaches high levels on the fellside. Only small areas of heather have survived.

The ravines support interesting woodland relict and montane communities, with saxifrages, alpine lady's mantle, wood sorrel, wood anemone and heathers. Elterwater Tarn (not owned by the Trust) and Little Langdale Tarn are valuable sites for wildfowl and goosander, and breeding sites for little and great crested grebes.

Throughout the summer swallow and swift swoop and feed over the water, and the surrounding reed beds, carr and woodland attract many nesting birds including nuthatch, tree creeper and warblers. A number of hay fields still have a wide range of flowers and grasses (betony, ox-eye daisy, cuckoo flower, heath spotted orchid, great burnet, wood crane's bill and lady's mantle).

ACCESS: By road (narrow roads unsuitable for caravans and congestion to be expected in Little Langdale); network of footpaths and bridleways; open access to fells.

PARKING: Car parks where signed; lay-bys; no parking on roadside or in gateways.

FACILITIES: WCS at Elterwater, Chapel Stile and Stickle Ghyll; information boards in car parks; viewpoint from Blea Tarn towards Langdale Pikes; canoeing; camping.

NOTE: No boating or fishing permitted on Elterwater or Little Langdale Tarn. The south screes are dangerously unstable because of erosion.

SANDSCALE HAWS

651 acres (263½ ha) 3m N of Barrow-in-Furness, off A595 Dalton to Askam road, Cumbria [96:SD1875]

Sandscale Haws is one of the best sand-dune systems in Britain. Within its very extensive area there are dunes of varying ages, from newly forming ones nearest the sea, high 'yellow dunes' with marram grass, to old stable grass-covered dunes inland. It also has a superb series of slacks, or wet depressions between the dunes. A large freshwater marsh with willow scrub behind the dunes, and developing saltmarsh on the foreshore add further valuable habitats.

The calcareous sand of the dunes and the slacks supports an exceptionally rich flora, with over 450 plant species recorded, including several orchids such as the rare coral-root orchid. The freshwater marsh has different species, such as yellow flag, meadowsweet, and numerous sedges and rushes. It is important, with the grassland behind, for nesting waders.

Sandscale has a thriving population of the rare natterjack toad. A

245

special pool has been constructed near the car park so that visitors can see the toads and hear the remarkable call of the males on evenings in April and May.

The Duddon Estuary is of international importance for its bird-life, with shelduck, mallard, merganser, eider duck, goldeneye, cormorant, dunlin, redshank, grey plover and ringed plover. Along the shoreline, plants able to establish themselves in the constantly changing conditions created by the tidal system include sandwort, sea rocket, saltwort, sea campion and knotgrass.

Grazing is essential for maintaining the rich flora of the dunes, slacks and grasslands. Some small fenced enclosures in the slacks, erected in 1970, illustrate what the effects of cessation of grazing would be.

Sandscale Haws holds a key to the importance of this coastal stretch throughout history. Stone axes from the Langdale axe factory sites have been retrieved from the area, and the word Sandscale comes from the Scandinavian *sandra* (beach) and *skali* (hut); *haws* is a Norse word for hills. Evidence of iron workings can be found over much of the area but in particular at Nigel Pit, next to the car park.

ACCESS: Bridleway along coast; Cumbria Coastal Way; Hawthwaite Lane leading to beach.

PARKING: Car park, signed Roan Head.

FACILITIES: Shop and WCs at car park; information board; leaflet; disabled access from car park to beach.

NOTE: There are dangerous gullies in the estuaries; check tides before venturing too far.

SILVERDALE: BANK HOUSE FARM, GEORGE'S LOT AND JACK SCOUT

82 acres (33 ha) 7m NW of Carnforth, W of Silverdale; 7m NW of Carnforth, 1m S of Silverdale, Lancashire   [97:SD460752 and 459737]

Bank House Farm is a working, organic farm set in an attractive situation overlooking Morecambe Bay and the salt marshes of the Kent Estuary. The surrounding farmland is crossed with light-grey limestone walls, reminiscent of the Yorkshire Dales, and a number of the fields are bordered by layered hedges. The whitewashed house has an unusual window facing the coast, through which it is thought a guiding light would shine for travellers crossing the dangerous sands.

Morecambe Bay is of international importance for its birdlife, with the biggest population of overwintering waders in Britain. Here it is fringed by clifftop grasslands and grazing marshes, lying within the shelter of a wooded limestone escarpment. The grassland supports flowers such as common rock rose, sea fern grass, hawkweed, crested hair and quaking grasses, small-leaved cotoneaster, green-winged orchid, autumn lady's tresses and a field of daffodils as well as some unusual whitebeams. Several small plantations provide shelter and additional tree cover; the wood between George's Lot and the grazing marsh includes oak, ash, wych elm and a few specimens of the rare Lancaster whitebeam.

Jack Scout is a wooded limestone cliffline on the southern point of the Silverdale peninsula, overlooking the Wharton Sands of Morecambe Bay, and was the first coastal property north of the River Ribble to be owned by the Trust. There are impressive views across the bay from the 'Giant's Seat' at the highest point.

The richness of these limestone habitats, with notable pockets of limestone pavement, woodland and grassland, make this an ecologically important site, and of historical interest is an old lime kiln, recently renovated by the Trust and now experimentally fired.

A varied scrub woodland of ash, birch, holly, hazel, juniper, yew, oak and guelder rose creates dense thickets in places, and soft-shield fern, lords and ladies, wood anemone and wood sorrel are among the many flowers to be found on the woodland floor. A number of self-coppiced small-leaved lime are of note. The grassland, which has been invaded by gorse and bracken in parts (now being cut and controlled) supports limestone-loving flowers and grasses, including crested hair grass, blue moor grass, salad burnet, carline thistle, small scabious, lady's bedstraw and early purple orchid.

ACCESS: From Silverdale; footpaths along cliffline and crossing Bank House Farm.

PARKING: Informal parking off road (avoid blocking gateways or lanes).

FACILITIES: Information panel at Jack Scout.

THE STUBBINS ESTATE

*436 acres (176½ ha) W of Stubbins, 5m N of Bury, 1m N of Ramsbottom,
each side of B6214, Lancashire*   [109:SD785177]

Perched above the Irwell Valley, this walled, improved pasture-
land links the industrial Pennine communities of Rossendale with
Holcombe Moor, a bleak open moorland typical of the Lancashire
Pennines. The countryside is made up of deeply incised and wooded
valleys, pastureland, low moorland and rushy hollows, characteristic of the acid soil overlying the Millstone Grit.

In the cloughs beech, oak and birch woodlands provide valuable
cover for a number of birds. There are several small areas of unimproved herb-rich grassland, and curlew, meadow pipit and skylark can be heard calling over the rough tussocky upland grassland
during the spring and summer months.

A network of footpaths crosses the farmsteads overlooking the
valley and leading up to the moorland. The buildings and drystone
walls are built from local gritstone and some farm buildings date
back to the seventeenth century.

ACCESS: Footpaths; Rossendale Way (route established by Ground-
work).

PARKING: Informal parking.

FACILITIES: Local facilities.

ULLSWATER

*12,500 acres (5059 ha) SW of Penrith, N of Windermere on A592 running
along N shore of lake, Cumbria*   [90:NY386170]

The second largest lake in the Lake District, Ullswater follows a
sinuous course along a glaciated valley with classic features such as
upland tarns, ridges, U-shaped valleys and screes. The Trust estate is
concentrated around the head of the valley at Brotherswater and to
the north and west of the lake around Glencoyne Wood, Park and
Farm, Gowbarrow Park and Aira Force (impressive waterfalls surrounded by a pinetum and landscaped parkland).

Beyond the steep valley sides lie the imposing fells of Helvellyn, Fairfield and Great Dodd. This historic landscape was divided into manors in medieval times, and has been strongly influenced by the large estates. Farming has continued to be the main land use, as can be seen from the traditional farmhouses, hogg houses and walls dating from the sixteenth century. Glencoyne Farmhouse dates back to at least 1629. There is probable evidence of medieval deer parks at Gowbarrow and Glencoyne.

Ullswater has a literary link with the poet Wordsworth: after a walk along the shore of the lake he wrote, 'I wandered lonely as a cloud'.

It was the success of the Trust in acquiring a stretch of shoreline at Gowbarrow that started a more concerted effort in preserving the beauty of the valley. The increased numbers of nesting birds, including goosander and cormorant on the lake are a result of limiting the use of power boats. Brotherswater is also of great value to over-wintering wildfowl, and the marginal reed vegetation attracts many breeding birds. Buzzard, raven and red grouse are also seen in the area.

The area contains a variety of other wildlife habitats of great interest. On the fell tops and mountain sides a good range of upland plants can be seen, including saxifrages, northern bedstraw and sedges. Dry and wet heaths occur in pockets, with heather, bilberry, *Sphagnum* moss and common and hare's tail cotton grasses. Excellent ancient woodlands and wood pastures occur above Brotherswater and at Glencoyne, Glencoyne Park and Gowbarrow. The last site includes some very fine old ash, elm, oak, yew and small-leaved lime. The oak woods are rich in mosses, ferns and lichens. This is a good area for red squirrels.

ACCESS: By road; network of footpaths and bridleways; steamers run on Ullswater (seasonal); station at Penrith.

PARKING: Car parks and lay-bys.

FACILITIES: Facilities at Glenridding and Patterdale; WCs at Glenridding, Aira Force and Patterdale; information boards at Cow Bridge car park (N of Brotherswater) and Aira Force; NT information vehicle at Aira Force (seasonal); caravan and camping sites; boating and fishing facilities (for further information contact regional office).

WASDALE

17,298 acres (7000 ha), access from A595(T) via minor roads NE of Santon Bridge, Cumbria [89:NY162066]

Wasdale is one of the few seemingly wild areas left in the Lake District, quiet, remote, yet dramatic. Wastwater, England's deepest lake (Arctic char still survive in the pure and nutrient-poor waters), is bounded on the south-east by impressive scree slopes (the main area of dramatic scree is from Whin Rigg to Illgill Head), and some of the highest peaks in the Lake District (Scafell Pike, Great Gable, Great End and Red Pike) form a striking horseshoe around the head of the valley, their grey shapes and steep fans of unstable scree reflected in the calm surface of the lake. With the exception of the 139 acres of Bowderdale Farm (over which it has covenants) the Trust owns all the valley land, including the 1000-acre Nether Wasdale Estate, the bed of the lake and all the surrounding fells. Wasdale Hall, at the foot of Wastwater, is let to the Youth Hostels Association.

The flood plain of Lingmell and Mosedale becks at Wasdale Head has an especially notable pattern of drystone walls, some several feet thick, while the screes are of particular importance for plants including dwarf juniper, alpine lady's mantle, purple saxifrage and a number of rare mountain plants.

The area contains a large expanse of upland grassland and grassy heath with mountain flowers and mosses. Bogs and mires are found in the hollows, with damp-loving plants such as sundew, cotton grasses, sedges and yellow mountain saxifrage.

Like much of the Lake District, the area contains a great deal of historic interest, with Bronze Age cairns, Iron Age and Roman settlements, and prehistoric field patterns.

ACCESS: By one road only (no through road); well-marked footpaths and bridleways; open access to fells.

PARKING: 3 NT car parks.

FACILITIES: Facilities in local villages; WCs at Wasdale Head; NT camp site; youth hostel; boating facilities (for further information contact regional office).

WINDERMERE

2356 acres (953 ha) on W side of B5286 Ambleside to Hawkshead road, on E side of A591, Cumbria
[89:SD397911, 90:NY414010, 90:SD410998, 96 and 97:SD404958 and
396964, 96:SD386951, 97:SD422996 and 424995]

In the centre of the Lake District, this is probably the busiest and most heavily populated valley. More mountainous in the north, it opens out to a wide lake, ten miles long, with sheltered bays, wooded islands and knolls, many in Trust ownership. The wildlife interests of the lake are threatened by pollution and disturbance from boating and water-borne leisure activities and are the subject of constant reviews by the Trust, together with the National Park Authority and various conservation organisations.

The Trust owns some of the most secluded, wooded shoreline and valley side along the west shore, from Wray Castle through Arthur's Wood, Heald Wood, Belt Ash Coppice to the ferry-crossing point to Windermere. From the early Middle Ages the coppice woodlands of oak, ash and alder clothing the lake's shore were cultivated for the production of charcoal, especially by the monks of Furness Abbey (the old monastic courthouse still stands near Hawkshead).

On the islands of Rampholme and Lady Holme are ungrazed broadleaved woodlands with an inland cormorant roost, and other important wildlife sites include Skelghyll Wood, an ancient woodland on base-rich rocks which contains snails and insects characteristic of its antiquity; Wansfell Pike, east of Ambleside which commands good views across the lake; Borran's Field (the site of the remains of a Roman fort) which has some important reed-beds with a wide range of plants, including rushes, marsh bedstraw, purple loosestrife, sneezewort, greater burnet, marsh marigold and bur reed. The woodlands along the east shore include ash, yew, oak and hazel, and good numbers of small-leaved lime trees.

The local farmland has some excellent traditional hay meadows, rich flushes and pastures, all with a very rich flora, and the lake itself is an important site for a variety of overwintering wildfowl which congregate in undisturbed sanctuaries, including pochard and tufted duck and the strikingly-marked goldeneye. Coot, moorhen, common sandpiper, goosander and mute swan can be seen along the shoreline.

Cockshot Point near Bowness-on-Windermere and Queen Adelaide Hill are popular and easily accessible sites on the shore of the lake, and nearby Troutbeck, with its village and farms centred on the stream of the same name, is well worth a visit. The farmhouse of Hill Top at Near Sawrey, between the lake and Esthwaite Water, was the home of Beatrix Potter and the setting for many of her stories. The house was bequeathed by her to the Trust in 1944.

ACCESS: Network of footpaths; access to lake by boat (several boat-hire companies); station at Windermere, and Lakeside and Haverthwaite Railway connected to Windermere station by boat trip across lake.

PARKING: Car parks at Ambleside for Borran's Field and Skelghyll; Wray Castle and Belle Grange for west shore; Bowness and Windermere for Cockshot Point and Queen Adelaide Hill.

FACILITIES: Facilities at Ambleside, Bowness, Waterhead and Windermere; café, WCS, rowing-boat hire; NT camping at Low Wray; NT Country Park at Fell Foot, near Newby Bridge; boating and fishing facilities (for further information contact regional office).

North-East England

COUNTY DURHAM · NORTHUMBERLAND
TYNE & WEAR · NORTH AND WEST YORKSHIRE

Extending from the remote, expansive hills of the Cheviots in Northumberland bordering with Scotland to the familiar limestone plateaux of the Yorkshire dales, this region holds some of the gems of the wilder English landscape, much of it protected as National Parks, AONBs and Heritage Coastlines.

A significant part of the Northumbrian Heritage Coastline is protected by the National Trust; the Farne Islands off the coast are a great refuge for the many nesting seabirds and seals.

The most famous archaeological spectacle is Hadrian's Wall. In its former glory it extended right across the island from the Solway Firth to Wallsend, east of Newcastle. The Trust owns some outstanding stretches of the Wall and fortifications, and has been central in a programme of excavation and consolidation with its own team of archaeologists. Typical Northumberland farmhouses bear witness to a pattern of farming over the centuries; agricultural development now poses a threat to the wealth of mires, raised and valley bogs, rough grassland, carrs and loughs which represent some of the richest wildlife habitats in the area. Remote from any major con-urbations, this seemingly immutable landscape has faced threats from extensive military use, afforestation, reservoirs and now the possibility of oil exploration.

Durham is a county of contrasts. The upper reaches of the Wear and Tees unfold into Pennine dales with characteristic whitewashed farmhouses, drystone walls, herb-rich meadows, relics of its industrial past and Wesleyan chapels located in the most remote of places. The Durham coastline has suffered in the past from the dumping of tons of colliery waste and sewage on the beaches. The Trust has recently acquired a large proportion of this popular coastline to ensure that the wildlife interest is protected and to demonstrate that it wants to make itself accessible to urban locations.

Overlooking the industrial backbone of England – Teesside and the south Pennine dales – the Yorkshire moors are best known for their unique heather, which in August and September covers the exposed tops. This peculiar habitat has resulted from changing land use and management. In some areas it is wet and boggy, elsewhere dry, resulting in a diverse wildlife interest. The grey and green landscape of the Yorkshire dales is characterised by the outline of the limestone plateaux, most notably around Malham: drystone walls, farm buildings and isolated field barns, flower rich hay meadows, prominent rivers, green lanes and ancient trackways. Once larger estates became smaller after the Dissolution of the Monasteries and the fragmentation of great medieval holdings. Dairy farming has shaped much of the landscape as well as grouse management on the higher moors, and these changing agricultural practices and the focus of local communities have changed the emphasis of the Dales landscape.

ALLEN BANKS AND STAWARD GORGE

500 acres (202 ha) 3m W of Haydon Bridge, ½m S of A69, near junction of Tyne and Allen rivers, Northumberland   [86 and 87:NY799630]

Surrounded by the characteristically exposed Northumbrian landscape, the River Allen, a tributary of the Tyne, carves its way through a deep ravine clothed in mature deciduous woodland. Most of the trees were planted during the eighteenth and nineteenth centuries when a large part of the property was laid out as 'wilderness' walks for Radley Hall. There are some conifer plantations.

A network of paths leads through the varied woodland of beech, oak, sweet chestnut, sycamore and ash, and a suspension bridge crosses the brown, peaty water of the river, offering the chance to catch sight of a dipper or grey wagtail flitting down the gorge. A longer walk, with beautiful views of the meadows and moorland, leads out on to the open landscape of the North Pennines.

Staward Gorge, to the south in the Allen Valley, contains the dramatic ruins of the SAM of Staward Pele, a medieval fortified tower-house and gateway. There are also extensive remains of old lead and coal mining with spoil tips, adits and old trackways.

The great variety of ground flora, including wood anemone, ferns, ramson and bluebell, suggests that parts of the woodland are of ancient origin. A number of mature trees are covered in lichen. Red squirrel, once holding its own in the north of the country, is becoming increasingly rare, but roe deer are common and the woods are some of the most northerly where nuthatch breed. Among the conifers, the high-pitched calls of goldcrest, tree creeper and coal tit can often be confused. The damp atmosphere of the ravine leads to mosses shrouding the rocks and dead wood.

ACCESS: Open all year (donation box); main entrance at northern end of property; footpaths including one from south side at Plankey Mill.

PARKING: Car park in old kitchen garden.

FACILITIES: WCs; 2 information boards; guided walks; picnic facilities; no caravans, coaches or camping.

BELLISTER

1120 acres (453 ha) S of A69, both sides of Haltwhistle to Alston road, Northumberland   [86:NY699631]

The ruins of Bellister Pele Tower and Castle, once the hub of a large agricultural estate, are prominent features of this historic countryside near Hadrian's Wall.

The varied soil-cover on the property gives rise to an interesting flora, and wildlife habitats range from open rough pasture and moorland to improved pasture and mixed woodland. A number of interesting earthwork remains have escaped modern agricultural improvement.

ACCESS: Footpaths; access to pele tower by written appointment with tenant.

PARKING: Informal parking.

FACILITIES: Leaflet for Hadrian's Wall walks; Burnside camp site.

BRIDESTONES MOOR, BLAKEY TOPPING AND CROSSCLIFF

1237 acres (501 ha) 12m S of Whitby, 1m E of A169, via toll road through Dalby Forest Drive, N. Yorkshire [94:SE8791]

Steeped in local folklore and legend, the Bridestones are curiously shaped ancient sandstone stacks rising above the moor (an SSSI managed by the Trust as a nature reserve). They overlook a landscape of heather moorland dissected by steep-sided ravines or 'griffs'. The heather was once more extensive, but agriculture and forestry over the past few decades have considerably changed the landscape.

Blakey Topping, the geological curiosity of a heather-covered conical hill rising above a sea of forest, stands to the east adjoining Crosscliff Moor. Both Bridestones and Crosscliff contain important heath communities, under pressure from changing land use.

Heather, crowberry, bilberry, sedges, grasses, mosses and lichens grow in the mixture of wet and dry heath on the open moor, and of particular interest are the pockets of mature heather which ensure the regeneration of this essential habitat for its associated insects, birds and lichens. Emperor moth feed on the heather, and can be seen occasionally, with lizards and slow worms found in the open patches. Maidenhair and black spleenworts, and wall rue grow in the rock crevices. The slopes are peppered with birch and rowan. The moor is being managed to protect the heath from fire, and to control scrub and bracken encroachment.

The ancient oak woodland of Dovedale Wood has a lush growth

of mosses, ferns, primrose, dog's mercury and honeysuckle, and birds such as greater spotted woodpecker, great tit and redstart can be seen. The dale grasslands have a rich flora and fauna, with grazing and mowing now established for their protection.

The Forest Drive follows the course of the Staindale Beck to the south of the property, which is bounded by forest to the east. Of historical interest are some prehistoric barrows hidden among the heather of Grime Moor.

ACCESS: Via Forestry Commission toll road; open access to moors; permitted paths to Blakey Topping and Crosscliff Moor; North Yorkshire Moors Railway runs from Grosmont to Pickering (seasonal).

PARKING: Forestry Commission car park off Dalby Forest Drive at Staindale Lake; car park at the Hole of Horcum.

FACILITIES: WCs and picnic site (Forestry Commission); NT information panel; leaflet (from Low Dalby Forest Centre); guided walks; viewpoint.

BRIMHAM ROCKS

387 acres (156½ ha) 8m SW of Ripon off B6265, 10m NW of Harrogate off B6165, N. Yorkshire [99:SE2165]

High on a windswept escarpment above Nidderdale, Brimham Rocks and Moor are a combination of spectacular rock formations (of national geological importance) dating back to prehistoric times and rugged heather moorland designated an SSSI, providing rich habitat for an array of plant and animal life.

Brimham House, built as a shooting lodge in 1792 and now housing an information centre and National Trust shop, is by virtue of its prominent position on the hillside the perfect spot to view the property and surrounding countryside.

The moor is dominated by ling and bell heathers, and bilberry is also present in large quantities. The less common cross-leaved heath is found in the wetter areas, as are bog asphodel, cranberry and the insectiverous sundew.

Grouse, snipe and curlew are frequently seen on the moorland, whilst jackdaw predominates in the main rock area and red deer can occasionally be seen. Pheasants, willow warbler, green woodpecker and chiff-chaff can be heard in the wooded areas.

Evidence suggests that the area was once heavily wooded, and natural regeneration still occurs, with silver birch, rowan, oak and crab apple present. Holly trees on the edge of the escarpment attract the holly blue butterfly, a rare visitor to Yorkshire.

ACCESS: Open access to moors; footpath to rocks; Nidderdale Way long-distance footpath passes through; stations at Ripon and Harrogate.

PARKING: Car parks at property entrance (no parking on roadside).

FACILITIES: NT shop and information centre in shooting lodge; refreshment kiosk (seasonal opening); WCS (including disabled); wheelchair access to rocks; leaflet; guided walks.

CAYTON BAY AND KNIPE POINT

88 acres (35½ ha) 3m S of Scarborough, E of Osgodby, N. Yorkshire
[101:TA063850]

The popular beach of Cayton Bay is sheltered by the sandstone headland of Knipe Point to the north, and surrounded by impressive cliffs and areas of landslip which create a wide range of interesting habitats in this SSSI, with herb-rich grassland, scrub, woodland, pools and wet flushes. Extensive woodland and grassland management schemes are being undertaken to improve the nature conservation interest.

The woodland on the drier upper slopes contains bluebell, ferns, orchids, wood avens and red campion, and on the grassland grow harebell, small scabious, yellow rattle, grass of Parnassus, woolly thistle and orchids. Meadowsweet, angelica, butterwort, sundews and sedges are found in the wet flushes.

ACCESS: Access to beach through woods; steps to the south; Cleveland long-distance footpath; station at Scarborough.

PARKING: Car park ½m S, off A165.

FACILITIES: Local facilities.

CRAGSIDE ESTATE

1000 acres (405 ha) 1m NE of Rothbury on N bank of River Coquet, off
B6344 Morpeth to Rothbury road, Northumberland [81:NU073022]

Situated in the secluded valley of the Debdon, a tributary of the
River Coquet, and surrounded by wild Northumbrian moorland,
is an unusual pleasure ground created by Sir William Armstrong,
the extraordinary Victorian inventor, engineer and industrialist
from Tyneside.

Established originally as a weekend retreat, and subsequently a
country mansion, the romantic and picturesque house stands on a
heathery hillside which was transformed into a park by planting
expanses of conifers (including some unusual varieties in the pinetum below the house) and rhododendrons, and the laying out of an
elaborate network of carriageways, footpaths and bridges. Streams
cut their way through deep ravines, with steep banks softened by
luxuriant ferns, which give glimpses of naturally wooded concealed
valleys.

Armstrong used his knowledge of engineering to create five large
lakes which supplied water, hydraulic power and hydroelectricity
for the house (Cragside was the first house in the world to be elec-
trically powered in this way); he built roads, dammed streams and
cleared the heather and scrub wilderness to plant a very large rock
garden and more than seven million trees, mostly conifers. These
woodlands harbour many birds, including woodcock, spotted and
pied flycatchers, wood warbler, siskin and tree pipit.

Sparrowhawk soar overhead, and red squirrel, roe deer and adder
can also be seen. There are still some remnants among the trees of the
former heathland cover, with plants such as heather (including the
cross-leaved species), bilberry and purple moor grass. Flocks of
goldcrest, tit and finch inhabit the conifers, young pioneer birch
woodland and rhododendron scrub. Some species of bat, including
the rare Leisler's, are found in the old buildings and trees. On the
moors above Cragside Woods seventy Bronze Age barrows can be
seen.

The long-established wetland vegetation (fragrant agrimony is
among the more unusual plants) beside the lakes attracts various

birds and insects, including dragonflies. Dipper are common along the streams, where it is possible to find plants associated with the old woodland.

ACCESS: House, garden and grounds open seasonally; entrance on Rothbury to Alnwick road; permitted paths; 40 miles of footpaths; bus service from Morpeth and Newcastle, alight Reivers Well Gate.

PARKING: Car and coach parks.

FACILITIES: NT shop and restaurant; WCs (including disabled); visitor centre; leaflets and guidebook; information centre and boards; power centre with tour of restored hydraulic and hydroelectric machinery; adventure playground; pinetum; rock garden and formal Victorian garden; concerts; guided walks; Tumbleton fishery; fishing pier; viewpoints suitable for wheelchairs.

CRASTER, EMBLETON LINKS AND LOW NEWTON-BY-THE-SEA

756 acres (306 ha) on coast between Craster and Beadnell, off A1 via B1339, Northumberland [75:NU258220, 236417 and 243235 to 243240]

This estate includes some of the finest scenery along the Northumberland coast, from the busy fishing village and kippering centre of Craster, with a sweep of grassland leading up to the spectacular ruins of the fourteenth-century Dunstanburgh Castle (under the guardianship of English Heritage) on an outcrop of the great Whin Sill, the precipitous cliffs behind, and much of the coastal strip as far as Newton Point on the other side of Embleton Bay.

There are some important historical remains, including interesting earthworks around the castle, with a medieval or post-medieval farmstead and impressive relics of former open-field cultivation preserved under permanent pasture, and some evidence of Romano-British settlements. Near Craster are the buildings of a Second World War radar station, part of the country's first early-warning system. There is also a Rocket Life-Saving Apparatus Post, used in the past to train the local volunteer life-saving brigade and once a common feature of all rocky coasts.

Embleton Bay, another potential landing beach, was heavily defended in the Second World War, and there is an interesting collection of wartime pillboxes which have survived by chance because the demolition squads were refused access across the golf course.

At Newton Pool and Point are remains of some probable post-medieval farmsteads or cottages, and at Low Newton, a picturesque eighteenth-century planned fishing village with a natural harbour protected by an offshore reef, there is a nineteenth-century coastal lookout (now a holiday cottage owned by the Trust).

The property includes a variety of habitats supporting a wide range of wildlife. The freshwater Newton Pool is a nature reserve of special ornithological interest which attracts many species including migrants, waders and breeding birds with sedge warbler and reed bunting in the fringes. It also harbours some interesting invertebrates. Snipe and water rail are attracted by the open pond margins, and short-eared owl breed in the area. The cliffs of the Whin Sill are home to sea birds such as fulmar, shag and at least 700 pairs of kittiwake. Eider duck inhabit the rock pools.

The castle is surrounded by herb-rich limestone grassland, with purple milk-vetch, field madder, spring squill, wild thyme, bloody crane's bill and clover. The sand dunes also support a variety of plants, with the newer ones stabilised by lyme and sea couch grasses. In the grassland between the established dunes grow bloody crane's bill, restharrow, burnet rose, harebell and primrose, with common butterwort and tufted centaury in the damp patches.

Newton Links, in the centre of Beadnell Bay, has an important series of coastal habitats which support dwarf mallow, orchids and burnet rose among the fine dune sward. A colony of Arctic tern, protected during the breeding season, just manages to survive here. The tidal zone, with its important beach and rock habitats, and the marine environment beyond are of great ecological interest and are protected as a marine nature reserve.

ACCESS: Footpaths.

PARKING: Car parks at Low Newton (vehicle access to Low Newton Square restricted to residents only), Craster and Embleton.

FACILITIES: WCs (including disabled at Craster) at all 3 sites; leaflets; information panels; guided walks (details from regional office); birdwatchers' hide at Newton Pool with access for wheelchairs (available from Warden).

THE DURHAM COASTAL PROPERTIES: NOSES POINT TO LIME KILN GILL

400 acres (162 ha) 5m S of Sunderland, 15m SE of Newcastle-upon-Tyne, Durham　　　　　　　　　　　　　[88:NZ437480 to 455408]

The Trust acquired these properties with a view to reclaiming the landscape from the scarring caused by mining over the years. With its raised beachlines, wooded denes or valleys, floristically rich magnesium limestone grassland and extensive broadleaved woodland, the area is of great ecological interest.

It includes Beacon Hill, the highest point on the Durham coast and used as a navigation aid for shipping from the Middle Ages, with impressive views across to the Pennines and along the coast. Some mesolithic worked flint has been found, and there is evidence of old field systems around the hilltop, with the remains of two post-medieval farmsteads.

Hawthorn Dene is one of the most extensive and varied areas of broadleaved woodland on magnesium limestone in the county. There is an eighteenth-century lime kiln on the beach and the ruin of a nineteenth-century coastguard station above the valley. The remains of Hawthorn Towers house and garden include an old greenhouse and boathouse. Blue House Farm is also of interest, and some old field boundaries can be seen. The acquisition of Warren House Gill near Easington marks a major landmark for Enterprise Neptune. Given for a nominal fee of £1 by British Coal in 1987, it was the 500th mile of coastline to come to the Trust. Now, more than one in every six miles of coastline in England, Wales and Northern Ireland is owned by the Trust.

There are some possible First World War clifftop trenches, and a Second World War pillbox at the head of the beach. A dramatic nineteenth-century railway viaduct (not owned by the Trust) crosses the dene and is still in use.

Despite the impact of industrial activities, the area has a wide range of wildlife. The woods are made up of ash, oak and sycamore, with alder, yew, wych elm and hornbeam also present. Foxes and roe deer can be seen, with birds such as kestrel and long-eared owl. Bluebell, wood anemone, cuckoo pint, ramson and sanicle flourish. The grassland includes the unusual dyer's greenweed, a small shrubby plant with narrow leaves and yellow flowers, so called because of its use over the centuries as a source of dye.

On the exposed clifftops the limestone vegetation is influenced by its closeness to the sea, and wild thyme, bloody crane's bill, rock-rose and pyramidal orchid can be found. There is a wide variety of sea birds, including fulmar and kittiwake. A number of damp fen areas, a scarce habitat in the county, add to the wildlife interest of the properties.

ACCESS: Via Easington on rough dirt tracks; network of footpaths from Easington Colliery, Hawthorn and Seaham, and along cliff-top; Durham coastal path.

PARKING: Small car park near Fox Holes Dene.

FACILITIES: Local facilities; line fishing from coast.

THE FARNE ISLANDS

81½ acres (33 ha) 2–5m off coast opposite Bamburgh, Northumberland
[75:NU230370]

The Inner and Outer Farnes are two in a scatter of about thirty virtually uninhabited basalt islands (an AONB and Heritage Coast) separated from the mainland by Inner Sound. They are renowned for their early Christian and medieval monastic settlement (the enclosure is an SAM), their history of shipwrecks, and their immense wildlife interest. The Farne Islands are accessible by boat only, and visits are dependent on weather and sea conditions.

Inner Farne, the largest island, is the site of St Cuthbert's hermitage in the seventh century, and the fourteenth-century chapel (restored in 1848) built in his memory can still be seen. The fifteenth-century pele tower, once used as a lighthouse burning coal on the roof, now houses the Farne Islands Bird Observatory (the islands have been protected as a nature reserve, and now a sea-bird sanctuary, since 1925). The island supports a wide variety of flowering plants.

There is also a nineteenth-century lighthouse (not open to the public), and on Brownstone Island the ruin of another coal-burning lighthouse and its replacement stump which was succeeded by the Longstone Lighthouse, made famous by Grace Darling who rescued survivors from the wreck of the *Forfarshire* in 1838. There are also some old ridge and furrow cultivation terraces, now obvious only from the air.

A good range of birds can be seen, with the cliffs of the resistant Whin Sill (encased in lichen and in places eighty feet high) used by thousands of breeding birds. More than twenty species have been recorded, with 6000 pairs of kittiwake, 12,000 pairs of guillemot and a smaller number of razorbill. Four species of tern (common, Arctic, roseate and Sandwich) arrive for the summer breeding season, and are famous for their dive-bombing of sightseers between mid-May and early July, as they protect their nests and young. Some 26,000 pairs of puffin nest in burrows and eider breed in any suitable habitat.

Atlantic grey seal, which can be seen all year round lounging on the rocks, use the islands as a breeding site in the autumn, with the pups born between October and December.

ACCESS: Seasonal, depending on weather, by boat daily only to Inner Farne and Staple Island from Seahouses (landing fee not included in boatmen's charges); footpaths.

PARKING: Car park in Seahouses.

FACILITIES: NT shop and information centre in Seahouses; WCs (including disabled) on Inner Farne; nature walks on Inner Farne; disabled access possible on Inner Farne, not recommended on Staple Island; local station at Chathill and bus service connecting Seahouses with trains.

NOTE: Hats advised mid May to early July when terns can be aggressive.

GIBSIDE

*14 acres (5½ ha) 7m SW of Newcastle, 20m NW of Durham, off B6314,
Tyne & Wear*   [88:NZ172583]

The core of the Gibside Estate was laid out by Sir George Bowes from 1720–1760, and is one of the finest surviving eighteenth-century landscapes in the North East. Trust ownership is restricted to the chapel, a fine 1760s Palladian building by James Paine, and the Avenue or Great Walk, which is lined with giant Turkey oaks and forms the principal axis of the grounds, designed by 'Capability' Brown.

The (dangerous) ruins of Gibside Hall and its orangery can still be seen, with the walled kitchen garden, stables and banqueting house.

In recent years seasonal access to a larger area has been agreed with the landowners, with a long circular walk allowing visitors to see from close up the striking statue to British Liberty, which stands on a column higher than that of Nelson's in Trafalgar Square. The walk returns along the River Derwent.

The parkland and the extensive woodlands, with recent plantings now reaching maturity, are of interest for their variety of wildlife, and an eighteenth-century plantation of beech, oak, ash and sycamore is an additional refuge for birds and mammals including red squirrel.

ACCESS: Open seasonally; circular walks and permitted footpaths; woodland walk; local station at Blaydon.

PARKING: Small car park.

FACILITIES: Shop; tea-room; WCs (including disabled); guided walks; picnic area in car park.

HADRIAN'S WALL ESTATE AND HOUSESTEADS FORT

2247 acres (909 ha) 4m NE of Haltwhistle, 2½m N of Bardon Mill on
B6318 (the Military Road), Northumberland   [87:NY790688]

Marching along the precipitous outline of the Whin Sill, Hadrian's Wall is a spectacular reminder of the Roman occupation of Britain. The wall was constructed between AD122 and 125 as the northern most frontier of the Roman Empire, to defend against the unruly tribes from the north. Flanked with a ditch and vallum (earth rampart), at intervals along the wall are milecastles and forts, one of the best-preserved of which is Housesteads, owned by the Trust and under the guardianship of English Heritage. The wall is a World

Heritage Site, an sssi and sam, and lies within the Northumberland National Park.

The Trust owns some four miles of the central sector of the wall, and has carried out much work over recent years in excavating, recording and consolidating the structure and two of the milecastles, which have suffered from erosion caused by the many visitors. It is also carrying out an archaeological survey of the estate alongside the wall.

While the history of the world-famous wall, which is seventy-five miles in length and links Wallsend with the Solway Firth, is well documented, the countryside around is often overlooked. Isolated farmsteads, in-bye fields enclosed by gritstone walls, expanses of grassy moorland, alder carr, shelter belts of windswept trees, damp hollows (mires) and glacial lakes include a range of habitats with associated wildlife.

The lakes offer a refuge for overwintering wildfowl; teal and tufted duck are common. The luxuriant, well-developed heathland and fen communities are the remains of shallow glacial lakes where the high rainfall and impeded drainage has resulted in a patchwork of *Sphagnum* moss concealing rare and beautiful plants and invertebrates. The open water, marsh, fen, raised bogs, alder carr and damp grassland supports an interesting range of plants, such as unusual sedges, grass of Parnassus, early marsh orchids and stag's horn club moss. The crags of the Whin Sill contain a rich flora which includes mountain male and parsley ferns, fir club moss, woodrush and a variety of lichens.

There are spectacular views across the open landscape to the Pennines in the south, and to the Kielder and Wark forests in the north.

ACCESS: Wall and Housesteads Museum and Fort open all year; shop and information centre open seasonally; path along wall; stations at Bardon Mill, Hexham and Haltwhistle, and seasonal bus service from Hexham and Haltwhistle stations.

PARKING: Car parks at Housesteads, Steel Rigg and Cawfields.

FACILITIES: Shop and refreshments at Housesteads; WCs (including disabled) at Housesteads car park; information centre at Housesteads (seasonal opening); Roman Wall display in information centre; leaflets; National Park centre at Once Brewed; guided walks by NT and National Park Authority.

HARDCASTLE CRAGS

430 acres (174 ha) 1½m NW of Hebden Bridge, off A6033, 5m NW of Todmorden, W. Yorkshire [103:SD988291]

In the heart of the Pennines the two wooded valleys of Hebden Dale and Crimsworth Dean lead down from Heptonstall and Wadworth moors. Hardcastle Crags, weathered stacks of gritstone, overlook a woodland of oak, birch, beech and rowan surrounding Hebden Water. On the south-facing slope is 'Slurring rock', where children used to slide down on wooden clogs carved out of alder or 'clog' wood. The local names, old mill ponds, stone packhorse routes ('causeys') and Gibson Mill (a former water-powered spinning and cotton-weaving mill) are evidence of the industries that once dominated the valleys. There are also some charcoal-burning platforms and remains of an old railway used in the construction of the reservoirs on the moors above.

A network of way-marked walks leads through the woods, along traditional paths and beside Hebden Water. Many of the woods have individual names, such as Foul Scout, Shackleton and High Greenwood, and old records suggest that part of the area is ancient woodland, although most was planted in the nineteenth century. Carpets of bluebells cover the ground in spring, and birds such as greater spotted woodpecker, tree creeper, spotted and pied fly-catchers and tawny owl have been recorded.

Piles of pine needles camouflage the chambers and tunnels of wood-ant nests. Gnawed cones are signs that squirrels are present, and although mostly grey, red squirrel can also be found. Dragonflies, grey wagtail and dipper are seen along the river.

Bilberry, ling and purple moor grass grow on the rough moorland on the valley sides and at Blakedean at the head of Hebden Dale.

ACCESS: Network of way-marked footpaths.

PARKING: 2 car parks.

FACILITIES: Facilities at Hebden Bridge; leaflet showing 3 way-marked walks and routes of varying lengths; list of monthly guided walks; information caravan open weekends during season; main track accessible for wheelchairs, otherwise steep ground.

THE LEAS AND MARSDEN ROCK

296 acres (120 ha) E of A183 South Shields to Sunderland road, 10m E of Gateshead, Tyne & Wear [88:NZ388665]

The 'flagship' of this property is now the recently acquired light-house complex at Souter Point, an example of what was in its hey-day a technologically very advanced aid to navigation just south of the busy entrance to the River Tyne. It also provides a focus for what is otherwise open clifftop space, although in the past there was a colliery village close by. The region has become famous through the novels of Catherine Cookson.

At the north end of the property there has been extensive lime-stone quarrying at Trow Point, and there are some remains of nine-teenth-century coastal defences with the mounting for an experi-mental 'disappearing gun' (it is hoped that a replica of this will be displayed), and the site of a gun battery overlooking Frenchman's Bay. There is also an impressive array of lime kilns from the nine-teenth and twentieth centuries next to Souter Lighthouse, the first lighthouse to be powered by alternating electric current.

The area has a long history based on fishing, and points of interest include the eighteenth-century Grotto Pub, and a cave in the cliff which was once inhabited by a hermit.

The stretch of unspoilt coastline with its broad band of grassland was given to the Trust in 1987 by South Tyneside Metropolitan Borough Council, and is famed for its classic features of coastal erosion. The natural rock arches, stacks, caves and platforms, with cliffs and bays carved from the limestone, are a haven for sea birds, with nesting ledges for fulmar and more than 5000 pairs of breeding kittiwake. Divers and guillemot can be seen offshore.

Marsden Bay is recognised as one of the most important main-land sites for breeding colonies between the Tweed and the Tyne, and Marsden Rock is particularly popular, with nesting cormorant which have been increasing in numbers since they were first seen to use the stack in 1955.

The rocky and sandy foreshore is rich in marine life, and purple sandpiper and turnstone can be seen darting across the rocks. The cliffs and grassland support a wide variety of plants such as cowslip, burnet saxifrage, thrift, sea plantain, rock-rose, wild thyme, small scabious and autumn gentian.

ACCESS: Open access; footpaths.

PARKING: 4 car parks.

FACILITIES: Local facilities; WCs at Marsden car park; restaurant, information, shop and video display at Souter Lighthouse (seasonal opening); steps and lift to shore; viewpoint; guided walks.

MALHAM TARN ESTATE

4187 acres (1694 ha) 6m NE of Settle in Upper Craven, midway between Ribblesdale and Wharfedale, N. Yorkshire [98:SD8966]

Malham Tarn, England's highest freshwater lake, lies within the classic limestone landscape of the North Yorkshire dales, and is an SSSI internationally important for the associations of wildlife based on the calcareous water draining from the surrounding rock. It is a nature reserve managed jointly with the Field Studies Council.

Trapped in a bowl of impervious shale, the tarn is bordered by willow carr, fen and raised peat bog which support a wide range of damp-loving plants, including cranberry, cloudberry, bog rosemary, cross-leaved heath, *Sphagnum* moss, round-leaved sundew, bog asphodel and meadowsweet. Great crested grebe, common sandpiper and coot nest along the shores.

The extensive estate includes expanses of typical karst scenery, a limestone pavement of clints and grikes (rock fissures), dry valleys and coves, and open moorland on the overlying blanket of peat. Ferns and lime-loving plants thrive in the fissures, and wild thyme, bird's foot trefoil, mountain pansy, eyebright, sedges and bird's eye primrose form a tight sward over the limestone outcrops. Blue moor grass and green spleenwort grow on the rocky ledges.

Kestrel and peregrine may be seen hunting, and the woodlands provide valuable shelter for birds. Upland breeding birds include curlew, lapwing, redshank, wheatear and golden plover.

A web of drystone walls covers the landscape, and evidence of prehistoric cultivation. There is also an old metal-smelting mill and a drovers' road.

ACCESS: Footpaths and bridleways cross tenanted land; Pennine Way long-distance footpath; Yorkshire Dales cycle path.

PARKING: Car park at Malham; informal parking.

FACILITIES: WCs at Malham; leaflet from regional office; guided walks; birdwatchers' hide at north-west corner of tarn; wheelchair access along estate road from Streetgate to Waterhouses.

THE MARSDEN MOOR ESTATE

5685 acres (2301 ha) W, S and E of Marsden, 8m SW of Huddersfield, both sides of A62, W. Yorkshire   [109 and 110:SE0210 and 0611]

Extending from Buckstones Moss in the north to Wessenden Moor in the south, this estate consists of large sweeps of bleak, undisturbed moorland dissected by steep-sided valleys or cloughs. The southern part falls within the Peak District National Park, and part of that within the North Peak ESA. The moor is divided into 'mosses', each with individual names; it is suffering from erosion caused by atmospheric pollution from the neighbouring cities, 'accidental' burning and the effects of the large numbers of grazing sheep.

The area contains much of archaeological and historical interest. The line of Standedge Canal Tunnel, an impressive nineteenth-century engineering feat which runs under the property, is marked by its construction shafts. There is a pre-Roman settlement, and a Roman road. In addition there are packhorse tracks and three old turnpike roads.

A blanket of peat covers the moor, waterlogged in the heavy rainfall, which provides an ideal habitat for mosses, heather and moorland grasses, including *Sphagnum* moss, cross-leaved heath, sedges, cotton grass and bog asphodel, as well as many birds of prey and breeding waders such as curlew, golden plover and lapwing. Summer visitors include whinchat, stonechat and wheatear, and skylark and meadow pipit can be heard overhead.

In the drier areas heather, grasses, bilberry and lichens cover the ground, and the steep valleys that have escaped heavy grazing are rich in ferns, mosses, sedges and bell heather.

ACCESS: Registered commonland; open access on foot.

PARKING: Car parks at Buckstones Edge and Wessenden Head; road-side parking.

FACILITIES: Leaflet; Tunnel End Canal and Countryside Centre with displays and information; information caravan open season-ally; guided walks.

ROSEBERRY COMMON

306 acres (124 ha) 8m SE of Middlesbrough, Cleveland

[93:NZ575124]

A popular venue for a day out, the striking angular form of Rose-berry Topping (a geological SSSI) rises above the Cleveland Hills, and is partly owned by the Trust along with Roseberry and Newton Commons, Newton Wood (an important expanse of natural oak woodland) and Cliff Ridge Wood.

Roseberry Common, part of the North Yorkshire Moors National Park, is dominated by bracken, although sheep-grazing is now being introduced. There are many archaeological remains, including some Bronze Age burial mounds, and the local names reflect the early Norse settlements in the area. There is a history of ironstone and whinstone mining.

Newton Wood is of particular interest for its birds, with greater spotted woodpecker, sparrowhawk, pied flycatcher and tawny owl. Great woodrush and wood sorrel are some of the many woodland plants.

The bent pinnacle of the Topping, which is over 1000 feet high, provides panoramic views across Cleveland to the North Sea. It is covered with a thick mat of coarse grasses and pockets of poorly developed heather. Mosses and sedges flourish in the damp flushes. Many of the paths are now suffering from erosion.

ACCESS: Network of footpaths; Cleveland Way long-distance foot-path. North Yorkshire Middlesbrough–Whitby line, nearest station at Great Ayton (good views of Topping from train).

PARKING: Car park.

FACILITIES: WCs; information panel; Captain Cook Monument (not NT) E of Great Ayton.

ST AIDAN'S AND SHORESTON DUNES

60 acres (24 ha) 2m SE of Bamburgh, just N of Seahouses, Northumberland
[75:NU204335]

This stretch of the sweeping Northumberland coast (an AONB and Heritage Coast) has magnificent views across to the Farne Islands, north to the dramatic profile of Bamburgh Castle two miles up the coast, and west to the Cheviot Hills.

A narrow ridge of dunes and rough dune grassland backs the foreshore which is of a considerable extent at low tide. The dunes are dominated towards the sea by the coarse spikes of marram grass, with a more varied range of plants inland. Wild clary and purple milk-vetch are among the more unusual, together with the typical dune grassland plants of rock-rose, restharrow, burnet rose, common centaury, sand sedge, harebell, bird's foot trefoil and lady's bedstraw.

Monk's House, which marks the northern boundary of the property, was once the mainland store house and ferry landing stage for the monks of the Farne Islands. Also of interest is an old lime kiln north of Seahouses and linked to the town by a disused railway line.

ACCESS: Open access; footpaths; local station at Chathill.

PARKING: Car park at Seahouses; informal parking on verges.

FACILITIES: NT shop, information centre and WCs at Seahouses; signs explaining dune restoration.

STAINTONDALE AND ROBIN HOOD'S BAY

860 acres (348 ha) 15m N of Scarborough on A171, N. Yorkshire
[94:NZ980013]

Lying within the North Yorkshire Moors National Park, these crumbling cliffs of sandstone, shale, limestone and ironstone (a Heritage Coast and SSSI) are of considerable botanical interest, with habitats ranging from dry heath and bracken, scrub, woodland and wet flushes. Herb-rich grassland covers the open crags.

The variety of flowering plants provides food for many bees, hoverflies and other insects, and birds such as stonechat, whinchat and linnet nest in the dense scrub. Part of the commonland is well-wooded, with a rich flora of sweet woodruff, mosses and ferns including soft-shield fern (at Hayburn Wyke). Spotted flycatcher and tree creeper are among the many woodland birds.

Much of the spectacular clifftop farmland is protected by the Trust. The fields of Bay Ness Farm run down to the cliffs overlooking Robin Hood's Bay to the north, and Rigg Hall Farm, between Hayburn Wyke and Ravenscar, also includes more than 1000 yards of cliffline. Hayburn Wyke is an attractive small bay with delightful walks through woodland, a nature reserve and a stream tumbling down to a boulder beach above the impressive undercliff of Beast Cliff (not owned by the Trust).

At Bay Ness, the steep hillsides and incised valleys include some grassland with many herbs and wild flowers, and the cliffs are used by nesting sea birds such as fulmar, herring gull, kittiwake and cormorant. Boggle Hole is a steeply incised inlet in the middle of Robin's Hood Bay, and from Bay Town there are impressive views of the headland of Ravenscar with its cliffs of eroded sandstone, gently sloping undercliffs and rough cover of scrub, heath, grassland and bracken.

The vegetation partly conceals old brickworks and quarries where shale was extracted during the sixteenth century for the alum used in fixing dyes and curing hides. The remains of alum works are now being consolidated by the Trust and represent the best surviving example in the country of this early chemical industry – an important monument to a way of life which once dominated this strip of the North Yorkshire coast.

ACCESS: Via Cleveland Way long-distance footpath; access by car to Ravenscar and Robin Hood's Bay; network of footpaths; bridleway and cycle path along disused railway line (owned by Scarborough District Council).

PARKING: Car parks at Robin Hood's Bay and Ravenscar; roadside parking.

FACILITIES: Shop and NT coastal centre at Ravenscar; WCs at Ravenscar and Robin Hood's Bay (town); 2 information panels beside Cleveland Way explaining alum industry.

UPPER WHARFEDALE

5200 acres (2104½ ha) N of Grassington, both sides of B6460, N. Yorkshire
[98:SE9477]

This large estate lies in the valley of the River Wharfe, within the Yorkshire Dales National Park, and is part of the Pennine Dales ESA. The attractive landscape of pale grey limestone outcropping crags, drystone walls and vernacular buildings is offset by green pastures, herb-rich meadows, wooded slopes and moorland. There are some prehistoric field patterns and remains of old lead mines.

Those river valleys that have escaped agricultural improvement support a variety of lime-loving plants, such as ox-eye daisy, yellow rattle, betony, knapweed, sedges, self-heal, orchids and many grasses.

The gill woodlands are particularly important for their rich bryophyte flora. Historical evidence, and studies of the lichen and invertebrate communities have shown that parts of the valley have been managed as pasture-woodland for centuries.

In the woods ancient oaks, ash, wych elm, hazel, bird cherry, rowan, holly and birch can be seen, and the ungrazed ledges on the crags are rich in mosses, ferns and tall-herbs. Above the valley sides the plateaux are covered in peat, with the resulting grassland and peat bogs of particular interest for their plant and bird communities.

ACCESS: Marked footpaths; Dalesway long-distance footpath; access across tenant farms by footpath only.

PARKING: Car parks at Kettlewell and Buckden.

FACILITIES: National Park interpretative material; guided walks.

THE WALLINGTON ESTATE

13,500 acres (5463½ ha) 12m N of Morpeth, 6m N of Belsay, E of A696 Jedburgh road, 1m S of Cambo off B6342, Northumberland
[81:NZ030843]

This superb estate spans several parishes, with evidence of a complex sequence of past agricultural and industrial landuse reflected in the varied landforms and the increase in elevation away from the Wansbeck Valley. It includes the extensive grounds, partly the work of 'Capability' Brown (who was born nearby and went to school on the estate), of a grand eighteenth-century sandstone country house, the former seat of the Trevelyan family. There is a fine conservatory in the walled garden, grandiose landscaped grounds with artificial lakes, enclosed farmland with small woodlands, sheltered river banks and exposed moorland beyond.

Two newly established walks lead across the estate, beside the river and along disused railway lines. There are views into Redesdale, to the slopes of Simonside and the Cheviot Hills to the north.

The woodlands around the house have good breeding populations of tree creeper, pied flycatcher, summer migrants and nuthatch (this is their most northerly breeding area). The woods next to the river are of interest for riverside birds such as grey wagtail, dipper and kingfisher.

The reduction in grouse-shooting has led to the deterioration and decline of the heather moors, but a number of unimproved meadows have a rich flora which includes the melancholy thistle, globeflower and northern marsh orchid.

The landscape holds much of archaeological interest, with many hundreds of sites dating from the Bronze Age to the recent past, including some SAMs. Of interest is the eighteenth-century Paine's Bridge (not owned by the Trust) over the Wansbeck, two prehistoric camps, old lime kilns and milestones, and the village of Cambo (now a conservation area), which was built as a model village in 1740 and is still almost unchanged. The oldest building, a medieval fortified vicarage, is now the post office, and there are some attractive houses and farmhouses. Winter's Gibbet, near Harwood, is a stark reminder of past events.

ACCESS: House open seasonally; grounds open all year; walks round estate open June to October (Wannie Line and Greenleighton Moor Walks); extensive network of rights of way; station at Morpeth and bus service from Newcastle.

PARKING: Car park at house.

FACILITIES: NT shop and restaurant; WCs (including disabled); leaflets; information centre; grounds and terrace of walled garden suitable for wheelchairs.

Northern Ireland

COUNTY ANTRIM · COUNTY ARMAGH · COUNTY DOWN
COUNTY FERMANAGH · COUNTY LONDONDERRY

Northern Ireland is blessed with remarkable diversity for such a small area – from the granite peaks of the Mourne Mountains and the wooded Glens of Antrim, to the famous bizarre shapes of the basalt columns of the Giant's Causeway, the flooded drumlin landscape of Strangford Lough and the spectacular Fermanagh lakeland.

The landscape has its origins in a strongly agricultural past, and the low level of urbanisation and industrialisation has left the countryside largely unspoilt. One of the most important historical relics is the Iron Age hill farmsteads or raths. Over 600 still exist today, showing how the land was cleared of woodland for subsistence farming.

The English and Scottish planters of the early seventeenth century radically influenced the traditional farming, leading to the establishment of grand estates, with demesnes or large manor houses surrounded by parkland and farmland as in England.

Ireland's extremity on the north-west of Europe has influenced the diversity of plants and animals – the number of plants present is half that of Britain, there are no snakes, Tawny Owls or wood-peckers and trees such as hornbeam, maple, lime and beech are not native. Records show that in 1650 no more than three per cent of the whole of Ireland was covered by woodland.

Fermanagh is a county of lakes and hills enjoying a moist and clean atmosphere dominated by the Atlantic. Limestone escarpments harbour a varied community of plants, while the hollows are rich bogs, marshes, loughs and fens. A plateau of basalt juxtaposed with white chalk dominates the land form of County Antrim leading to spectacular coastline and a diversity of wildlife habitats. Floristically rich grasslands, once a common sight along the coastline, have now suffered the same fate as farmland in England and Wales with increased agricultural activity. This in turn has affected populations of the rare chough that feed and nest along the clifftops and coastline, reliant on traditional farming practices to survive. The Giant's Causeway is heavily visited, its spectacular beauty recognised in its designation as a World Heritage Site. The Causeway coast continues as a series of headlands and intervening bays with small communities strung out along the coast.

Strangford Lough is a gem of Northern Ireland – internationally important as an overwintering site for thousands of waders and wildfowl, and its tidal waters support abundant marine life. The Mourne Mountains, with their core of twelve peaks, the highest being Slieve Donard, can be seen for miles – a granite landscape incised by deep ice-formed valleys.

THE ARGORY

315 acres (127½ ha) 4m from Moy on Derrycaw road, 3m from Junction 14 of M1, Co. Armagh   [H872580]

Overlooking the River Blackwater, this house dating from 1824 is an example of the lifestyle of the Irish gentry during the nineteenth and early twentieth centuries. The original gas lighting can still be seen.

Beyond the lawn and yew arbours, woodlands of oak (including evergreens), beech and sycamore cover much of the estate. Some of these, particularly in the south, contain interesting plants such as wood sanicle, common dog violet, lords and ladies, and yellow pimpernel, although rhododendron and laurel are causing problems by overshadowing the woodland floor. Willow warbler, wood-cock, jay and chaffinch are some of the many woodland birds.

Argory Moss, a raised bog partially cut over for peat, is a valuable wetland rich in mosses, including *Sphagnum* moss, heather, notably the cross-leaved variety, lichens, cranberry and sedges, managed jointly by the Trust and the Ulster Wildlife Trust. The encroaching birch and Scots pine will need repeated clearance. The drainage ditches which lead to the river support many flowers and are the haunt of dragonflies (nine species have been recorded). The peatland areas attract many moths such as emperor, pebble hook-tip, drinker, double dart and brindled beauty; lapwing, snipe and curlew can be seen feeding here and on the meadows.

ACCESS: Several walks around the house; Ulster Way along banks of the Blackwater; house open seasonally; station at Portadown and bus service from Portadown, alight Charlemont.

PARKING: Car park.

FACILITIES: NT shop and tea-room; WCs (including disabled); drive-ways and special parking for disabled; adventure playground.

BALLYKEEL, ISLAND MAGEE

36 acres (14½ ha) on outer east-facing shore of Island Magee, just south of Gobbins Cliffs, off B150, Co. Antrim [J485965]

This very attractive property, with its strong feeling of remote-ness, overlooks Scotland to the east and the Copeland Islands at the mouth of Belfast Lough. It consists of coarse semi-improved agri-cultural grassland, bracken-dominated grassland, landslip faces sup-porting some interesting flowers, and undercliff scrub. The rocky shore varies from eroding boulder cliff faces to outcrops of cret-aceous limestone, with small areas of boulder and shingle beaches.

A small part of the property is situated on the upper level of the basalt cliffs, accessible from a grass trackway leading to an old stone cottage. Two fields of coarse, cattle-grazed grassland lie near the house. At the northern end, furthest away from the cottage, the grassland is unimproved and more diverse in character, despite being colonised by bracken. Rose bay willowherb occurs in patches, with many primroses and a wide variety of grasses including false oat grass, cock's foot, creeping soft-grass, crested dog's tail and species of sedge.

There are several wet flushes, with small overgrown streams rising from the base of the cliffs, which support plants such as yellow iris, angelica, marsh thistle, meadowsweet and devil's bit scabious.

The face of the cliffs is mainly covered with thickets of fuchsia, blackthorn, elder and hawthorn scrub, with hazel now mostly confined to the northern end. Ash is one of the few trees in the area, and there is an undergrowth of brambles and ivy. Whitethroat are particularly numerous among birds breeding in the scrub.

Below the cliff face lies an uneven area of boulder clay, with semi-improved agricultural grassland and a small wet flush. Most of the land is accessible to grazing cattle, and in places is heavily poached. The boulder clay runs down to the shore, and sometimes forms undercut cliff faces at the top of the beach. These, and other small landslip features, support a rich and interesting flora, with kidney vetch, harebell, greater burnet-saxifrage, wild carrot, fairy flax, sea campion, eyebright, thyme, stonecrop, mouse-ear hawkweed, field scabious and lady's bedstraw. Six-spot burnet moths are abundant.

ACCESS: Pedestrian access only.

PARKING: Informal parking.

FACILITIES: Local facilities.

BALLYMACORMICK AND ORLOCK POINT

58 acres (23 ha) 1–3m NE of Bangor, off A2 on S side of entrance to Belfast Lough, Co. Down   [J525837]

This low rocky shore along the mouth of the lough, a nature reserve and ASSI, has escaped encroachment by nearby Bangor. A network of paths leads through rocky outcrops covered in maritime heath and gorse.

Common pearlwort, sea aster, wild thyme, spring squill, rock spurrey, buck's horn plantain, bird's foot trefoil, thrift and many other more common plants are scattered among the rough grassland and heath of the clifftop and in the rock crevices. Butterflies include the small heath, common blue and wall brown. Stonechat, rock pipit, reed bunting and linnet breed among the scrub and gorse, and there are large flocks of eider.

The property also includes areas of salt and freshwater marsh, as well as a tidal lagoon which attracts a number of migrant birds. The saltmarsh supports sea purslane (its northernmost occurrence in Ireland), lax-flowered sea lavender and saltmarsh flat sedge. In winter, cormorant and shag can be seen off the point, and turnstone, oystercatcher, purple sandpiper and greenshank are among the many waders feeding on the mudflats.

The low cliffs of cleft rock are interspersed with shingle and sandy beaches. Cockle Island in Groomsport Harbour, an attractive place full of boats and framed by whitewashed cottages, has the sixth largest breeding population of Arctic tern in Ireland. Throughout the summer months they can be seen screeching overhead and diving for sand eels.

ACCESS: Open access to saltmarshes; footpath along shore (poor in places), part of North Down coastal path; station at Bangor.

PARKING: Car parks at Groomsport and Ballyholme.

FACILITIES: Local facilities.

BARMOUTH

26 acres (11 ha) on S side of River Bann, 1½m E of Castlerock and 5m NW of Coleraine, Co. Londonderry [C792355]

The muddy sand and salt marshes of the Bann Estuary, sheltered from harsh weather by Portstewart Strand, a narrow strip of land on the south side of the estuary, are rich feeding grounds for waders and wildfowl, and the area is now protected as a bird sanctuary.

In spring and autumn Bar Mouth is an important refuge for migrating birds, and the river provides a passage in May each year for elvers making their way to Lough Neagh for the summer, to return by the same route fully grown in the autumn. In summer, salmon have for many centuries travelled upstream to spawn (remains of fish-bones have been excavated from a nearby mesolithic camp).

The estuary mouth is of great historic interest, with the oldest occupied sand dune site in Europe. Many ancient dug-out canoes have also been found in the river mud.

The saltmarsh is covered in the grey and green of sea aster, sea milkwort, common saltmarsh grasses and sea rush. From November to January lapwing, golden plover, dunlin, redshank, curlew and oystercatcher rest and feed, and offshore great crested grebe, merganser, shelduck, divers and auks can be seen. An ecologically important assortment of plants and insects flourish in an area where the saltmarsh merges with a freshwater marsh.

ACCESS: Open all year; access via path from car park to hide; station at Coleraine.

PARKING: Car park next to level crossing.

FACILITIES: Birdwatchers' hide with wheelchair access (key available from Warden).

CARRICK-A-REDE, LARRYBANE AND SHEEP ISLAND

99 acres (40 ha) 5m W of Ballycastle, 55m from Belfast, Co. Antrim
(D062450)

Gaelic for 'Rock in the Road' (the road is the path of salmon on their westerly migration to the Bann and Bush rivers), Carrick-a-Rede has been the site of a salmon fishery for many centuries. During the season fishermen sling a precarious rope bridge across the sixty-foot-wide and eighty-foot-deep chasm between the mainland and the Island.

Those bold enough to cross the void are rewarded with views of the sea-bird colony on the sides of the island. It is a site of complex and fascinating geology (designated an ASI) with some volcanic rock and chalk deposits.

Larrybane Bay, wide and backed by cliffs, links the headlands of Carrick-a-Rede and Larrybane Head. There are magnificent views from all the coastline around here, to the island of Rathlin and to the Hebrides beyond.

The craggy rocks, covered with guano, form ideal nesting sites for fulmar, kittiwake, razorbill and guillemot. Off Larrybane Head, Sheep Island (recently designated an ASSI) supports large numbers of sea birds, including cormorant, black guillemot and eider. A colony of house martin and swift nest in the old chalk quarry.

A number of enclosed fields and the clifftop grassland, particularly on the mainland, support some interesting coastal plants, with spring squill, harebell, kidney vetch and several species of orchid, although pressure from grazing is reducing the quality of the meadows.

Carrick-a-Rede is one of the earliest (and most famous) purchases by the Trust in Northern Ireland, bought with Enterprise Neptune funds in 1967.

ACCESS: From Larrybane only; rope bridge to island open seasonally in good weather.

PARKING: Car park at Larrybane.

FACILITIES: WCs; small visitor centre; picnics; disabled access; dogs on leads only.

CASTLE COOLE

423 acres (171 ha) 1½m SE of Enniskillen on A4 main Belfast to Enniskillen road, Co. Fermanagh   [H260430]

Built between 1789 and 1795, this massive white palace lies within a fine wooded parkland surrounded by a landscape of rounded hillocks with scattered small lakes. The park is influenced by the eighteenth-century English style of naturalistic landscaping.

The woodlands attract a number of unusual birds, with blackcap, long-eared owl and jay. The glades in Flaxfield Wood are particularly important for invertebrates, including a number of uncommon hoverflies. Flaxfield and Lough Yoan woods also contain some interesting plants such as twayblade and broadleaved helleborine. These damp deciduous woodlands are also rich in bryophytes and lichens.

Breandrum Lough and Lough Coole are important wetland habitats, with cowbane, an unusual umbellifer, growing along the lake margins. The surrounding damp grassland is dominated by yellow flag, and provides valuable insect food for the many dragonflies hovering about the alder carr, reed beds and fens. Lough Coole, the largest lake, has a varied shoreline with tussocks of sedge, bird cherry and spindle in the alder carr. Breeding ducks, red-breasted merganser and greylag geese inhabit the lough. A keen eye may spot the elusive water rail as it picks its way through the reeds, and curlew, snipe and lapwing can be seen on a small pocket of marshy grassland.

ACCESS: House open seasonally; grounds open to pedestrians all year during daylight hours (access for cars only when house is open); local bus service from Enniskillen.

PARKING: Car park (seasonal charge).

FACILITIES: WCs (including disabled) at visitor centre; picnics.

CASTLE WARD

794 acres (321 ha) 7m NE of Downpatrick, 1½m W of Strangford village on A25, on S shore of Strangford Lough, entrance by Ballyculter Lodge, Co. Down [J752494]

One of the great Irish country houses owned by the Trust, Castle Ward is located on the shores of Strangford Lough and was built on the site of the earlier fortified Old Castle Ward (the tower can still be seen). During the late nineteenth century it was the home of Mary Ward, a remarkable woman who pioneered the microscope as well as being a naturalist, astronomer and artist.

The Gothick façade of the house overlooks an eighteenth-century landscaped park in the English style, with beeches and oaks leading down to the water's edge. The old quay was used to export lead and import the coal used to fuel the gas lighting. There is also an old ice-house in the grounds.

The farmyard contains evidence of the once-flourishing agricultural estate, with a sawmill (driven by the water which fed Temple Water), barn, drying kiln and slaughterhouse. It was once a centre for the development of the linen industry and for innovative agricultural practices under Judge Michael Ward.

A number of walks, many in existence since the nineteenth century, lead through the farmyard to the woods of Old Castle Ward, and along the loughside past the square tower of the fifteenth-century Audley's Castle, built by an Anglo-Norman family.

The estate's close proximity to the lough and the variety of its landscape features have led to an interesting range of wildlife, although this has been reduced by large areas of improved pasture and conifer plantations. The blocks of woodland, which in spring are carpeted in bluebells, are important for birds, with butterflies and hoverflies in the clearings. Wood sanicle and enchanter's nightshade flourish on the woodland floor. Temple Water, a man-made lake north of the house, attracts a number of birds from the lough.

Plants such as white water lily, spiked water milfoil, mare's tail and broadleaved pondweed grow in the nine freshwater ponds, as well as in Temple Water. At Mallard Pond seven species of dragonfly have been recorded. A grassland at the end of Temple Water supports nipplewort, ox-eye daisy and common spotted orchid. There is also a colony of pipistrelle bats in the estate buildings.

ACCESS: House open seasonally; ground open all year during daylight hours; footpaths; bus service from Downpatrick to Strangford.

PARKING: Car park.

FACILITIES: NT shop and restaurant; WCs (including disabled); interpretation of house and estate in stable yard; educational study pack; guided walks organised by Wardens at estate office; headquarters of Strangford Lough Wildlife Scheme on estate (Strangford Barn); interpretation centre with audio-visual displays (seasonal opening); playground; Victorian pastimes centre; caravan site; base camp.

COLLIN GLEN

39 acres (16 ha) running from Glen road, 1m SW of Falls Road boundary of Belfast, to foot of Collin Mountain, Co. Antrim [J270720]

Contiguous with the west side of Belfast, the River Glen cuts a dramatic course through a great variety of rock types, descending in a series of impressive waterfalls between the Collin and Black mountains on the edge of the Antrim plateau. The glen is situated at the north-western upper end of the river, and the lower slopes have been developed by the local community as a linear country park.

The upper glen, owned by the Trust, can be reached on foot from the country park, and is now under negotiation to be included as a nature reserve.

Of particular interest to geologists, this richly wooded gorge contains one of the Trust's most important broadleaved woodlands in Northern Ireland, and is especially of benefit because of its close proximity to the heavily populated city of Belfast. Despite recent modification with the planting of non-native trees, evidence of the wood's ancient origin remains in the abundant and varied wildlife.

Beneath the beech, wych elm and oak canopy, the woodland floor is lush with ferns, sweet woodruff, wood sanicle, wood sedge, early dog violet and broadleaved helleborine, with shrubs of blackthorn, hazel, holly and ash. There is a variety of rare molluscs and beetles, only associated with such ancient woodlands.

Dipper, grey wagtail and kingfisher inhabit the course of the river, and the exposed rock faces of the gorge harbour many ferns, sedges, mosses and liverworts in the cracks and crevices. The silverwashed fritillary, rare in the east of the country, has been recorded.

ACCESS: Easily accessible from Belfast; network of well-made paths; access to river steep and difficult (impossible in places).

PARKING: Car park next to Glen Bridge.

FACILITIES: Viewpoints; limited access for disabled.

THE CROM ESTATE, LOUGH ERNE

1630 acres (660 ha) 3m W of Newtownbutler on the Newtownbutler to Crom road, Co. Fermanagh   [H36328, 361245 and 381232]

This romantic landscape of islands, wooded peninsulas and ruins (including Crom Castle and Crichton Tower) lies on and around the tranquil waters of upper Lough Erne. Areas of deciduous woodland on Inishfendra, in Reilly and Gole Woods (among many others) are of great nature conservation value for their extent, the range of structure and age of the trees, and the numbers of breeding populations of birds. The woods are rare in Ireland as ancient sites, and over the millennia have developed special wildlife interest.

Oak and ash dominate the woodlands, with hazel, holly and spindle forming a dense shrub layer below the canopy. Rare mosses and lichens cloak the trees and the woodland floor. Woodland herbs and flowers are abundant, with wild garlic, wood sanicle, wood goldilocks, violets, twayblade and early purple orchid.

The oak woodland is the only known locality in Northern Ireland for the scarce purple hairstreak butterfly. Spotted flycatcher, garden warbler, blackcap and tree creeper all nest in the woods, and there is a heronry among the trees on Inishfendra. Many mammals also make their homes in the woodland: badger, fallow deer and red squirrel can be seen.

Alder, willow and downy birch are common in the marshy fringes of the lough, with club rush, watermint, gipsywort, flowering rush, water horsetail, marsh marigold, yellow flag, yellow pimpernel and summer snowflake. Buckthorn, an uncommon shrub in Ireland, can be found along the lakeshore and provides food for the brimstone butterfly.

Great crested grebe are common; flocks of whooper swan feed on the improved pasture and cormorant roost in the winter months. The damp grasslands are important for breeding waders such as snipe, curlew and lapwing.

A study of the lichen and invertebrate communities has added to the national importance of the estate's historic parkland, wood pasture and lough shore, with the mixture of land and water leading to the many and varied habitats to be found. The area, which in many respects parallels the Norfolk Broads, is threatened by land drainage and agricultural pollution.

ACCESS: Crom Estate open seasonally; footpaths; bus service from Enniskillen–Clones (with connections from Belfast), alight Newtownbutler.

PARKING: Car park.

FACILITIES: WCs (including disabled); estate partly accessible to wheelchairs; nature trail; interpretation room with panels and guide to walks and trails; coarse fishing (day tickets by arrangement with Warden); picnics; dogs on leads only.

CUSHENDUN

64½ acres (26 ha) 23m N of Ballymena, on east Antrim coast, on B92
[D248327]

The picturesque village of Cushendun is a small settlement of slate-hung whitewashed cottages, lying in the shelter of Glen Dun where the river carves its way to the sea through one of the loveliest of the Nine Glens of Antrim, which dissect this wild, hilly countryside. The village has for long been a centre for poets and painters, and has attracted many legends and folk tales.

The Trust owns most of the village, with some of its buildings designed by Clough Williams-Ellis in the Cornish style as a memorial to Maud, first wife of Lord Cushendun. It also owns the dunes (an unusual feature on the east coast) which have unfortunately suffered from the effects of sand extraction and erosion, but they are now being restored under an innovative programme supported by the local community.

The ruins of Castle Carra are near the Regency house of Rockport, the childhood home of Moira O'Neill, the poet of the Glens, and about three miles from the village is a Bronze Age passage grave, said to be the burial place of the poet Oisin.

On the north side of the glen, Craigagh Wood conceals an old stone altar within the mixture of broadleaved trees and pines. Raised beaches and clifflines are evidence of a previously higher sea level.

ACCESS: Via an undulating road; footpaths.

PARKING: Car park in village.

FACILITIES: WCs (including disabled); dogs on leads only; picnics; wheelchair access.

DOWNHILL

141 acres (57 ha) 1m W of Castlerock, 5m W of Coleraine on A2,
Co. Londonderry   [C758363]

The ruins of the eighteenth-century Downhill Castle can still be seen on this bleak headland overlooking the Atlantic Ocean, and the rotunda of Mussenden Temple, built in 1785 by Frederick Hervey, the Earl-Bishop of Derry, stands romantically poised on the edge of the cliffs complete with its impressive ashlar stone Corinthian columns and domed roof.

Midway between the mouth of the Bann and Magillan Point, the site commands good views of Donegal, Portstewart Strand and the Antrim coast. A walled garden, dovecot, ice-house and storm-damaged mausoleum are further remains of an opulent lifestyle, although the headland is as dramatically wild as ever.

Remnants of the former heathland can be found among the farmland, and the maritime grassland of the clifftops is scattered with spring squill and heath spotted orchid. Sea birds such as fulmar and kittiwake nest on the cliffs. On the eastern border of the estate is a wooded glen with bluebell, wild garlic and ferns, which harbours spotted flycatcher, willow warbler, goldcrest and whitethroat. Jackdaw and tree sparrow inhabit the ruins.

ACCESS: Grounds open all year; temple open seasonally; footpaths through woods and along cliff; limited access for coaches; station at Castlerock.

PARKING: Car park next to entrance on main A2 road.

FACILITIES: Leaflet; picnics; facilities for disabled and paths through garden; dogs allowed on leads.

FAIR HEAD AND MURLOUGH BAY

764 acres (309 ha) 3m E of Ballycastle, Co. Antrim
[D185430 and 199419]

This exceptionally beautiful and wild stretch of coast (an ASI) has a great variety of landscape and wildlife. The sheer, volcanic cliffs of the Fair Head promontory contrast strongly with the chalk and sandstone landslips of Murlough Bay.

The haunt of peregrine, buzzard, raven and the increasingly scarce chough, Fair Head is a landmark for miles around, with a wide range of vegetation resulting from its varied geology. There is a spectacular and steep path, known as the Grey Man's Path, down the centre of the promontory.

The plateau is covered with the dry and wet heath and grassland typical of acid soils. The small heath butterfly is common on the moorland, and wood tiger and emperor moths feed on the heather. Meadow pipit, skylark, linnet and stonechat inhabit the scrubby heather and bog myrtle, and the emergent and marginal vegetation around the three small lakes includes bog bean, white water lily, lesser spearwort and marsh marigold. A carpet of sedges and mosses covers the surrounding hollows.

The wooded slopes of Murlough Bay are notable for their rare lichens, mosses and ferns, characteristic of this damp western climate. The 'hanging' woodlands are dominated by rowan, downy birch, ash and hazel, with great wood rush, Wilson's filmy fern and bilberry. Other woodlands important in the landscape are plantation woods of ash, sycamore and beech. Chiff-chaff and spotted flycatcher are among the many species of birds to be found in the woods.

Springs at the base of the cliffs are surrounded by damp-loving plants such as yellow flag, bog asphodel, bog cotton and *Sphagnum* moss. Damselflies and dragonflies dart over the damp hollows.

The chalk grassland in the south of the bay is rich with thyme, harebell, early dog violet and wild strawberry. The cliff scree is scattered with a number of rare plants such as spring sandwort, harebell, sheep's bit, bladder campion, stonecrop and St John's wort. Jackdaw, house martin, swift, rock and stock doves, kestrel and raven inhabit the cliffs, eider nest in the bay, and gannet dive off the shore. It is a good place to watch for whales, with occasionally pilots and killers as well as porpoises passing through the north channel into the Irish Sea.

Relics of the area's industrial past include scattered lime kilns, coal mines and derelict cottages. Also of historical interest is a late Bronze Age defence settlement in the centre of Lough Na Cranagh (not owned by the Trust).

ACCESS: Network of footpaths; circular waymarked path on Fair Head; paths in Murlough Bay.

PARKING: 3 car parks.

FACILITIES: Leaflet available from Causeway or Larrybane information centres; guided walks (contact regional office); picnic areas.

FLORENCE COURT

*388 acres (157 ha) 8m SW of Enniskillen, via A4 and A32 Swanlinbar road,
1m W of Florencecourt village, Co. Fermanagh*   [HI75344]

Celebrated for its elaborate rococo plasterwork, this impressive eighteenth-century house is situated against a backdrop of the imposing Cuilcagh Mountains. The surrounding parkland, designed by the Irish landscape gardener John Sutherland, is planted with clumps of oak, beech, sycamore, rhododendron and magnolia.

A saw mill, driven by a Victorian waterwheel, is a relic of the early woodland management. Other outbuildings include a forge and a carpenters' workshop. Whiskered bats and long eared bats are known to roost around the house.

Of particular interest for their wildlife, the damp, deciduous woodlands are contiguous with the Forest Park (managed by the Forest Service of the Department of Agriculture). The luxuriant lichen, fern and moss communities include many rare species, and a number of uncommon plants such as bistort and broadleaved helleborine flourish in the rides and glades. Blackcap, woodcock and long-eared owl are among the many birds, and silver-washed fritillary, a woodland butterfly, has been recorded.

Grasses, sedges and flowers border the paths around the estate, and the wetlands support breeding waders.

ACCESS: House and estate open seasonally; footpaths and bridleways; local bus service from Enniskillen.

PARKING: Car park at house; Forest Service car park by driveway.

FACILITIES: NT shop and restaurant; WCs (including disabled); wheelchair access to ground floor of house.

THE GIANT'S CAUSEWAY

*239 acres (97 ha) 9m from Portrush on B146 Causeway to Dunseverick
road, 2m from Bushmills, Co. Antrim*   [C952452]

Immortalised in Irish folklore and legend, this geological phenomenon is internationally renowned for its impressive columns of exposed layers of basalt, the result of volcanic activity millions of years ago, on the Antrim coast. Fanciful names such as the Giant's Eyes, Chimney Tops, Onion Skins and Amphitheatre reflect the unusual formations. The towering, sculptured pillars, mainly hexagonal in shape, create an imposing landscape which has now been designated a World Heritage Site, and is also an AONB, ASI and National Nature Reserve.

As well as the rock structure itself, there are some beautiful bays overlooked by headlands from which there are good views of the north coast and the Hebridean Islands. Port-na-Spaniagh, off Lacada Point, is the site of the wreck of the Spanish galleass *Girona* which sank in 1588 after the ill-fated Armada was dispersed.

Affected by sea spray and driving winds, the clifftop vegetation includes maritime heath and grassland, two habitats which support a range of plants such as heathers, mountain everlasting, heath spotted orchid, creeping willow, heath bedstraw and devil's bit scabious. Sea pink and bladder campion carpet the slopes, and the occasional delicate sky-blue flowers of spring squill can sometimes be seen. The scarce sea spleenwort also occurs.

The rocks are encrusted with lichens in shades of black, yellow and grey-green, and at the shady base of the cliffs woodland plants such as great woodrush, bluebell, wood stitchwort and red and white campion flourish. In the bays, wet flushes emerge from the cliff base, and grade to a mixture of sand, boulders and saltmarsh on the shore, which supports some rare northern plants such as oyster plant and Scots lovage.

The area is regionally important for its populations of breeding chough, peregrine, fulmar and buzzard.

The rocks have attracted tourists for many years, including famous travellers such as Sir Walter Scott, and in the eighteenth and nineteenth centuries they were studied by geologists trying to find out about the origins of the earth. In the past, seaweed was dried on the old stone walls, and burnt in crude kilns to produce a residue rich in potash and iodine which was exported to Scotland.

ACCESS: Open all year; network of footpaths along coast; start of North Antrim coastal path; station at Portrush and bus service from Portrush and Ballycastle.

PARKING: Car park with special area for disabled.

FACILITIES: NT shop and tea-room in visitor centre (owned by Moyle District Council); WCs (including disabled); leaflets; audio-visual displays; guided walks; mini bus with hoist for disabled; ramps.

KEARNEY AND KNOCKINELDER

43 acres (17 ha) 3m E of Portaferry, Co. Down   [J650517]

This property includes two miles of coastline looking towards the Isle of Man on the east side of the Ards Peninsula around the former fishing village of Kearney.

The green, rounded forms of drumlins (hills shaped by the retreating glaciers of the last Ice Age) give way to a plateau in the south and form a backdrop to the foreshore. Beyond the village, the coast includes cliffs, a low rocky foreshore, the eight-acre sandy beach of Knockinelder, and a small pocket of saltmarsh.

The path leads through lichen-covered slaty rocks and coastal grassland studded with spring squill on the promontories. The small, sheltered bays are made up of shingle and saltmarsh, with the yellow horned poppy, an unusual plant of the area. Breeding birds along the coast include oystercatcher, rock pipit, shelduck and stock dove. The dramatic white form of the gannet can be seen diving out to sea, and tern, eider and wintering waders are common. Turnstone feed around the seaweed-covered rocks.

ACCESS: Footpaths.

PARKING: Car park in village.

FACILITIES: WCs; information centre.

THE MOURNE COASTAL PATH

53 acres (21 ha) S of Newcastle, E of Mourne Mountains, Co. Down
[J389269]

Leading through heathland, scrub and across wet flushes, the coastal footpath runs along a rocky shoreline at the base of boulder clay cliffs, with views across Dundrum Bay to the Murlough Dunes and

St John's Point. The mountain path follows the Bloody River Valley, a narrow glen leading up to Slieve Donard with a breathtaking panorama. Another section of the path runs south from Bloody Bridge along the coast. Over the years, the Trust has acquired two miles of this very popular footpath.

The heathland is dominated by western gorse and bell heather which attracts a diverse population of invertebrates, including a number of grasshoppers and butterflies, with marsh fritillary feeding on the devil's bit scabious. Bog myrtle, black bog rush, bog pimpernel and pale and common butterworts grow in the wet flushes. Yellowhammer, now scarce in Ireland, have been seen on the heath, and the viviparous lizard, the only terrestrial reptile native to the country, is present but uncommon.

A boulder beach, where yellow horned poppy and oyster plant can be seen, runs from William's Harbour to Dunmore Head. The rocks are covered in lichen, with some maritime grassland. There is a small fulmar colony, and black guillemot breed in holes in the rocks. Tern, gannet, Manx shearwater and common seal can be seen offshore. St Mary's Ballaghanary, a Celtic church, stands on the clifftop.

ACCESS: Open access from A2.

PARKING: Car park at Bloody Bridge.

FACILITIES: Local facilities; WCs.

THE MOURNES: SLIEVE DONARD AND SLIEVE COMMEDAGH

1300 acres (526 ha) S of Newcastle, Co. Down [J365285]

The rounded granite masses of Slieve Donard and Slieve Commedagh form the highest peaks in the Mourne Mountains massif of south Down, which tower over the holiday resort of Newcastle, and true to the song really do 'sweep down to the sea'.

The Trust's holdings on the northern flanks of the mountains, together with the hills of Thomas' Mountain and Shan Slieve, are included in the Mourne AONB. The mossy heath of the summit is of particular interest, and the lower slopes support a wide range of montane vegetation, with rare flowering plants and ferns. In late summer these slopes are ablaze with purple heathers. The jagged cliffs of Eagle Rock, overlooking the infant Glen River, were the last Northern Irish home of the sea eagle.

Prehistoric burial cairns are found on the summits of both mountains. Those on Slieve Donard are also associated with Saint Domangard, a disciple of St Patrick, who is reputed to have lived the life of a hermit on the mountaintop. No doubt he too enjoyed the spectacular views to the Isle of Man and to the English Lake District, which today reward the visitor for the climb from sea level to 2796 feet.

These splendid views, together with the thrill of climbing the highest peaks in Northern Ireland, attract many thousands of walkers. Their impact on the floor of the Glen River valley has led in the past to uncontrolled erosion which the Trust intends to alleviate with paving techniques pioneered in the Lake District.

ACCESS: Open access; main point from Glen River path from Donard car park in Newcastle.

PARKING: Large car park in Newcastle.

FACILITIES: Local facilities.

MURLOUGH NATURE RESERVE

697 acres (282 ha) 2m NE of Newcastle, 28m S of Belfast on Dundrum to Newcastle road, Co. Down [J410350]

The village of Dundrum lies within a beautiful landscape of dunes and a tidal estuary overlooking the Mourne Mountains. The dunes and heathland of Murlough contain many interesting botanical and archaeological specimens; the dunes have been a site of human settlement over thousands of years, with archaeological remains from the neolithic and Bronze Ages to early Christian Iron Age and medieval times.

The dunes were once the site of a vast warren where rabbits, introduced by the Normans, were farmed for meat and fur for the Dublin hatters.

The complex network of dunes, grassland and scrub harbours an immense variety of wildlife, although sadly the twentieth century has brought with it increasing threats to this fragile landscape, and in 1967 Murlough was designated Ireland's first Nature Reserve for its continued protection.

Today the mudflats and saltmarshes are an important wintering site for dunlin, redshank, oystercatcher, curlew, wigeon and Brent geese. During the summer, it is an important breeding site for shelduck. Overwintering sea duck, grebes, divers, auks and shag can be seen offshore, the majority having journeyed from Iceland, Scandinavia and the Arctic regions, and in summer there are concentrations of feeding terns, gannet and gulls.

The oldest dune has been dated at over 6000 years old, and the highest reach 120 feet. Concealed within the dunes are post-glacial 'raised' shingle beaches, and there are some fine examples of dune heath, a scarce and declining habitat. The dune grasslands support a wide range of plants which include carline thistle, Portland spurge, pyramidal orchid and burnet rose. The scrub attracts many birds, with stonechat, whitethroat, linnet and willow warbler.

ACCESS: Main access point on A24; access to certain areas restricted April to September; network of footpaths open all year.

PARKING: Car park at access point next to A24.

FACILITIES: Visitor facilities and information centre open seasonally; guided walks (seasonal); education and special interest tours all year by arrangement; schools video on sale to teachers; boardwalk suitable for wheelchairs.

NOTE: Military activity at north end of beach is indicated when flags flying. Dogs on leads only and prohibited in fenced areas.

PORTSTEWART STRAND

197 acres (80 ha) ¾m NW of Coleraine, off A2, Co. Londonderry
[C720360]

Protecting the mouth of the River Bann, this elongated sand spit is backed by one of the few dune systems in Northern Ireland. The beach is very popular, especially in the summer when it is crammed with cars. The undesirable extraction of sand, used for a number of purposes, is difficult to control, and the dunes, already naturally mobile, are subject to much activity by ecologists and conservation groups to safeguard this vulnerable wildlife haven.

Many features of a mature dune system, an increasingly threatened coastal habitat, can be seen, with mobile and stable dunes, hollows (dune slacks) containing herb-rich grassland, dune scrub and saltmarsh. Some of the larger dunes are over 100 feet high, and the continuing movement of the sand has exposed old raised beach deposits. There are remains of some Bronze Age settlements.

The mobile dunes are colonised by sand couch and marram grass, and sand sedge. The established dune grassland is rich with flowers such as kidney vetch, bulbous buttercup, creeping thistle and wild pansy, with the calcareous nature of the sand encouraging a wide range of plants. The oldest dunes support bee and pyramidal orchids, and common centaury.

More than fourteen species of butterfly have been recorded, including small heath, dark-green fritillary and grayling. Mosses and lichens are also important in the more stable dunes. Sea buckthorn, although not native to Ireland, has been planted to help stabilise the dunes and is now widespread. It provides an ideal habitat for warblers and reed bunting, and shelter for foxes and badgers.

A pocket of saltmarsh in the Bann Estuary attracts small numbers of waders and wildfowl which feed on the tidal flats within the Bar Mouth bird sanctuary.

ACCESS: From Portstewart; station at Coleraine.

PARKING: Parking on beach (at a charge).

FACILITIES: WCs; information at Warden's office on beach; horses and dogs controlled (dogs to be kept on leads on beach, dog litter area).

STRANGFORD LOUGH

5400 acres (2185 ha) SE of Belfast via A22, A21, A20 and A25, car ferry from Portaferry to Strangford, Co. Down [J560615]

Linked to the Irish Sea by a narrow channel less than a mile wide, this great sea lough is not only a most beautiful landscape of islands, water and rounded drumlins or glacial hills, but it is also of international importance for its wildlife. The Trust owns or leases Gibb's, Bird, Salt (where there are some old agricultural field patterns), Green, Dunnyneill, Taggart, Darragh, Horse, Ballyhenry and Nugent's islands, as well as Glastry Ponds, Jane's Shore, Ballyquintin Point and Walter Meadow and Woods. It is also responsible for most of the foreshore.

The 80,000 million gallons of sea water which rush through the 'Narrows' on each tide bring in marine life which feeds thousands of overwintering and summer-breeding birds. Two-thirds (more than 15,000) of the world population of pale-bellied Brent geese spend the winter on the lough after summers in the Arctic Circle.

Over 2000 species of marine animals have been recorded in several unique marine communities in the lough, and include starfish, corals, sea anemones, molluscs and crustaceans and worms. Among the large and varied populations of birds are whooper and mute swans, shelduck, teal, oystercatcher, godwit, knot, curlew, redshank, wigeon, red-breasted merganser, cormorant and mallard. The abundance of sand eels attracts flocks of tern (one-third of all terns in Ireland breed on the islands). Common and grey seals rest on the isolated rocky shores, and basking sharks and porpoises can be seen on the incoming tide. The coastal rocks are encrusted with lichens and seaweeds.

Around the shoreline, the variety of habitats depends on the tide and on the rivers feeding the lough. Coastal grassland of thrift and campion merges with heathland, shingle and sandy beaches, tidal mudflats and saltmarsh, with the sheltered islands, reefs and deep waters adding to the range. The lack of temperature extremes in this sheltered environment allows both southern and northern species to coexist.

ACCESS: Darragh, Taggart, Ballyhenry and Salt islands unrestricted access except where bird colonies are protected; footpaths around shore; bus service from Downpatrick to Strangford with connections from Belfast.

PARKING: Car parks at Castle Ward; several car parks around the lough.

FACILITIES: WCs (including disabled) at Castle Ward; visitor and interpretation centre at the Barn, Castle Ward; bothy on Salt Island for yachtsmen and groups; picnics allowed on some properties (prohibited on nesting islands during breeding season); other activities (not necessarily NT), sailing, yacht and cruising clubs, base camp at Castle Ward, birdwatchers' hides.

WHITE PARK BAY

179 acres (72½ ha) 1½m W of Ballintoy, 7m NW of Ballycastle off A2, Co. Antrim   [D023440]

A sweep of golden sand flanked by chalk cliffs marks a distinct change from the dark, tilted basalt stacks at the eastern edge of the bay and the cliffs of the Causeway coast to the west, and the variation in the underlying rock structure is reflected in the many plants flourishing in the soil which ranges from calcareous on chalk and neutral on clays. As with Portstewart, sand extraction is a problem here.

A broad stretch of lumpy grassland, wet flushes and scrub lies between the beach and the cliffs, and a narrow band of sand dunes is a refuge for some uncommon plants such as sea sandwort, fragrant agrimony, and Portland and sea spurges. The ancient chalk grassland contains a wide range of wild flowers and grasses, with orchids, lady's mantle, bird's foot trefoil, thyme, purging flax, lady's bedstraw and meadow crane's bill. Moonwort and adder's tongue are two unusual ferns to be found.

Bees, ants, grasshoppers and molluscs are among the many invertebrates which thrive on the coarser grassland, and brambles, hawthorn, elder and hazel scrub provide important nesting sites for willow warbler, whitethroat, sedge warbler, linnet and stonechat. The shaded slopes below the cliff, with conditions similar to woods, harbour a variety of woodland plants such as wood anemone, primrose and common twayblade. Yellow flag, meadowsweet, water mint and marsh marigold flourish in the marshy pockets.

There is much of archaeological interest, including some megalithic tombs above the bay, and a Bronze Age burial mound along the sand hills.

ACCESS: Network of footpaths; North Antrim Coastal Path.

PARKING: Car park on clifftop.

FACILITIES: WCs; nature trail.

Useful Addresses

London Office: 36 Queen Anne's Gate, London SW1H 9AS
(071-222 9251)

London Information Centre: Blewcoat School, 23 Caxton Street, London SW1

Membership: PO Box 39, Bromley, Kent BR1 1NH (081-464 1111)

Finance; Internal Audit; Enterprises; Volunteer Unit: Heywood House, Westbury, Wiltshire BA13 4NA (Westbury, Wilts (0373) 826826)

The National Trust for Scotland: 5 Charlotte Square, Edinburgh, EH2 4DU
(031-226 5922)

1 **Cornwall:** Lanhydrock, Bodmin PL30 4DE (Bodmin (0208) 74281)

2 **Devon:** Killerton House, Broadclyst, Exeter EX5 3LE (Exeter (0392) 881691)

3 **Wessex** *(Avon, Dorset, Somerset, Wiltshire)* Eastleigh Court, Bishopstrow, Warminster, Wiltshire BA12 9HW (Warminster (0985) 847777)

4 **Southern** *(Hampshire, Isle of Wight, South-Western Greater London, Surrey and West Sussex)* Polesden Lacey, Dorking, Surrey RH5 6BD
(Bookham (0372) 453401)

5 **Kent & East Sussex** *(includes South-Eastern Greater London),* The Estate Office, Scotney Castle, Lamberhurst, Tunbridge Wells, Kent TN3 8JN
(Lamberhurst (0892) 890651)

6 **East Anglia** *(Cambridgeshire, Essex, Norfolk, Suffolk)* Blickling, Norwich NR11 6NF (Aylsham (0263) 733471)

7 **Thames & Chilterns** *(Buckinghamshire, Bedfordshire, Berkshire, Hertfordshire, London north of the Thames, and Oxfordshire)* Hughenden Manor, High Wycombe, Bucks HP14 4LA (High Wycombe (0494) 528051)

8 **Severn** *(Gloucestershire, Hereford & Worcester, Warwickshire, part of West Midlands)* Mythe End House, Tewkesbury, Glos GL20 6EB
(Tewkesbury (0684) 850051)

9 **South Wales:** *(Dyfed, Gwent, West Glamorgan, southern part of Powys)* The King's Head, Bridge Street, Llandeilo, Dyfed SA19 6BB
(Llandeilo (0558) 822800)

10 **North Wales:** *(Clwyd, Gwynedd, northern part of Powys)* Trinity Square, Llandudno, Gwynedd LL30 2DE (Llandudno (0492) 860123)

11 **Mercia** *(Cheshire, Merseyside, Shropshire, Greater Manchester, most of Staffordshire, part of West Midlands)* Attingham Park, Shrewsbury, Shropshire SY4 4TP (Upton Magna (074 377) 343)

12 East Midlands *(Derbyshire, Leicestershire, Lincolnshire, Northamptonshire, Nottinghamshire, South Humberside and those parts of Cheshire, Greater Manchester, Staffordshire, South Yorkshire and West Yorkshire within the Peak National Park)* Clumber Park Stableyard, Worksop, Notts s80 3be (Worksop (0909) 486411)

13 Yorkshire *(includes North, South and West Yorkshire, Cleveland and North Humberside)* Goddards, 27 Tadcaster Road, Dringhouses, York yo2 2qg (York (0904) 702021)

14 North-West *(Cumbria and Lancashire)* The Hollens, Grasmere, Ambleside, Cumbria la22 9qz (Ambleside (05394) 35599)

15 Northumbria *(Durham, Northumberland, and Tyne & Wear)* Scots' Gap, Morpeth, Northumberland ne61 4eg (Scots' Gap (067 074) 691)

16 Northern Ireland: Rowallane House, Saintfield, Ballynahinch, Co. Down bt24 7lh (Saintfield (0238) 510721)

Regional Offices Map

SCOTS' GAP

16

SAINTFIELD

NORTHERN IRELAND

15

14

AMBLESIDE

13

● YORK

● CLUMBER

LLANDUDNO

11

10

ATTINGHAM

12

BLICKLING

6

8

7

TEWKESBURY

HUGHENDEN

LLANDEILO

9

BISHOPSTROW

POLESDEN LACEY

SCOTNEY

3

4

5

KILLERTON

1

2

LANHYDROCK

Definitions and Glossary of Terms

PROTECTED AREAS IN THE UNITED KINGDOM

National Parks

There are eleven National Parks in England and Wales designated by the Government to include areas of unspoilt beauty. They are mainly in upland or coastal areas although the Norfolk Broads, recently designated, diverges from this original concept and includes a populated lowland area. Land ownership varies, with much being privately owned. Development control is strict to ensure the traditional appearance of the landscape is protected.

Areas of Outstanding National Beauty (AONBs)

The forty-six AONBs include many scenic areas of England, Wales and Northern Ireland. Most of the land is in private ownership.

Environmentally Sensitive Areas (ESAs)

In ESAs farmers are offered financial incentives to farm in a traditional way for the benefit of the landscape, wildlife and the historic interest of these areas. There are ten in England, two in Wales and two in Northern Ireland.

Heritage Coasts

Forty-three lengths of unspoilt coasts have been defined by local authorities and the Countryside Commission covering thirty-three per cent of the total coastline of England and Wales – a substantial amount is in the Trust's ownership.

National Nature Reserves (NNRs)

A total of 238 reserves have been designated in England, Wales and Northern Ireland, representing some of the most important and threatened habitats; they are managed for protection and research.

'Ramsar' Sites

These are wetlands designated by governments in accordance with the provisions of the Convention on Wetlands of International Importance signed at Ramsar, Iran in 1971.

Scheduled Ancient Monuments (SAMs)

Sites of national importance, protected by the current ancient monument legislation (the Ancient Monuments and Archaeological Areas Act).

Sites of Special Scientific Interest (SSSIs)

SSSIs are areas of land or water identified by the Nature Conservancy Council as being of outstanding value for their wildlife or geology. The Trust owns about nine per cent of all SSSIs in England and Wales. In Northern Ireland these sites are either Areas of Special Scientific Interest (ASSIs) or Areas of Scientific Interest (ASIs), eighteen of which are owned by the Trust.

World Heritage Sites

Natural and cultural sites of exceptional interest and universal value are drawn up on a World Heritage List under the UNESCO World Heritage Convention of 1972. The Giant's Causeway in Northern Ireland is an example in the natural category; National Trust sites on the cultural list include Stonehenge, Avebury and Hadrian's Wall.

GLOSSARY OF TERMS

acid: refers to the low pH of soil; acid soil has few basic minerals and is generally formed on rocks such as sandstone; peaty soils are usually acid.

alkaline: refers to the high pH of the soil; alkaline soil often occurs on chalk and limestone.

ancient woodland: woodland that has had a continuous tree cover since 1600.

bog: an area of acid, wet, spongy ground consisting largely of decayed of decaying vegetation, which eventually turns into peat.

bourne stream: an intermittent stream, occuring mainly in the chalk regions of southern England; usually dry, except in winter when the water table rises above its level.

cairn: a mound of stones erected as a marker or memorial.

clearance cairn: a pile of stones built up from clearing fields.

calcareous: made of or containing calcium carbonate and hence alkaline; occurs on chalk and limestone.

canopy layer: the trees which have the highest layer of leaves.

carr: shrub or woodland growing in water-logged conditions.

clint: a ridge of bare rock between 'grikes' in a limestone region; a classic example is seen at Malham Cove in Yorkshire.

coppicing: a method of periodically cutting trees or bushes close to the ground, enabling new shoots to grow from the stump.

copse: a thicket or dense growth of small trees or bushes.

covert: a thicket providing shelter for game.

diversity: the number of species within a particular habitat or the number of habitats in an area.

dyke: a ditch or water course; a bank made of earth beside a ditch; in Scotland, a drystone wall.

earthworks: soil-covered archaeological remains visible as undulations on the land surface.

ecology: the study of the relation of plants and animals to each other and to their surroundings.

fen: low-lying, flat marshy land in which peat is being formed beneath the surface; the soil is generally alkaline.

flow: a flat, moist tract of land; a moorland pool.

glade: a clearing or open space in a woodland.

grike: a fissure between 'clints' in the surface of rock in a limestone region, formed when limestone dissolves in rain water containing carbon dioxide.

ground layer: the closest layer of vegetation to the ground in a woodland.

habitat: the natural environment of plants and animals.

hammerpond: an aritificial pond at a water-mill.

heathland: an open area of uncultivated ground dominated by small shrubs such as heather and ling, usually on sandy soil at lower altitudes. Vegetation varies according to water table.

improved grassland: grassland that has been treated with chemical fertilisers and sometimes herbicides to improve productivity.

intake field: enclosed tract of land.

knoll: a small, rounded hill.

lichens: small plants formed by the symbiotic association of a fungus and an alga.

lynchet: a terrace or ridge formed in prehistoric or medieval times by ploughing a hillside.

marsh: a community on low-lying, wet ground, but not on peat.

moorland: an upland area of open, unenclosed ground usually dominated by heather, coarse grasses, bracken and moss.

neutral: soil and water that is neither acid nor alkaline.

pillow mounds: low, oblong mounds of earth and stones often with a shallow ditch round them, constructed as rabbit warrens in the Middle Ages.

ramparts: surrounding embankments of a fort.

Red Data Book: national reference books of data listing rare species of flora and fauna in Britain.

secondary woodland: woodland growing on land that has previously been used for some other purpose.

semi-natural: used to describe an assemblage of native plants that is apparently natural but has been modified by human activities.

settlement pattern: the distribution of archaeological sites within a particular geographical area.

shieling: northern term for a seasonal hut for shepherds or herdsmen. Sometimes with enclosures for stock.

unimproved grassland: grassland that has not been re-seeded, treated with chemical fertiliser and is a rich wildlife habitat.

South-West England

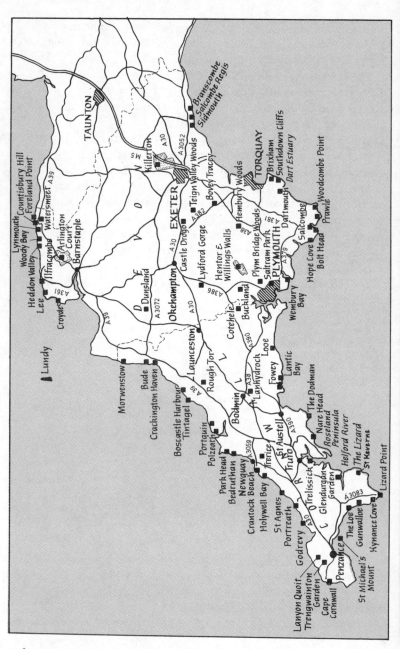

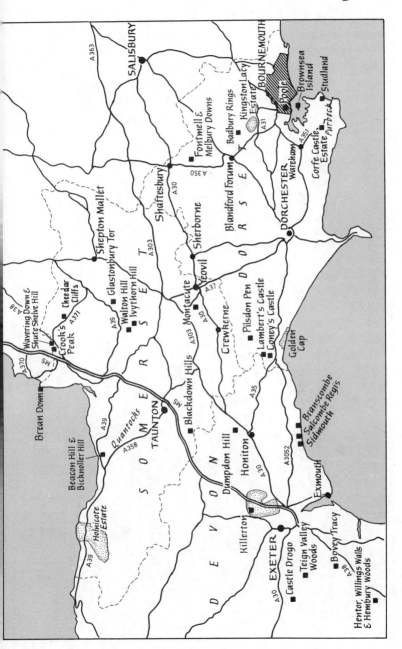

Wales and the Welsh Borders

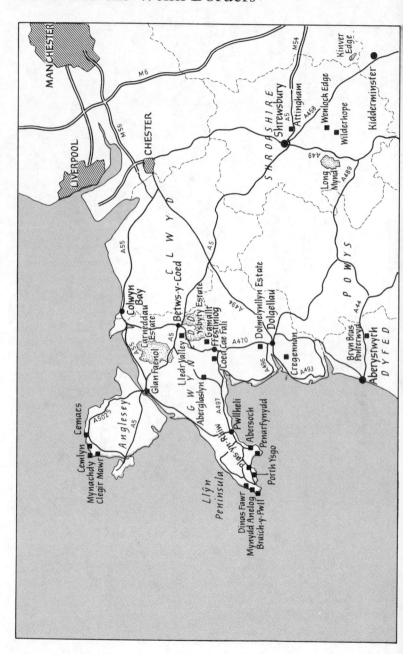

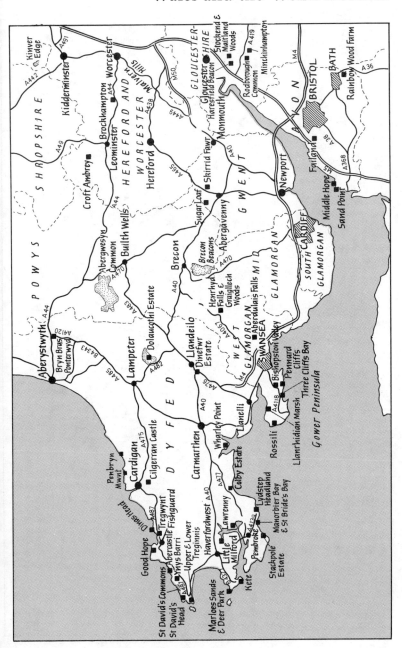

Southern England

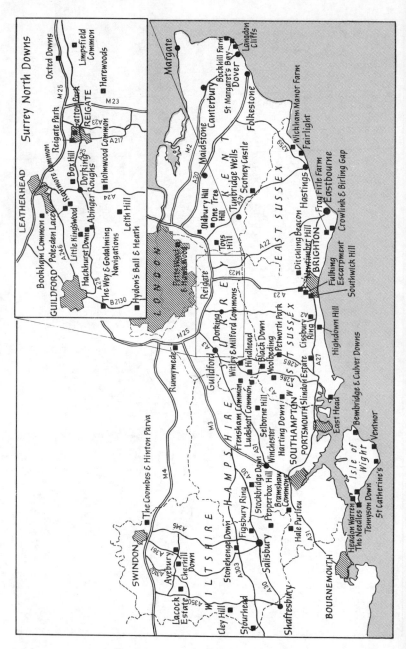

London, Thames Valley and the Chilterns

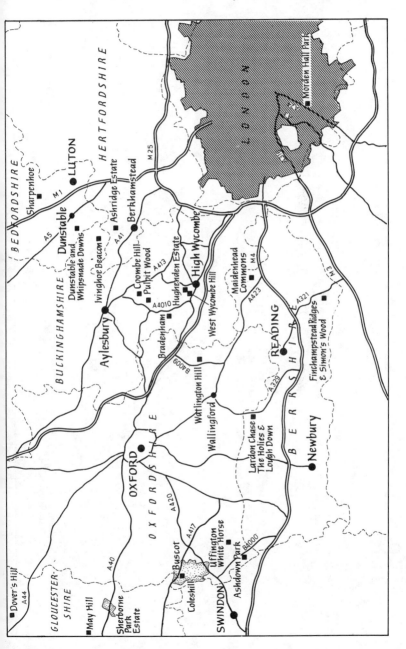

Central England

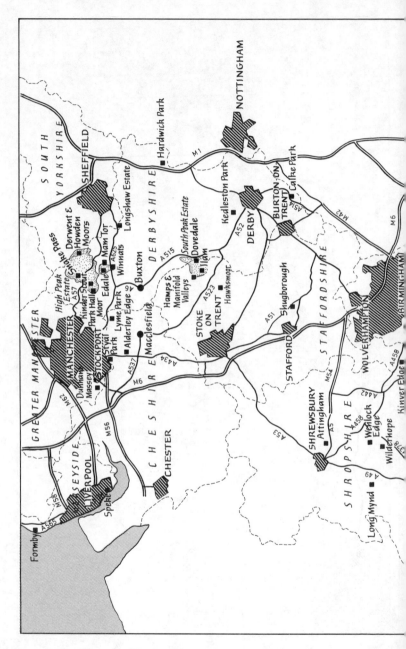

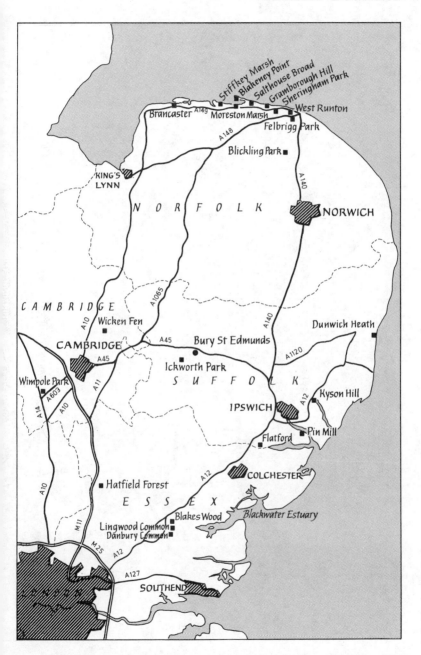

North-West England

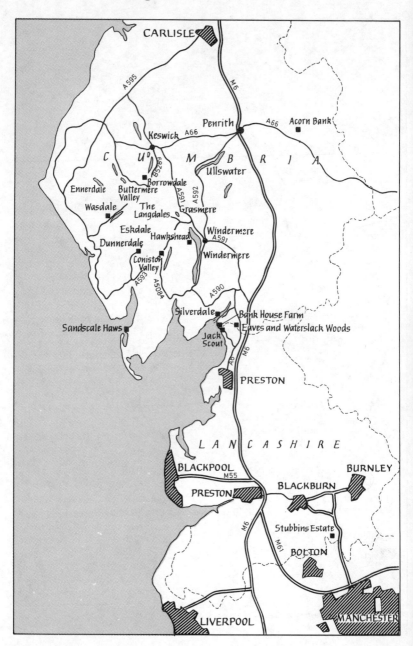

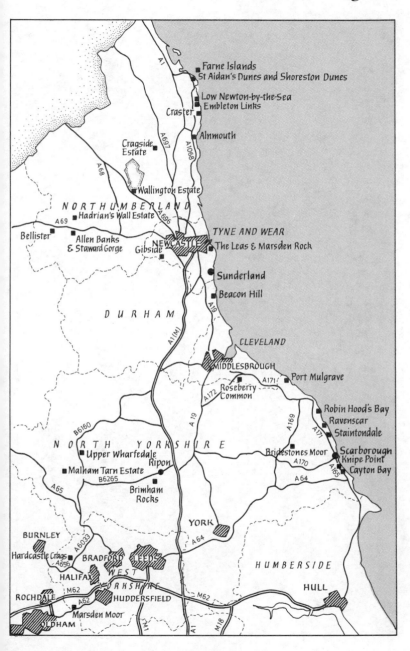

Farne Islands
St Aidan's Dunes and Shoreston Dunes
Low Newton-by-the-Sea
Embleton Links
Craster
Alnmouth
Cragside Estate
Wallington Estate
N O R T H U M B E R L A N D
Hadrian's Wall Estate
A69
Bellister
Allen Banks & Staward Gorge
Gibside
NEWCASTLE
TYNE AND WEAR
The Leas & Marsden Rock
Sunderland
Beacon Hill
D U R H A M
CLEVELAND
MIDDLESBROUGH
Port Mulgrave
A171
Roseberry Common
A172
Robin Hood's Bay
Ravenscar
Staintondale
Bridestones Moor
N O R T H   Y O R K S H I R E
Upper Wharfedale
Ripon
Scarborough
Knipe Point
Cayton Bay
Malham Tarn Estate
Brimham Rocks
YORK
BURNLEY
Hardcastle Crags
BRADFORD
LEEDS
H U M B E R S I D E
HALIFAX
W E S T   Y O R K S H I R E
ROCHDALE
HUDDERSFIELD
HULL
Marsden Moor
OLDHAM

Northern Ireland

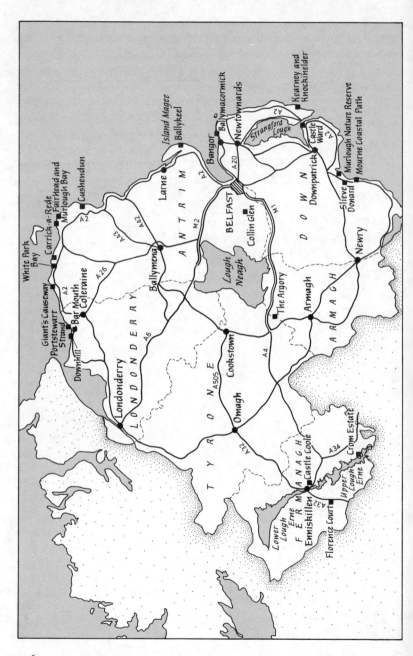

National Trust Countryside Publications

Britain's Countryside Heritage; a guide to the landscape, by Phil Colebourne & Bob Gibbons, 1990. Blandford Press.

The Butterflies of Britain & Ireland, by Jeremy Thomas & Richard Lewington, 1991. Dorling Kindersley.

Figures in a Landscape; an illustrated history of the National Trust, by John Gaze, 1988. Barrie & Jenkins.

In Search of Neptune, by Charlie Pye-Smith, photographs by Joe Cornish, 1990. The National Trust.

The National Trust Atlas, 3rd edition, 1989. George Philip.

The National Trust Handbook, annual publication for members and visitors. The National Trust.

The National Trust Guide, 4th edition, compiled by Lydia Greeves & Michael Trinick, 1988. The National Trust.

The National Trust Guide to Exploring Unspoilt Britain, edited by Derrick Mercer, 1991. Bounty Books.

The National Trust Nature Companion, by John Harvey, Keith Alexander & David Russell, illustrated by Sandra Fernandez, 1990. Dorling Kindersley.

Properties of the National Trust; details of all National Trust land (except that held for investment purposes). The up-dated edition (1992) is available on request from the Membership Department, Bromley, price £2.50 (including post and packing).

Strangford Lough; wildlife of an Irish Sea Lough, by Robert Brown, 1990. The Queen's University of Belfast.

Traditional Buildings and Life in the Lake District, by Susan Denyer, 1991. Victor Gollancz.

Wales, by William Condry, 1991. Gomer Press.

Index